MW01126258

Halley's

Bible
Handbook
for Kids

Dr. Henry Halley
and Jean E. Syswerda

Discovery House.
from Our Daily Bread Ministries

Discovery House is affiliated with Our Daily Bread Ministries,
Grand Rapids, Michigan.

Requests for permission to quote from this book should be directed to:
Permissions Department, Discovery House, P.O. Box 3566, Grand Rapids,
MI 49501, or contact us by e-mail at permissionsdept@dhp.org.

All photographs by Terry Bidgood © Our Daily Bread Ministries except
p. 23 © iStock.com/GlobalP; p. 42 © iStock.com/iceninephoto; p. 45 by Terry
Bidgood © Our Daily Bread Ministries; p. 80 © iStock.com/seread; p. 137 ©
iStock.com/Andyworks; p. 215 © iStock.com/akiwi; p. 225 © iStock.com/
ruvanboshoff; p. 230 © iStock.com/ezza116; p. 320 © iStock.com/spyder24.

Interior design by Sherri L. Hoffman

ISBN: 978-1-62707-411-7

Printed in Italy
First printing of this edition in 2016

CONTENTS

Maps

INTRODUCTION

Battling giants! Surviving a fiery furnace! Fishing for men! The Bible is one exciting adventure after another. But what does it all mean? Why was it written?

Well, have you ever been on a treasure hunt where you go from place to place searching for the next clue to find the surprise at the end? The Bible is like a treasure hunt. While you search for clues to understand what it is all about, God reveals himself to you and answers questions about your own life.

But it helps to have a treasure map like *Halley's Bible Handbook for Kids* to show you the way. Now let's see how many clues you can find to see what God has in store for you!

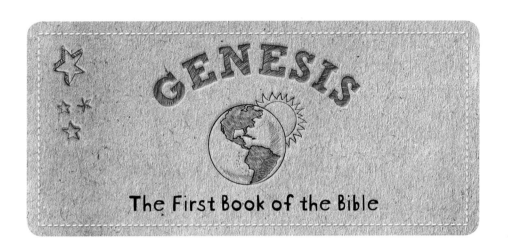

GENESIS

The First Book of the Bible

Like a band concert that begins with drums rolling and cymbals crashing, Genesis rocks into action. With the very first verse, God begins to create. Just the sound of his voice makes the sun, moon, stars, water, animals, and plants appear. God creates people too and breathes life into them.

God then chooses the best of the best of all he's created and makes a beautiful garden. He puts the first man and woman, Adam and Eve, in it. They eat the garden's lush fruits, including the one fruit God clearly told them not to eat. Foolish first people! With that one bite of forbidden fruit, sin enters the world. The rest of Genesis sets the stage for God's plan to save his people from sin and bring them back to himself.

Writer:
Moses

Place:
Near the Tigris and Euphrates Rivers

People:
Adam and Eve, Noah, Abraham, Isaac, Jacob, and Joseph

Why Is It Important?
The book of Genesis describes the beginning of God's relationship with human beings.

Some Stories in Genesis:
A World Is Created: Genesis 1–2
A Flood Destroys Land and People: Genesis 6–8
New Languages Are Formed in an Instant: Genesis 11
Abraham's Covenant with God: Genesis 12–17
Cities Destroyed by Fire: Genesis 19:15–29
A Son Almost Sacrificed: Genesis 22:3–14
A Brother Dumped in a Well: Genesis 37:12–36
A Famine Predicted!: Genesis 41:25–27

Genesis 1:1–2:3 The Creation

The Bible begins with a beautiful poetic description of the creation of the world. God took seven days to create:

Light and dark (day 1)
Sea and sky (day 2)
Oceans, lands, plants, and trees (day 3)
Sun, moon, and stars (day 4)
Fish and birds (day 5)
Animals and people (day 6)

On the seventh day, God rested. That doesn't mean he was tired—it just means he did not work on the final day of creation.

> **Be Wise—Memorize!**
> **Genesis 1:1** In the beginning, God created the heavens and the earth.

Create Genesis 1:1

To make something out of nothing. God created the world out of nothing. Just his voice speaking the words made everything come into being.

Genesis 2:4–25 God Creates a Man and a Woman

This is sometimes called the "second creation story." It's another account of the same events. God made the first man in his own image by forming Adam from the dust of the earth. Then God breathed life into the man. God put Adam in the Garden of Eden to work in it and take care of it. Adam spent his time in the garden naming the animals and visiting with God. But God knew that Adam needed another *person* to be around. So God put Adam to sleep, took one of his ribs, and created a woman. Adam named her Eve.

Here, we see that the start of the human race is also the start of marriage. From the beginning, marriage was God's idea—one man, one woman, together for life.

Garden of Eden Genesis 2:4–17

We don't know for sure where the Garden of Eden was located. But the Bible does give us a couple of hints. It was between the Tigris and Euphrates Rivers, which still have the same names today! They flow through the country of Iraq.

Genesis 3 The Start of Sin

That sneaky Satan, disguised as a snake, persuaded Eve, then Adam, to eat from "the tree that gives life forever" (Genesis 2:9). Yum. It may have tasted good, but God had said no. They might as well have eaten poison! Disobeying God is

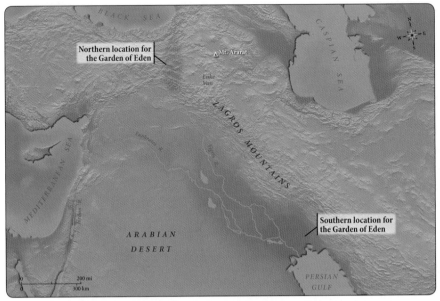

Map 1. Possible Locations of the Garden of Eden

called sin, and it has consequences. God told Adam and Eve to leave the garden, but he still loved them very much—even though they had sinned.

Genesis 4 Cain and Abel

We're only to the fourth chapter of the Bible, and already we have a family feud. Abel's sacrifice to God was accepted, because he offered a proper sacrifice. His actions were right with God (1 John 3:12), and he had faith in God (Hebrews 11:4). Cain did not. Cain was *mad*—so mad he killed his brother, Abel. God put a curse and a mark on Cain to punish him (Genesis 4:11, 15). We don't know what the mark was, but people then must have understood what it meant.

Genesis 5 The Family Line from Adam to Noah

Take a look at the ages of the people in this family. Adam lived 930 years; Seth, 912 years; Methuselah, 969 years (he's the oldest person in the Bible!); Noah, 950 years. Wow! Now that's *old!*

Enoch Genesis 5:21–24

One of the best of the first people on earth. When all those around him were horribly wicked, Enoch "walked with God." He didn't die like other people. The Bible says, "God took him from this life." The only other person to be taken by God without having to die was Elijah (2 Kings 2).

Genesis 6:1–8 Wickedness before the Flood

What a difference between verses 5 and 8. Verse 5 talks about how sinful the people were, and then verse 8 talks about how good Noah was. No wonder God decided to destroy the world but save Noah.

Genesis 6:9–10:32 The Story of Noah

When the flood came, Noah and his family and hundreds of animals spent over a year on the ark—a kind of floating zoo. When the rains finally stopped, the ark came to rest on the mountains of Ararat (Genesis 8:4). Noah sent out a raven first, and then a dove to see if the water was going down. The dove flew around and came back two times. The third time it didn't return to the ark. Noah then knew the bird had found dry land and that the waters were going down.

Finally, Noah and his family and the animals left the ark. What did they do first? Offer thanks to God. A rainbow streaked across the sky as God's promise that he would never again destroy the earth by a flood (Genesis 9:11–14).

The Ark Genesis 6:14–16

The ark was 450 feet long (that's one and a half football fields), 75 feet wide (that's about as wide as a six-lane highway), and 45 feet high (about as tall as a building with five floors). Has anyone ever discovered the remains of Noah's ark? Well, lots of people have made claims. But no one so far has offered proof that it's been found.

Raven Genesis 8:7

A large bird. Noah sent one out from the ark to see if dry land was near. He forgot that a raven will continue to fly and search for food without returning to where it started.

Dove Genesis 8:8–12

A medium-sized bird that remembers where it started out flying and returns there. Noah sent one out from the ark. It flew around and came back two times. The third time it didn't return to the ark. Noah then knew the bird had found dry land (Throw a party!) and that the waters were going down.

Genesis 11:1–9 A Babble of Languages

About one hundred years after the flood, people decided they would build a huge tower to prove how powerful they were and get closer to God. This did not please God. So he mixed up their languages to make people move away from each other and settle other parts of the earth.

Tower of Babel Genesis 11:4
The tower of Babel could also be called the tower of *babble*. The people sounded like they were *babbling* when God mixed up their languages. The ruins of many tall towers, called *ziggurats* (ZIG-ur-ots), are still found today. The tower of Babel was probably much more primitive.

Genesis 11:10–32 The Family of Shem
The family line of Noah's son Shem brings us to the next hero in the Genesis story, Abraham.

Genesis 12–15 God Chooses Abram
About four hundred years after the flood, God called Abram to be the founder of a nation. Through that nation, God would bring salvation from sin. Abram believed in God, not in the idols those around him worshiped. Because Abram was faithful, God promised that Abram's family would own the land of Canaan, become a great nation, and be a blessing to other nations.

> **Be Wise—Memorize!**
> **Genesis 15:6** Abram believed the LORD. The LORD accepted Abram because he believed. So his faith made him right with the LORD.

God called Abram to leave his land and family. "So Abram left" (Genesis 12:4). Abram not only *believed* in God, but every time God told him to do something, Abram *obeyed*. Abram and his family stopped first at Haran and then moved on into the land of Canaan. Because of a famine, Abram made a side trip down to Egypt, where he got himself into trouble because of his beautiful wife, Sarai (Genesis 12:10–20).

Abram/Abraham Genesis 12:1–4
God promised Abram, later called Abraham by God, that his family would be as many as the stars in the sky. Now that's a huge family! Through Abraham, several nations were formed, including the nation of Israel. It still exists today. Jewish people live in Israel as well as in other countries throughout the world.

Tents Genesis 13:5
Don't picture your little two-person backyard tent. These tents were often huge and were made of animal skins. Poles and cords with stakes held the tents in

place. Open sides let the cool evening breezes blow through. These tents could be taken down, packed up, and put on an animal for quick moves.

Covenant Genesis 15:18

A promise between people. God made a covenant with Abraham—and through him with all the Israelites—to give them a land to live in.

Genesis 16 Abraham's Son Ishmael

When a wife couldn't have children, she sometimes gave her servant to her husband. The servant's children were then family members. Sarai was so desperate for children that she gave her servant Hagar to Abram. Hagar had a son named Ishmael. The situation caused nothing but trouble.

Hagar Genesis 16:1–10; 21:8–21

Sarai's slave Hagar had a baby. As soon as she knew she was pregnant, Hagar started to look down on Sarai, her owner. Sarai in turn was mean to Hagar. So Hagar ran away into the desert. But God was watching, and he took care of Hagar.

Genesis 17 God Renews His Promises to Abraham

God came to Abram and gave him a new name (Abraham) and a sign (circumcision). Circumcision marked a male as part of Abraham's family and, therefore, God's family. God also changed Sarai's name to Sarah and promised to bless her with a son. God said that through this son, Sarah would become the mother of nations (Genesis 17:16).

Genesis 18–19 Two Cities Destroyed

The people of Sodom and Gomorrah were about as disgusting and wicked as they come. Abraham begged God to spare the cities if only ten good people could be found there (Genesis 18:32). But not even that many could be found. God destroyed the cities. But he did save Abraham's nephew, Lot, and his family by sending angels to rescue them.

Sodom and Gomorrah Genesis 18:20; 19:24–25

One cloudy morning God sent down a rain of *fire* on Sodom and Gomorrah. He punished the people for their terrible sins. Some people think these cities were at the northern end of the Dead Sea. Others think they were at the southern end. No one knows for sure.

Lot Genesis 19:15–16

Lot wanted a lot. He took the best land from Abraham. He grew rich in the wicked cities of Sodom and Gomorrah. God destroyed those wicked cities. But because Abraham asked that Lot be saved, God sent an angel to rescue Lot and his family.

Genesis 20–21 A Baby for Very Old Abraham and Sarah

God promised Abraham and Sarah that they would have a son, and he kept his promise. Even though they were both too old to have kids (almost one hundred!), they did have a son and named him Isaac. *Nothing* is too hard for God (Genesis 18:14).

Sarah Genesis 21:1–7

Sarah had a baby. It's true! Sarah was about ninety years old (and Abraham was a hundred) before she had her first baby. Sarah was so happy when Isaac was born that she couldn't stop laughing.

Genesis 22 Abraham Offers Isaac

God had promised that Abraham would have many children through Isaac, and they would become a great nation (Genesis 17:16). Yet God commanded Abraham to sacrifice Isaac (that means to kill him!) when he was just a young man. So Abraham took Isaac up Mount Moriah, tied him onto an altar, and raised a knife to kill him. But God never intended for Abraham to kill Isaac. This was God's way of testing Abraham's faith. Abraham believed that God would keep his promise no matter what—even if that meant bringing Isaac back to life (Hebrews 11:19). When God saw Abraham's faithfulness to obey, he called out for him to stop. Then God provided a ram for Abraham to sacrifice instead of Isaac. Isaac lived, and his descendants became the nation of Israel.

Mount Moriah Genesis 22:2

This is where Abraham went to sacrifice his son Isaac. Later Solomon built the temple on that same spot (2 Chronicles 3:1). Today the Dome of the Rock, a Muslim shrine, stands in that same area in the city of Jerusalem.

Altar Genesis 22:9

A place where sacrifices are made to worship gods. Some altars were made to worship the one true God; others were made by those who followed false gods. Some are made of piles of rocks, others are carved from stone or wood.

Genesis 23–25 A Wife for Isaac

Sarah had died, and Abraham was old. He sent his servant back to the land where he had once lived to find a good wife for Isaac among his relatives. Isaac could not marry a Canaanite woman who worshiped false gods or idols. Abraham's servant returned with Rebekah, and Isaac married her.

Isaac and Rebekah had two sons, Esau and Jacob. Knowing before they were born what these men would be like, God chose Jacob. Even though he was born after his twin brother, Esau, Jacob would be the next father of the nation of Israel. Instead of letting God do the work, however, Rebekah and Jacob used lies and trickery to gain the blessing for Jacob.

Rebekah Genesis 24:61, 67

Rebekah loved her husband, Isaac, and comforted him when he was sad because his mother had died. But Rebekah also thought she needed to do things her own way instead of waiting for God. Her schemes only brought her unhappiness.

Genesis 26–27 Jacob Gets His Father's Blessing

Jacob had already tricked his brother and bought the rights of the firstborn son from Esau (Genesis 25:31–34). Now Jacob wanted to be sure to get the blessing from his father that proved he had the rights. With his mother, Rebekah, Jacob tricked his father into giving the blessing to him instead of Esau. Esau said he would kill Jacob for stealing his blessing. Jacob didn't wait around to see if Esau was serious. After Jacob stole Esau's blessing, he ran to his Uncle Laban. There, he would marry two sisters, Leah and Rachel. The sons of these marriages would lead the future tribes of the nation of Israel.

Genesis 28 A Vision for Jacob

Jacob received a promise from God. A vision assured Jacob that the nation of Israel would be founded through him and his descendants. He dreamed of a ladder reaching to heaven. It was a hint that God would send someone to create a bridge between heaven and earth—Jesus!

Bethel Genesis 28:18–19

While Jacob slept with a stone for a pillow, God came to him in a dream. Jacob named the place Bethel, which means "house of God." The city is important throughout the history of Israel.

Genesis 29–30 Jacob Marries and Has Children

Jacob lived in Haran for twenty years. Just as Jacob had tricked his father, his Uncle Laban tricked him. Jacob fell in love with Laban's daughter Rachel and worked seven years for his uncle in order to marry her. After the wedding, he discovered that his uncle had somehow snuck Rachel's sister, Leah, into the wedding—and he had married the wrong girl! Laban also allowed Jacob to marry Rachel, but he had to agree to work another seven years. These two wives and their maids, Zilpah and Bilhah, gave Jacob twelve sons, who would be leaders of the "twelve tribes of Israel":

Leah—Reuben, Simeon, Levi, Judah, Issachar, and Zebulun
Rachel—Joseph and Benjamin
Zilpah—Gad and Asher
Bilhah—Dan and Naphtali

This family, though far from perfect, was accepted by God to become a great nation of people blessed by God.

Rachel Genesis 29:16–18, 21–30

Known for her beauty, Rachel didn't seem to have much else going for her. Jacob spent years of his life working for her father in order to gain permission to marry her. Rachel spent most of her life competing with her sister for his love. She died while giving birth to her second child, Benjamin (Genesis 35:17–18).

Leah Genesis 29:16–18, 21–30

Jacob was in love with Rachel but was tricked into marrying Leah first. While Leah was able to give Jacob several sons, as well as a daughter, she spent most of her life knowing her husband loved her sister, Rachel, more.

Genesis 31–33 Jacob Has a Wrestling Match with God

Jacob left his home alone and empty-handed. He returned as a rich man with many sons, flocks, and herds. But he was still afraid of his brother, Esau, so he sent a peace party on ahead with many gifts.

The night before he crossed over into Canaan, God came to Jacob in the form of a man. They had a wrestling match and fought all night! But God showed Jacob who was more powerful. He touched Jacob's hip, and from then on Jacob walked with a limp. Jacob still refused to give up until the "man" blessed him. The man gave Jacob a blessing and changed his name to Israel, which means "he struggles with God."

Genesis 34–35 Jacob Worships God

Jacob returned to Bethel and built an altar on which to worship God. He destroyed all the idols still worshiped by his family. He wanted to be sure they worshiped only the one true God.

Genesis 36 Esau's Family Line

Esau's family is outlined here. His family would become the nation of Edom. They were enemies of the Israelites for many centuries—almost until the end of the Old Testament (see the book of Obadiah).

Genesis 37 Joseph Sold into Slavery

When Jacob gave his son Joseph a special robe, Joseph's ten older brothers grew jealous. They wondered if Jacob intended to give Joseph the family blessing. The dreams that God gave Joseph, showing he would rule over his brothers one day, only made matters worse. Joseph was hated so much by his brothers that they sold him into slavery. They took Joseph's robe, tore it, splattered blood on it, and then told their father that Joseph had been killed.

Joseph Genesis 37:3

Joseph was the first son of Jacob and Rachel, Jacob's eleventh son overall. His brothers hated him. They sold him into slavery in Egypt. When Pharaoh, the Egyptian king, had a dream, Jacob told him the dream's meaning. Pharaoh made Joseph a ruler in Egypt. When a famine came, Joseph was able to help the Egyptians survive. He was able to help his own family as well, the ten brothers who had mistreated him plus a baby brother, Benjamin, the other son of Jacob's wife Rachel.

Egypt Genesis 37:28

Egypt is located in the northeast corner of Africa. Its kings, laws, and buildings have been famous throughout history. Egypt is mentioned more than six hundred times in the Old Testament. Joseph went there as a slave and became a king. Jacob's family went there as guests and became slaves. In the New Testament, we read that Jesus went there with his father and mother to escape Herod.

Genesis 38 The Family of Judah

This chapter is probably inserted because Jesus was born from the family line of Judah. All through the Bible, Jesus' family line is recorded, even when the people and events were not respectable.

Genesis 39–41 From Slavery to Power in Egypt

Although enslaved and imprisoned, Joseph never forgot the God of his father, Jacob. Joseph gained the attention of Pharaoh by telling him what his dream meant. Through the dream, God gave Pharaoh, who didn't know God, a warning about a coming famine. With Joseph's help, Egypt got ready for the famine by storing up food during the good years. Pharaoh was so impressed with Joseph that he put him in charge of the whole land of Egypt.

Famine Genesis 41:27–36
A time when for one reason or another (not enough rain, too much rain, bugs, war) very little food is available.

Genesis 42–45 A Beautiful Story
Joseph's reunion with his brothers and later his father, Jacob, has been called one of the most beautiful stories in history. A really touching scene is when Judah, who many years before had suggested selling Joseph into slavery (Genesis 37:26), offered to become a hostage for Joseph's younger brother, Benjamin (Genesis 44:18–34).

Genesis 46–47 Jacob Settles His Family in Egypt
All the events that took place between Joseph and his brothers were part of God's plan to have his people settled and protected for a time in Egypt. Egypt was the most advanced culture in the world at that time. As Jacob left Canaan, however, God gave him a promise that his family would one day return (Genesis 46:3–4).

Goshen Genesis 46:28
Joseph invited his father, Jacob, and his whole family to come to live in Goshen. The Nile River dropped rich soil and moisture there, making it one of the best places in Egypt.

Genesis 48–49 Jacob's Blessing
Jacob split up the family blessing, giving Judah the promise of being the line through which Jesus would come into the world, and telling Ephraim, Joseph's son, that his tribe would become one of the most prominent in Israel.

Genesis 50 Jacob and Joseph Die
When Jacob died, his body was taken back to Canaan for burial. Joseph wanted to be buried in Canaan as well. He made his family promise that when they returned to Canaan, they would carry his bones with them. The belief that Canaan would again be their homeland was never forgotten. More than four hundred years later, when the Israelites were finally freed from Egypt, they carried Joseph's bones along with them (Exodus 13:19).

EXODUS

Freeing God's People from Slavery in Egypt

The book of Exodus is filled with action and adventure. From a baby rocking in a basket in a crocodile-infested river, to frogs in beds and bowls, to hundreds of thousands of people walking between walls of water, Exodus jumps from one amazing act of God to the next. Using a man who survived a childhood boat ride in a basket, God forced Pharaoh to let the Israelites go free. They may have left Egypt, but they didn't leave their troubles behind. Egyptian soldiers, hunger, thirst, and sin were chasing them. But each time God had a plan to save them. Exodus is not so much the story of the Israelites as it is the story of their astounding, all-powerful God.

Writer:
Moses

Place:
Egypt and Sinai

People:
Moses; his brother, Aaron; his sister, Miriam; and the pharaoh of Egypt

Why Is It Important?
The book of Exodus shows how much God is willing to do for his people.

Some Stories in Exodus:
Baby Survives Trip Down River in Basket Exodus: 2:1–10
Fiery Bush Doesn't Burn Up: Exodus 3:1–4
Plagues Fall upon Egypt: Exodus 7:14–12:30
Water Divides to Let People Through: Exodus 14:21–22
People Donate Jewelry to Make Idol: Exodus 32:1–8

Exodus 1 The Israelites in Egypt

Genesis ended with the death of Joseph. Exodus begins three hundred years later with the birth of Moses. During that time, the descendants of Abraham had become a huge nation and had been forced into slavery in Egypt. At first, the Egyptians welcomed the Israelites, but as the years went by, they began to treat them like slaves. The Israelites were forced to work very hard, and the Egyptians were often cruel to them. And at one point, Pharaoh ordered that every baby boy should be killed by throwing him in the Nile River! The Israelites prayed that God would free them from their slavery. God heard their prayers and led them out of Egypt. When they left Egypt, there were six hundred thousand men above the age of twenty, plus women and children (Numbers 1:44–46). That's about three million Israelites!

> **Pharaoh** Exodus 1:8, 11
>
> *Pharaoh* was a title given to the rulers of early Egypt. The famous ones are remembered for their fantastic building projects, especially the pyramids.

Exodus 2 Moses

Moses was born to Israelite slave parents and raised as a royal prince by Pharaoh's daughter. He took a nation of slaves and led them to freedom in the Promised Land, where they were transformed into a powerful nation that has changed the whole course of history.

Moses was from the tribe of Levi (Exodus 2:1). His real mother, Jochebed (Exodus 6:20), kept baby Moses for three months. When the wicked pharaoh ordered all of the Egyptian babies to be killed in the Nile River, Jochebed put Moses in the river as she had been ordered—except she put him inside a floating basket! The pharaoh's own daughter found the baby in his basket and felt sorry for him. Moses' sister, who was watching, stepped in to suggest that Moses' own mom could care for the baby, and Pharaoh's daughter said yes. So Jochebed took care of Moses in his early years before he was sent to Pharaoh's palace. She loved him and taught him all about his people and their God. All the riches and temptations of Egypt's royalty couldn't take away those early teachings. Moses had the best education in Egypt, but it did not turn his head or make him lose his childhood faith.

> **Nile River** Exodus 1:22; 2:3–5
>
> The Nile is a large river that flows northward through Egypt. It flooded every year and poured rich soil and water on the farmers' fields. When this yearly flood didn't happen, crops couldn't grow without that water, so there was very little food.

Miriam Exodus 2:4; 15:20–21

Miriam was Moses' sister. She watched as baby Moses floated away down the river in his basket. Miriam saw Pharaoh's daughter find Moses. Miriam arranged for Moses' real mother to care for baby Moses until he was older. Later Miriam, along with her brother Aaron, helped Moses lead the Israelites.

Exodus 3–4 A Burning Bush

Moses was eighty years old when God called him to lead his people out of Egypt. Moses was unsure of himself and made all kinds of excuses. But in the end he went. He knew God would help him and give him the power to work miracles.

Aaron Exodus 4:14–16; 28:3

Aaron was Moses' brother. He was also Moses' helper, speaking to Pharaoh and leading the Israelites when they wandered in the desert. Aaron was from the tribe of Levi and became the first high priest.

Exodus 5 Moses' First Demand

Moses and Aaron made their first visit to Pharaoh. The king was so angry when he heard their words that he ordered the Israelite slaves to make the same number of bricks while finding their own straw (Exodus 5:10–19). The slaves quickly blamed Moses for the harder work they had to do.

Bricks Exodus 5:6–9

Blocks of sun-dried or baked mud, often with straw mixed in for strength. The Israelites had to make bricks for Pharaoh's building projects.

Exodus 6 Moses' Family

The families of leaders are always important to Israelite history. Moses' family line is recorded in this chapter.

Exodus 7 Plague 1

The Nile River flowed with blood instead of water. The fish died, and people could not drink the water. The Nile was a god to the Egyptians. Without the Nile, Egypt would be a lifeless desert.

Plague Exodus 7:14–11:10

An event that causes suffering or death. God sent ten plagues to Egypt to force Pharaoh to let the Israelites leave Egypt. The Israelites were protected from the plagues.

Exodus 8 Plagues 2, 3, 4

Frogs swarmed out of the Nile and into the houses. Gnats, small biting insects, filled the air. Then swarms of flies covered the people and filled the houses of the Egyptians. Still Pharaoh wouldn't let the Israelites leave Egypt.

Exodus 9 Plagues 5, 6, 7

The animals of the Egyptians died in huge numbers. Then large, painful sores called boils appeared on the Egyptian people and their remaining animals. God gave a warning before the seventh plague so people would have time to prepare. Some of the Egyptians listened and were spared. When the hail of the seventh plague hit, it killed many Egyptians and their animals and destroyed crops.

Exodus 10 Plagues 8, 9

The plague of locusts was one of the worst. They came in mammoth clouds and covered the ground, eating everything in sight. Locusts were everywhere—in jars, baskets, and beds. The ninth plague was the plague of darkness. It was as dark as the middle of the night all over Egypt for three long days.

By now the people of Egypt were convinced (Exodus 10:7). The sudden appearance and disappearance of the plagues—at just one word or action from Moses—were accepted as miracles from the Israelites' God. They urged Pharaoh to free the Israelites, but stubborn Pharaoh said no.

No one knows for sure how long the ten plagues rained down on Egypt. No doubt it would have given Pharaoh great pleasure to put Moses to death. But he didn't dare. With each plague, Moses became more and more famous (Exodus 11:3).

Locusts Exodus 10:13–19

Locusts are large grasshoppers. "The locusts covered the ground until it was black. . . . There was nothing green left" (Exodus 10:15).

Exodus 11–13:16 Plague 10

God ordered the Israelites to prepare for the tenth plague. He instructed them to kill a lamb and brush its blood over the doorways of their houses. When the Lord saw the blood, he passed over their houses. But in each house that didn't have blood on the doorway, the oldest son died.

The cries of the Egyptians that night must have been horrible. Throughout the land, all the oldest sons of the Egyptian families were dead, including the son of the Pharaoh. Finally, Pharaoh agreed to let the Israelites leave. In fact, the Egyptians were so eager to send them on their way that they gave them clothes and articles made of gold and silver (Exodus 12:35). Once the Israelites were gone, the Pharaoh had second thoughts and sent his army to bring them back.

Passover Exodus 12:1–30

This event in Egypt, when the Lord *passed over* the homes with blood on the door frames, was the first Passover. God commanded the Israelites to celebrate Passover every year from then on.

Yeast Exodus 12:8

Yeast is the ingredient in bread dough that causes the dough to rise and become soft and fluffy. Bread made with yeast (also called leaven) takes time. At the Passover, the Israelites didn't have time to let their bread rise, so they made it without yeast. Each year they celebrated the feast of unleavened bread (or bread without yeast) just before Passover.

Passover Lamb Exodus 12:21–23

God told the Israelites to kill a lamb and put its blood on the doorways of their houses. When the Lord sent the tenth plague to kill the firstborn of Eygpt's families, the Lord would "pass over" the Israelites' houses where the doorway was covered with blood. They were saved by the blood of the lamb. Jesus is called the "Lamb of God" (John 1:29). He is our Passover Lamb (1 Corinthians 5:7). Because of Jesus' blood shed on the cross, those who believe in him are rescued from the penalty of their sins.

Exodus 13:17–14:31 The Israelites' Journey Begins

The route God directed the Israelites to take out of Egypt was not the most direct route to Canaan. The most direct way would have been along the shores of the Mediterranean Sea. Going that way, the Israelites would have run into groups of Egyptian and Philistine soldiers. God, in his wisdom, took them instead through the desert of Sinai.

When they reached the Red Sea, the Israelites must have felt like a mammoth red stop sign had been placed right in front of them. Now what? The Israelites saw only water in front of them and Egyptian soldiers behind them. But God had a miracle planned. The waters parted so the Israelites could walk right through the middle on dry land, and then they closed again just at the right time, saving the Israelites and destroying the Egyptians.

Red Sea Exodus 13:18

The large body of water that forms the eastern edge of Egypt. Can you imagine marching out of Egypt, knowing the armies of Egypt are behind you, then seeing only water in front of you? No wonder they "were terrified" (Exodus 14:10)! No bridges or boats for this mass of people. God had other things in mind. He drove all the water back and made a path right through the water. The Israelites walked through, and the ground wasn't even muddy! What an outstanding place for God to (again!) show the Israelites his power.

Pillar of Cloud and Pillar of Fire Exodus 13:21–22

The Israelites didn't need maps or lamps! God led them in his own special way. A huge pillar of cloud moved along in front of them during the day. If they traveled at night, a huge pillar of fire burned in front of them to lead the way.

Exodus 15 Moses and Miriam Write a Song

Moses and Miriam led the people in a song that praised God for saving them from the Egyptians. Then Miriam picked up her trusty tambourine and led the women in a dance.

> **Be Wise—Memorize!**
> **Exodus 15:2** The Lord gives me strength. I sing about him. He has saved me. He is my God. I will praise him.

Tambourine Exodus 15:20

A musical instrument for keeping rhythm. Miriam beat on a tambourine when she danced in praise to God after the Israelites made it safely through the Red Sea.

Exodus 16–17 God Provides

After traveling in the desert for a month, the Israelites weren't in the best mood. They began to complain about what they missed about their old way of living in Egypt instead of thinking about what God had promised to give them in their new life where he was leading them.

Manna for Food Exodus 16:2–4, 31

There were no grocery stores or farms in the desert. The Israelites grumbled and complained all the time about how hungry they were. At least in Egypt they had had enough to eat.

As usual, God had a plan. Food rained down from heaven. The ground was covered with fresh manna every morning when they woke up. All they had to do was pick it up, grind it, and cook it. The Israelites had never seen manna before (and no one has ever seen it since), so when it appeared, they all said, *"Manna?"* which in Hebrew means, "What is it?"

Water from a Rock Exodus 17:1–8
Next the Israelites complained because they were thirsty. God told Moses to hit a rock with his staff. Moses obeyed, and water came gushing out.

Exodus 17:8–16 Amalek
The Amalekites were the first army to try to stop the Israelites after they left Egypt. Joshua led the Israelite soldiers, while Moses stood on a nearby hill and raised his hands to God. As long as Moses kept his arms raised, the Israelites continued to win. Aaron and Hur helped Moses keep his tired hands up, and the Israelite soldiers won the battle.

Exodus 18 Jethro Gives Advice
Moses was an amazing and gifted leader. But he still needed help at times. His wife's father, Jethro, could see that Moses was trying to do too much himself. He helped Moses see that more could be done for the people if leaders were trained to work under Moses.

Exodus 19 God's Voice
Fire, dark clouds, thunder, earthquakes, and the sound of a trumpet came with the voice of God on Mount Sinai (Exodus 19:16).

Sinai Exodus 19:1–2
The desert of Sinai is a triangle of land that lies between the two arms of the Red Sea. Mount Sinai is also called Mount Horeb. No one is sure today which mountain in that area is actually Mount Sinai.

Exodus 20 The Ten Commandments
The Ten Commandments are God's basic rules of life for his people. He wrote them on two stone tablets and gave them to Moses. The first four commandments had to do with the Israelites' relationship with God, and the last six dealt with their relationships with each other. Jesus shortened these commandments into two: "Love the Lord your God with all your heart and with all your

Exodus

soul. Love him with all your mind. . . . Love your neighbor as you love your-self" (Matthew 22:37, 39).

Exodus 21–24 Laws for the Israelites

The laws recorded in these chapters covered every aspect of life. Some exam-ples include laws that required kindness to widows and orphans, the death penalty for murder, and care for strangers. Although many of these laws related to situations we no longer deal with today, the principles they teach—fairness, justice, and mercy—can be applied in every life.

Exodus 25–31 Instructions for the Tent of Meeting

God gave detailed instructions on how to build this tent, which would be the center of Israelite worship and life. The details are repeated in Exodus 35–40 to show that the Israelites followed God's instructions carefully.

Ark of the Covenant Exodus 25:10–22

The Ark of the Covenant was not like Noah's ark. This was a wooden box, cov-ered inside and out with pure gold. Two golden cherubim, which are winged heavenly creatures, faced each other on its top. It contained a jar of manna, Aaron's staff, and the tablets of the Ten Commandments (Hebrews 9:4). The ark was the place where God's presence lived with the Israelites.

Incense Exodus 30:7–8

A recipe of sweet spices that the priests burned in the Tent of Meeting. The sweet-smelling smoke of incense drifted slowly upward just as the priests' prayers moved up to God. Another more practical reason for burning incense may have been to cover up the smell of blood from the animals killed for sacrifice.

Be Wise—Memorize!
Exodus 34:6 "I am the LORD, the LORD. I am a God who is tender, and kind. I am gracious. I am slow to get angry. I am faithful and full of love."

Exodus 32–33 A Calf of Gold

This act of idol worship—so soon after God had spoken to the Israelites from the mountain, so soon after all his miracles in Egypt—revealed just how much the Israelites had begun to believe in the gods of Egypt. This event was a crisis in their relationship with God. He knew this would make them vulnerable to their enemies and lead them away from what he had promised them. They would be safe and prosperous when they listened only to his voice and wor-shiped only him. He ordered a quick and hard punishment.

Moses, reared as royalty in Egypt, now loved his nation of former slaves so much that he offered to take their punishment for them (Exodus 32:31–32), if only God would forgive them. What an amazing man!

Golden Calf Exodus 32:3–4

While Moses was up on Mount Sinai meeting with God, his brother, Aaron, took gold jewelry from the people and formed it into an idol for the people to worship. Worshiping an idol was terribly wrong. God wants people to worship only him—not other false gods or idols.

Exodus 34 New Stone Tablets

When Moses saw the Israelites worshiping the golden calf, he was so surprised and angry that he broke the first tablets of the Ten Commandments. He had to go back up the mountain to receive new tablets from God.

Exodus 35–40 Building the Tent of Meeting

The Tent of Meeting could be taken down and moved as the Israelites traveled through the desert. It served as the center of Israelite worship until Solomon built the temple in Jerusalem. It stood fifteen feet tall, taller than anything else in the camp of the Israelites. It rose above the sea of tents as a continual reminder that God was present with the people.

The Courtyard Exodus 35:17–18

The *yard* in which the tent stood was about the size of one quarter of a football field. The walls were made of brass posts from which linen curtains hung. The entrance, on the east, had colorful curtains of blue and red. The first thing an Israelite saw when entering the courtyard was the *bronze altar*, where animals were sacrificed. Next was the *bronze bowl*, where Aaron and all the priests washed their hands and feet before bringing a sacrifice to God.

The Tent of Meeting Exodus 40:34–35

The Tent of Meeting served as the Israelites' church. When they set up camp, they set up the Tent of Meeting—the Bible calls it a "holy tent"—right in the center of the campground.

The Tent of Meeting had two rooms. Only priests could enter the first room, the *Holy Room*. The sweet smell of incense filled this room. The Holy Room contained three items of furniture:

1. The incense altar was small. Incense was burned there, and the smoke that rose from it stood for the prayers of God's people rising to him.

2. The *lampstand* had to be kept burning throughout the night. It had seven lamps and stood about five feet tall.
3. The *table* was where twelve loaves of bread were placed each week. These loaves reminded the people of how God took care of them each day.

The second room in the Tent of Meeting was the *Most Holy Room*. Only the high priest could enter. This was the place where the holy presence of God resided. A beautiful curtain of blue and purple and red separated the Most Holy Room from the Holy Room.

Only one item stood in the Most Holy Room, the *Ark of the Covenant*. The lid of the ark was made of pure gold and was the place that the high priest sprinkled blood on the Day of Atonement. The lid was known as the atonement cover, or "the place where sin is paid for" (Exodus 37:6).

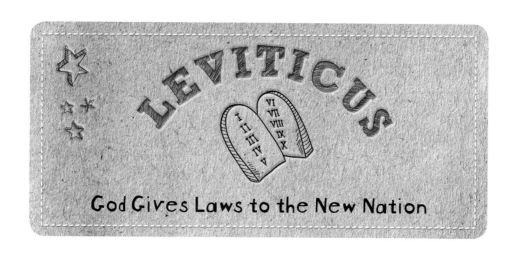

LEVITICUS

God Gives Laws to the New Nation

After all the action and adventure of Genesis and Exodus, Leviticus might seem pretty boring. But don't think that for a minute! As a new nation, Israel had no laws or rules to live by. For many years, the pharaohs had directed every part of the Israelites' lives. They really didn't know how to take care of themselves without someone telling them what to do. So God gave them rules or laws—hundreds of them.

The laws of Leviticus cover everything from soup to nuts. Well, actually, more like rules for worship, rules for being clean, rules for what to eat, rules for what not to eat, rules for how to treat others, rules for how to punish those who disobey—you get the picture. God wanted to teach the Israelites how to care for themselves and how to live good, healthy lives. The laws he gave them revealed that God was interested in every part of their lives. They weren't God's way of making life hard for the Israelites. They were his way of making life *good*.

Writer:
Moses

Place:
Mount Sinai

People:
Moses and Aaron

Why Is It Important?
The book of Leviticus shows that God is interested in you and wants to be involved in every part of your life.

Some Stories in Leviticus:
Aaron Named to Highest Religious Position: Leviticus 8
Sons of High Priest Convicted of Wrongdoing: Leviticus 10

Leviticus 1–7 Rules for Offerings

God gave the Israelites specific offerings for specific reasons and occasions. He knew the Israelites would sin and need his forgiveness. These offerings and sacrifices gave them forgiveness for their sins under the Old Testament law. All of them pointed ahead to the sacrifice Jesus would make on the cross.

Burnt Offering Leviticus 1:1–17; 6:8–13

Burnt offerings were acts of worship. They showed a person's love for God and total surrender to him. A bull, a ram, or a goat could be brought. Even a male bird could be offered if someone was poor. But the animal had to be perfect. The priests burned up the entire offering on the altar.

Grain Offering Leviticus 2:1–16; 6:14–23

A grain offering was made up of flour, olive oil, incense, or bread, but no yeast. It showed a person's thankfulness to God for his daily care.

Friendship Offering Leviticus 3:1–17; 7:11–34

A friendship offering could be a perfect male or female animal. The person making the offering as well as the priests could eat some of the meat. The friendship offering showed the person was thankful to God.

Sin Offering Leviticus 4:1–5:13; 6:24–30

A sin offering was brought to pay for sins and gain forgiveness from God. What kind of animal was offered depended on the worshiper's place in the community. The high priest brought a young bull. A leader in the community brought a male goat. Regular people brought a female goat or a lamb. A poor person could bring a pigeon or a dove. A very poor person could bring a bit of flour.

Guilt Offering Leviticus 5:14–6:7; 7:1–6

A ram or lamb was the sacrifice for the guilt offering. This offering removed a person's guilt for a sin or made the person clean and worthy to worship God.

Leviticus 8–9 Aaron Is Made High Priest

Israel was now an organized nation with an organized religion. Before that time, the head of a household would offer the necessary sacrifices. But now God set aside the family of Levi as priests to oversee the offerings and sacrifices. Aaron was selected to be the high priest. His oldest son would be high priest after him.

Urim and Thummim Leviticus 8:8

Try to say that ten times fast! No one knows for sure what the urim and thummim were. The high priest wore them as part of his holy dress. He used them to discover God's will about important Israelite decisions.

Jesus, A Perfect Sacrifice Leviticus 9:7

All the sacrifices of Leviticus—and the whole Old Testament—pointed ahead to the sacrifice of Jesus on the cross. The Old Testament sacrifices had to be made over and over again. But when Jesus died, all that became unnecessary. What the animal sacrifices couldn't do, Jesus did once and for all.

Leviticus 10 Nadab and Abihu

These two sons of Aaron were sinful. They disobeyed God's rules about burning incense. God's punishment was quick and terrible.

Leviticus 11 Clean and Unclean Animals

Even before the flood there was a difference between "clean" and "unclean" animals (Genesis 7:2). Something that was clean was acceptable to God. It was holy and sacred. Something that was unclean was just the opposite. It was not acceptable, and it was to be kept far from God. Now this difference became part of God's law—the law about what the Israelites could and could not eat. These laws set them apart as God's holy people and distinct from other nations. These laws were also rules or safe boundaries that God used to protect them from harm.

Cud Leviticus 11:3–7

Cud is the food that some animals spit back up and chew again. Whether an animal chewed cud or not was one of the ways God said the Israelites could determine if they could eat the animal's meat. An animal that chewed cud was to be considered clean and safe to eat. God also gave them other instructions on how to determine if food was clean or unclean.

Leviticus 12 Cleansing after Having a Baby

Because there is blood involved in childbirth, a mother needed to go through cleansing after she had a baby. God gave specific rules for how she was to do that. No clear reason is given for why the time of separation was forty days for a boy and eighty days for a girl.

Leviticus 13–14 Tests for Skin Diseases

These rules were put in place to control the spread of infection. These diseases could be anything from simple rashes to the horrible and feared disease of leprosy. Leprosy ate away at a person's skin and caused much suffering.

> **Hyssop** Leviticus 14:49–53
>
> Hyssop is a plant with lots of fuzzy parts to its stem. When it was dipped in the blood of an animal offering, blood hung on those fuzzy parts. The priest could then shake the branch of hyssop and sprinkle the blood.

Leviticus 15 Rules for Being Clean

These rules not only helped the people stay physically clean but also made them clean and holy before God.

Leviticus 16 The Day When Sin Is Paid For

The Day of Atonement is still celebrated by Jews today. It is called Yom Kippur. The ceremonies on that day covered all the sins of the people for the past year. They also pointed forward to the time when such sacrifices would no longer be needed.

> **Sacrifices and Offerings** Leviticus 16:3
>
> These two words appear hundreds of times in Leviticus. An offering is what a person brought to God to gain forgiveness for sin or cleansing from being unclean. The offering was then sacrificed to God, usually by burning it up.

Leviticus 17 Don't Eat Blood

These verses gave specific instructions for draining the blood from meat that would be eaten. God explained to the people of Israel that the life of all creatures was in their blood. This was why blood was used in sacrifices as a payment for sin.

Leviticus 18 Sexual Sins

The people of Canaan lived wicked lives and committed sins that God wanted his people to stay far away from.

Leviticus 19–20 More Laws

God was (and is!) interested in every part of our lives. These verses cover many life situations like taking care of poor people (Leviticus 19:9–10), showing kindness to people with disabilities (Leviticus 19:14), and being honest when measuring things to sell (Leviticus 19:35–36). God wanted his people to live in a way that was obedient and healthy. That was very different from all the people around them (Leviticus 20:26).

Ram Leviticus 19:21–22
An adult male sheep. A ram was brought to the priest for some sacrifices. As with any other sacrifice, it had to be perfect, without any flaws.

Leviticus 21–22 Priests and Sacrifices
Both priests and sacrifices had to be free of physical defects—no flaws or blemishes allowed.

Lamb Leviticus 22:28
A perfect lamb was the most common animal brought for sacrifice. In the New Testament, Jesus is called the Lamb of God (John 1:29). He became the perfect sacrifice when he died on the cross for our sins.

Leviticus 23–24 Feasts and Other Laws
The feasts of Israel were designed to separate the Israelites and their lifestyle from the lifestyles of their neighbors.

Sacred Leviticus 23:2
Something sacred is something that is holy. It is set apart from everyday things and belongs to God.

Sabbath Leviticus 23:3
The Sabbath day was a day for resting. The Hebrew word itself means "to stop, to rest." God commanded the people of Israel to rest on the seventh day of every week. He also said that the land should have a Sabbath—a rest (Leviticus 25:2–4). The Sabbath rest began when God created the world and rested on the seventh day (Genesis 2:2–3).

Goat Leviticus 23:19
Goats are part of the sheep family. They have horns and were used for some sacrifices.

Leviticus 25 The Sabbath Year and the Year of Jubilee

The Sabbath year came every seven years. The people were not to farm their fields that year, giving the land an opportunity to rest. And the Year of Jubilee came every fifty years. That year the people also didn't farm their land, all slaves were set free, debts were forgiven, and all land went back to its original owner.

Leviticus 26 Obedience or Disobedience

God here gave the people a clear promise that he would bless them if they obeyed, and he would punish them if they disobeyed.

Be Wise—Memorize!
Leviticus 26:12 "I will walk among you. I will be your God. And you will be my people."

Leviticus 27 Vows and Tithes

Vows were promises made to God. God wanted his people to be careful to make only vows they could keep. God also wanted his people to give back to him a tenth of everything they earned through the tithe. The clear lesson of tithing is that God is to be first in our lives.

Tithe Leviticus 27:30

A tithe was a tenth of something. A tenth of everything the people earned, whether money, land, or crops, belonged to God. If a person earned ten dollars, the first thing he or she was supposed to do was give one dollar to God. Through the tithe, God was asking the people to always remember that everything they had came from him.

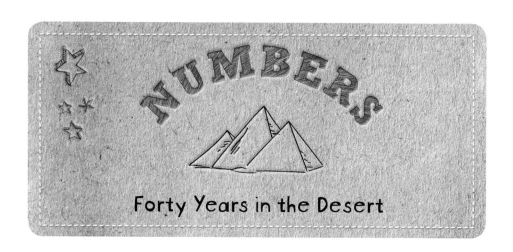

NUMBERS

Forty Years in the Desert

The book of Numbers is just what it says it is: numbers. God numbered (or counted) the Israelites as they began their trip through the desert to Canaan. He began to organize the new nation into an army so they could conquer Canaan. All through the book, the Israelites grumble and rebel against God. God gets angry at them for being so foolish and shortsighted and for risking the incredible plan he has for them. Then he disciplines them to get them back on track before they blow everything. Most of all, he never gives up on them. Again and again, God lovingly forgives their sin.

Writer:
Moses

Place:
In the desert around Mount Sinai

People:
The Israelites and their leaders

Why Is It Important?
The book of Numbers reveals not only God's willingness to reward his people when they obey but also his vow to punish them when they sin.

Some Stories in Numbers:
Food Appears Like Dew on the Ground: Numbers 11:4-9
Millions of Quail Fly over the Camp: Numbers 11:31-35
Twelve Spies Return: Numbers 13:26-33
Snakes Kill but Bronze Snake Saves: Numbers 21:4-9
Donkey Speaks!: Numbers 22:21-35

Numbers 1 Counting the Men

All of the men of Israel above the age of twenty were counted while they camped at Mount Sinai. There were 603,550 men who would be able to serve in the army (Numbers 1:3). This number did not include women and children or the tribe of Levi, the men who served as priests and cared for the Tent of Meeting, also called the Tabernacle (Numbers 1:45–50).

Numbers 2–4 Camping and Marching

These chapters give instructions about where each tribe was to camp and about each tribe's place in the marching order. The tribes camped all the way around the central Tent of Meeting. When they marched, the Levites, with the Tent of Meeting and its furniture, marched between the tribes—probably around two and a half million people! So the Tent of Meeting was protected whether the Israelites were camped or marching.

Tribes of Israel Numbers 2

The people of Israel were divided into twelve tribes; well, actually thirteen. Here's how it worked: The twelve sons of Jacob—with a couple of adjustments—formed the tribes: Reuben, Simeon, Levi, Judah, Issachar, Zebulun, Joseph's sons Ephraim and Manasseh, Benjamin, Dan, Naphtali, Gad, and Asher.

Joseph, who had died in Egypt many years before, had two sons who became leaders of tribes: Ephraim and Manasseh. That adds up to thirteen tribes. The tribe of Levi was the tribe in charge of the worship of Israel. The priests came from this tribe. They received no land in Israel but lived off the offerings of the people. Therefore, the tribe of Levi is usually not counted with the twelve tribes of Israel. Take that one away and you again have the twelve tribes of Israel.

Numbers 5–6 Some Laws

These two chapters record a variety of laws, some dealing with unfaithful wives and others with the specifics of making a Nazirite vow.

Be Wise—Memorize!
Numbers 6:24–26 "May the LORD bless you and take good care of you. May the LORD smile on you and be gracious to you. May the LORD look on you with favor and give you his peace."

Nazirite Numbers 6:1–21

Nazirites were men or women who took a vow to separate themselves for some special religious reason. Three things were common for Nazirites: they didn't drink wine, they didn't shave or cut their hair, and they didn't touch a dead body.

Numbers 7 Leaders Bring Gifts

A leader from each tribe brought gifts to the Lord. Each one brought the same gifts, and each is listed separately here. When you look at this chapter, you may think it's a bit silly to list each one separately, repeating the same things over and over again. But try to focus on the beauty of this twelve-day ceremony. Each tribe is listed. Each tribe's gift is listed. And then all the gifts are added together and brought to God. It's an awesome example of how important each person and each gift is to God.

Numbers 8–9 Levites Are Set Apart

The Levites were set apart from the other men of Israel. They served as priests and leaders in the people's worship of God. When the people traveled, the Levites walked between the tribes and carried the Tent of Meeting and its furniture. Numbers 9:15–23 explains how the people followed God's visible presence in a pillar of cloud and a pillar of fire. Sometimes they only camped overnight and sometimes they camped in one place for a whole year.

Numbers 10–11 The March Begins

The Israelites camped at Mount Sinai for one year. Then the cloud lifted, the silver trumpet blew, and they were on their way. It didn't take long for the people to start complaining about manna. God sent quail for them to eat, but he also sent a plague to punish them for grumbling.

Quail Numbers 11:31–32

A quail is a small bird that flies short distances close to the ground. On this day the Israelites didn't have a hailstorm, they had a "quail" storm—so many quail they could just reach up and pick them out of the air.

Numbers 12 Miriam and Aaron Rebel

The Bible doesn't say exactly why Miriam and Aaron rebelled against Moses' leadership. They blamed his foreign wife, but they also acted quite jealously. Miriam's rebellion was punished when the Lord covered her body in leprosy, a disease of the skin. Aaron pleaded with Moses to ask the Lord for forgiveness and healing. Moses cried out to the Lord, asking him to heal her. The Lord replied that Miriam should be sent outside the camp for seven days in disgrace for her rebellion. After that time, she would be clean and could be brought back into camp.

Leprosy Numbers 12:10

At that time, leprosy was a horrible and frightening disease with no known cure. It made a person's skin scaly and numb. As the leprosy got worse, the skin would fall off and the person would look deformed. To keep the disease from spreading, people with leprosy were not allowed to live in the camp or in towns with healthy people.

Numbers 13–14 Spying Out Canaan

How exciting to be chosen for *this* job! Twelve men got to go on ahead and check out the land of Canaan. After forty days, they came back with glowing reports of the wonderful plants and fruits there.

But then ten of the spies, forgetting the miracles God performed to get them out of Egypt, became afraid of the huge and powerful people who lived in Canaan. They encouraged Moses to turn the Israelites around and head back to Egypt. The other two spies, Caleb and Joshua, disagreed. They knew God would help them conquer the land.

The Israelites were in a serious spot. They were within sight of the land God had promised them, but they were too afraid to go in. God could no longer ignore their rebellion. Because they refused to trust God to protect them, they would never have the chance to enter Canaan. They were condemned to live out their lives and die in the desert. Only their children would experience the wonderful land God had promised. Caleb and Joshua, the two spies who wanted to go forward, were the only ones of the six hundred thousand men over the age of twenty who lived to enter Canaan.

> **Be Wise—Memorize!**
> **Numbers 14:18** "I am the LORD. I am slow to get angry. I am full of love. I forgive those who sin."

Canaan Numbers 13:16–33

Canaan, the land God promised to Abraham (Genesis 13:12–14), was located along the eastern end of the Mediterranean Sea. Anyone going just about anywhere had to pass through or near the land of Canaan.

Numbers 15–19 More Laws and Korah

The story of Korah's rebellion stands right in the middle of a whole list of laws. Korah and 250 of his followers rebelled against Moses' leadership. Moses went straight to God, and the matter was settled quickly. The earth opened, and the rebels fell in.

Numbers 20 The Start toward Canaan

After thirty-eight years of wandering around in the desert, the time finally came to go into Canaan. Right after starting out, when there was no water, Moses hit a rock with his staff instead of speaking to it as God had commanded. His punishment for disobeying God was that he would not be allowed to enter the Promised Land. Moses had rebelled in his own way and had to be punished. He had been faithful for many years, so God did not punish him with death, but Moses did lose the privilege of living in the Promised Land.

Water from a Rock Numbers 20:1–11

It was a miraculous, rocky drinking fountain. When there was no water to drink in the desert, Moses hit a rock and water gushed out from it. Can you imagine that first drink? How wonderful it must have tasted!

Numbers 21 From Kadesh to the Jordan River

Moses led the people away from enemy nations in a long and roundabout route to Canaan. Along the way, the people rebelled *again* and were bitten by snakes. God commanded Moses to make a snake and put it on a pole. Moses followed God's command and made an image from a yellowish metal called bronze and put it on a large pole. When the people looked up at the bronze snake, they were healed of their snakebites.

The Bronze Snake Numbers 21:4–9

Moses lifted up the bronze snake he had made, and those who looked at it were healed of their snakebites. Moses' action pointed forward to a time when Jesus would be lifted up on the cross (John 3:14–15). All those who look to Jesus in faith are forgiven of their sins.

Numbers 22–25 Balaam

Balaam's prophecies were an amazing prediction of how famous the nation of
Israel would become.

Balaam Numbers 22–24

Balaam was a wizard who claimed to speak for the gods, a man with an inter-
national reputation for having the power to curse or bless people. He was also
the owner of a talking donkey (see below)! King Balak ordered Balaam to curse
the Israelites. Balak hoped the curse would keep the Israelites from defeating
his people. Instead, God instructed Balaam to bless the Israelites.

Curse Numbers 22:12

To wish harm or hurt on someone. God didn't want his people to curse him
and ordered severe punishment for those who did (Leviticus 24:10–14). He
also didn't want anyone to curse those he had blessed, as Balaam was asked
to do in this verse.

A Talking Donkey
Numbers 22:21–35

Imagine how surprised you would be if your
dog or cat spoke to you! God wanted to get
Balaam's attention, so he caused the donkey to act crazy—and then made it speak
(v. 28)! The donkey first went off the road
into a field. Then it crushed Balaam's leg
against a wall. Then it sat down in the middle
of the road. Nothing worked—until it spoke.
Only then did Balaam get the message that he
was going in the wrong direction.

Numbers 26 Counting the Men Again

Life in the desert was hard. Only two (Joshua and Caleb) of the more than
six hundred thousand men counted years before had survived. These younger
men, hardened by life in the desert, were different from their fathers. Their
fathers had come from hard but predictable lives as slaves in Egypt. These men
were free, tough, and prepared for whatever lay ahead.

Numbers 27 Brave Daughters and a New Leader

Zelophehad had no sons, only five daughters. These confident and brave
women asked Moses for land in Israel. Only men owned land at that time. But

God showed himself to be above any human tradition when he told Moses the women should be given a share of the land.

Moses, under God's direction, now turned the leadership of the people over to Joshua.

Numbers 28–31 Offerings and Laws

The list of offerings that must be made to God at certain times was very specific. God also gave instructions for special feast days.

Number 32 East of the Jordan River

Some tribes (Gad, Reuben, and half of Manasseh) decided they would settle on the east side of the river. The land was good for grazing animals, and they had flocks of sheep. Moses agreed. But before they were allowed to settle there, they had to go to war and help the Israelites win the land on the west side of the Jordan.

Numbers 33–34 Camps

Each place the Israelites camped while they wandered in the desert was listed in careful detail.

Numbers 35–36 Levites

Unlike the other tribes, the Levites weren't given land in a specific place in Canaan. Instead, they were given certain cities throughout Canaan. The Levites would live spread out among the people.

Moses Gives a Farewell Speech

The title of the book of Deuteronomy means "second law" or "repeating the law." Many laws had been given to the Israelites in Exodus, Leviticus, and Numbers. Now, as they prepared to enter Canaan, Moses reminded them of these laws. The Israelite adults who had been freed from slavery in Egypt were all dead. The people about to enter Canaan were their sons and daughters. Moses wanted to reinforce the laws in their minds. He also wanted to help them understand how they would be expected to fulfill the laws once they were settled in Canaan.

Writer:

Moses

Place:

In the desert east of the Jordan River

People:

Moses

Why Is It Important?

The book of Deuteronomy shows God's love and interest in every part of his people's lives. If they obeyed his laws, God promised to bless them.

Some Stories in Deuteronomy:

Blessing for Obedience: Deuteronomy 11

New Leader Appointed: Deuteronomy 31

Great Leader Dies: Deuteronomy 34

Deuteronomy 1–3 Remembering

Moses recalled the highlights of their trip from Egypt to Canaan and the forty years of wandering in the desert. He made one last request of God. He wanted to be allowed to go into Canaan. But God said no.

Deuteronomy 4–5 Moses Urges Obedience

Moses urged the people to love God, obey his commands, and teach their children his ways. He directed them to stay as far away from idols as possible. And he reminded the Israelites that if they obeyed God, he would bless them. The Ten Commandments are repeated here.

Deuteronomy 6 The Great Commandment

The great commandment was about love. Moses reminded the Israelites that they needed to love God with all their heart, soul, and strength. He repeated this commandment several times (Deuteronomy 10:12; 11:1, 13, 22). Jesus later repeated this commandment (Matthew 22:37).

The Israelites were told not to rely only on public teaching to keep God's word alive. They were to teach their children at home. Because few books existed at that time, God told the people to write his commandments on their doors, to tie them on their arms and foreheads, and to talk about them constantly.

Be Wise—Memorize!
Deuteronomy 6:5 Love the LORD your God with all your heart and with all your soul. Love him with all your strength.

Deuteronomy 7 Destroying Canaanite Idols

When they entered Canaan, the Israelites were supposed to destroy every idol they found. God commanded them to stay away from the Canaanites. He didn't want them to marry the Canaanites or make agreements with them. God's people were to keep themselves separate from all the other peoples of the world. God loved Israel—not because they were better or more important than other nations—but simply because he had chosen them to be his own.

Deuteronomy 8 Amazing Desert Happenings

Can you imagine it? You walk around in a desert for forty years. Food miraculously appears on the ground every morning, your feet never get sore, and your shoes never wear out. Sound impossible? That's what God did for the Israelites.

Deuteronomy 9–10 Constant Rebelling

Moses reminded the people three times that God's goodness to them was not because they were such a righteous people. Far from it. They were constantly rebellious and stubborn.

Deuteronomy 11 Blessings for Obedience

God promised to bless his people if they would only obey him. His blessings were very specific. He promised to give them lots of rain for their crops, good food, and long lives. If they obeyed his commands, he would make sure they won all their battles and gained plenty of rich land.

Deuteronomy 12–15 Some Laws

Moses warned the people that punishments would follow if they failed to destroy all the idols they encountered in Canaan. Sadly, the Israelites did not follow this commandment and brought great suffering on themselves. Moses also reminded the people about eating clean and unclean animals.

Deuteronomy 16 Feasts

All Israelite men were supposed to appear before God three times a year—at the feasts of Passover, Weeks, and Booths. Of all the feasts, the Day of Atonement was the most important. During this feast, the high priest entered the Most Holy Room of the Tent of Meeting, or Tabernacle. It was the only time anyone went in there.

The feasts helped the people of Israel stay focused on God and his rule in their lives. The feasts were religious times, but they were also family and community holidays (sort of like Christmas is for us today). During the feasts, the Israelites rested, celebrated, and enjoyed being together.

Deuteronomy 17 A King Will Come

God said that Israel would one day have a king. He added some instructions and some warnings. King Saul, the first king of Israel, didn't arrive on the scene until several hundred years later.

Deuteronomy 18 A Prophet Like Moses

God told his people about a prophet who would follow Moses. This points not only to all the prophets who later came as God's messengers to Israel but also to Jesus (see John 5:46). God founded the Hebrew nation, Israel, so that he could one day bless all nations through Jesus, who was a Hebrew.

Deuteronomy 19 Cities of Refuge

Six cities were set aside where a person could seek safety (see Deuteronomy 4:41–53; Joshua 20:1–9). Someone who accidentally killed another person could run to one of these cities and would be safe from punishment by the dead person's family. But these cities were a safe place only for those who had killed by accident.

Moses set aside three cities east of the Jordan, and Joshua later set aside three cities west of the Jordan (Joshua 20). All six of these cities belonged to the Levites and were part of the total of forty-eight cities given to them (Numbers 35:6–28).

Deuteronomy 20 Rules for War

These rules covered those who did and didn't have to go into war. Those who had built a new house, planted a new vineyard, or were about to be married didn't have to go into battle. Also, those who were afraid were excused. When the Israelite armies destroyed the Canaanites, God told them to leave the fruit trees alone. A good plan, don't you think? The Israelites would go to live in the conquered towns and could eat the fruit from the trees they had saved.

Be Wise—Memorize!
Deuteronomy 20:4 "The LORD your God is going with you. He'll fight for you. He'll help you win the battle over your enemies."

Deuteronomy 21–26 More Laws

These laws cover all sorts of things, including unsolved murders, what to do with disobedient children, and even railings around roofs on houses. God was concerned with every part of Israelite life. He even wanted to protect little birds sitting on their nests of eggs (Deuteronomy 22:6–7).

Deuteronomy 27 Recording the Laws

Moses commanded the people to write his laws on large stones for everyone to see. Joshua made sure this was done (Joshua 8:31–32). Since there were no books at that time, important information was often recorded on stones.

Amen Deuteronomy 27:15–26

The word *Amen* appears fifty-two times in the Bible. It appears more in the book of Deuteronomy in this one chapter than in any other place. "Amen" is like saying, "Yes, Lord, I agree." Each time the Levites spoke a law that God wanted the people to obey, they answered by saying, "Amen."

Deuteronomy 28 Blessings and Curses

This couldn't be clearer. If God's people obeyed him, he would bless them. If they disobeyed him, he would punish them.

Deuteronomy 29–30 Moses Continues

"Today I'm giving you a choice. You can have life and success. Or you can have death and harm" (Deuteronomy 30:15). It doesn't seem like it could be much plainer, does it? Serving God leads to life; serving idols leads to death.

Deuteronomy 31 Joshua, the New Leader

God chose Joshua to take Moses' place as the leader of the Israelites. Moses turned the leadership role over to him and then reminded him and the people of the importance of reading the law. Moses had recorded the law of God and encouraged the priests and people to read it often. Reading the law brought about great reformation under King Josiah (2 Kings 23) and Ezra (Nehemiah 8). We are all changed when we read the Bible. God's Word is powerful!

Be Wise—Memorize!
Deuteronomy 30:17
Don't let your hearts turn away from the LORD. Instead, obey him.

Deuteronomy 32 Moses, the Songwriter

Moses wrote a song when the Israelites were freed from Egypt (Exodus 15), and he also wrote Psalm 90. He wrote the song recorded here for the people to sing. This song praised God in beautiful and honest language.

Deuteronomy 33 The Blessings of Moses

Moses gave a blessing to each tribe of Israel. This is a lot like the blessings Jacob gave his sons just before he died (Genesis 49).

Deuteronomy 34 Moses Dies

Moses was 120 years old when he died, but he was still as strong as a young man. Not quite superman, but almost! He climbed Mount Pisgah, and God showed him the Promised Land from a distance. When he died, God buried Moses' body in a valley in Moab, but no one ever knew exactly where. The people of Israel mourned him for thirty days. They had never had a leader as strong and awesome as Moses.

Old Testament Feasts and Sacred Days

Sabbath

Exodus 20:8–11; Deuteronomy 5:12–15

God rested on the seventh day when he created the world (Genesis 2:2–3). He also commanded his people to rest and do no work on the seventh, or Sabbath, day. Jews today visit their synagogues on Saturday, the seventh day of the week.

Sabbath Year

Exodus 23:10–11; Leviticus 25:1–7

Every seven years God wanted his people to let the land have a rest. They were not to plant any crops.

Year of Jubilee

Leviticus 25:8–55; 27:17–24

The Year of Jubilee was to be celebrated every fifty years in order to help the people who were poor and make Israelite society steady and stable. In that year, all debts were canceled, all slaves were set free, and all land was returned to its original owner.

Passover

Exodus 12:1–14; Leviticus 23:5; Numbers 9:1–14; Deuteronomy 16:1–7

Passover was celebrated on the fourteenth of Abib, the first month of the Hebrew calendar (March/April today). God wanted to be sure that the Israelites never forgot how he freed them from slavery in Egypt. Just as they had done right before they left Egypt, each family ate roast lamb and bread without yeast. Jewish families still celebrate the Passover today.

Feast of Unleavened Bread

Exodus 12:15–20; 13:3–7; Leviticus 23:6–8; Deuteronomy 16:3–4, 8

The Feast of Unleavened Bread was to be celebrated for seven days following Passover. It was to help the Israelites remember how they had left Egypt so quickly when God brought them out. They were to eat bread made without yeast, get together to worship, and do no work.

Feast of Firstfruits

Leviticus 23:9–14

At the Feast of Firstfruits, the people offered to God the first ripe barley. The celebration helped the Israelites remember that God had given them this rich land to live in.

Feast of Weeks

Leviticus 23:15–21; Numbers 28:26–31; Deuteronomy 16:9–12

The Israelites celebrated the Feast of Weeks by bringing in offerings to God, including the first ripe wheat. It was a time of joy and thanksgiving.

Old Testament Feasts and Sacred Days

Feast of Trumpets
Leviticus 23:23–25; Numbers 29:1–6

The Israelites blew trumpets to announce the start of the Feast of Trumpets! They rested and got together to worship. The purpose of this feast was to present the people before God for his blessing.

Day of Atonement
Leviticus 16; 23:26–32; Numbers 29:7–11

The Day of Atonement was a very special day of rest, fasting, and sacrifices for the sins of the priests and the people. It was held once a year. Today this feast is called Yom Kippur. It is one of the most important Jewish holidays.

Feast of Booths
Leviticus 23:33–43; Numbers 29:12–34; Deuteronomy 16:13–15

It's a campout! During the Feast of Booths, the Israelites lived for seven days in little buildings made of leaves and branches. It reminded them of the way they lived when they left Egypt. It was held after all the crops were brought in, so it was also time to celebrate and thank God for his goodness.

A New Leader and Land for the Israelites

After working as Moses' right-hand man during the years in the desert, Joshua became the leader of the people of Israel. They were ready to enter the land of Canaan—the land God had promised to Abraham almost five hundred years before (Genesis 12:1–3). Many people were already living in Canaan, and God promised to help the Israelites defeat them. God wanted total defeat of these people because they were idol worshipers. The Israelites weren't to quit and allow even a few of these people to live among them. They weren't to marry them or begin to worship their idols. Unfortunately, the people of Israel did not obey God's commands.

Writer:
Unknown, but he probably lived and wrote during the time of the judges

Place:
Canaan, also known as the Promised Land

People:
Joshua, Rahab, and the armies of Israel

Why Is It Important?
The book of Joshua shows how willing God is to give his people strength and courage to do difficult things.

Some Stories in Joshua:
Jordan River Stops Flowing: Joshua 3
Huge City Walls Come Crashing Down: Joshua 5–6
The Sun Stands Still!: Joshua 10:1–15

Joshua 1 God's Promise to Joshua

Joshua must have been pretty scared. He saw how hard Moses had to work as the leader of the crabby, grumpy, stubborn Israelites. Now it was Joshua's turn. No wonder God tells him four times in this chapter to be "strong and brave" (Joshua 1:6, 7, 9, 18). God promised that he would be with Joshua just as he was with Moses (Joshua 1:5). God would help Joshua lead the people of Israel into Canaan.

Joshua Joshua 1:1–8

Joshua became leader of the Israelites after Moses died. Joshua and Caleb had been in the spying party that went into Canaan for Moses. They were the only two who brought back a good report and trusted God. Because of their faithfulness, God honored them. He let them outlive all the others who wandered in the desert, so they were the two oldest men in Israel at that time.

The Jordan River Joshua 1:2

The Jordan River was the main river in Canaan. It still winds back and forth between the Sea of Galilee and the Dead Sea. The tribes of Israel lived on both sides of this river.

> **Be Wise—Memorize!**
> **Joshua 1:9** "Be strong and brave. Do not be afraid. Do not lose hope. I am the LORD your God. I will be with you everywhere you go."

Joshua 2 Two Spies and Rahab

Rahab had heard about the miracles God had done for the people of Israel. Although everyone around her served idols, she was convinced that the Israelites served the only true God (Joshua 2:10–11). When Israelite spies came into the city, she hid them from the city officials and helped them escape.

When the Israelites conquered Jericho, Rahab hung a red cord out of her window. That red cord was a signal to the Israelite army that she and her family were not to be harmed.

Flax Joshua 2:6

A plant with blue flowers. Its stems were used to make linen cloth for clothing. The cloth was cool to wear, something good in that hot land.

Wall Houses Joshua 2:15

Important cities had walls built around them. These walls were so large that houses could be built on them. Rahab lived in a house on a city wall.

Joshua 3 Crossing the Jordan River

The Israelites reached the Jordan River at flood time. Bad timing? Not at all! As soon as the feet of the Levites carrying the Ark of the Lord touched the river water, the water stopped flowing at a place upriver called Adam (Joshua 3:16). The water drained off and left the stony river bottom dry enough to walk on. The Levites carried the ark across the dry riverbed ahead of the people of Israel. God was leading his people into the Promised Land!

Joshua 4 Memorial Stones

Joshua ordered a leader from each tribe of Israel to pick up one large stone in the middle of the river. They carried the stones to the other side and piled them there. The stones reminded the people of what God had done for them as they crossed over into Canaan. When their children saw the pile of stones, they would ask their parents what they stood for—and their parents could tell them how God had helped his people.

Joshua 5 The First Passover in the Promised Land

Finally! The Israelites were in the Promised Land. But they still had to defeat the people living there. On the fourth day after they crossed the Jordan River, they celebrated the Passover. The very next morning, no manna fell on the ground. After forty years, they would no longer need this miracle food.

Jordan River

Joshua 6 Jericho Falls

No battering rams or ladders were required. The Israelites only had to march around the city as God ordered, and he made the walls surrounding the city of Jericho come roaring down. What a way for God to impress on the Israelites that he really and truly was with them!

Jericho Joshua 5–6

Jericho was the first big city the Israelites had to defeat. It had huge, thick walls all around it. It must have been a frightening sight. Even more frightening must have been the way God wanted them to fight against Jericho. *We're going to do what? March around it for seven days? That's no way to fight a battle!* But it was God's way.

These two chapters tell the story of Jericho's mighty walls crashing down. Jericho was about six miles from the Jordan River. Its wall enclosed about ten acres (that's about fourteen or fifteen football fields). All the people who lived in the area would go inside Jericho for safety when an enemy (like the Israelites) attacked.

City Walls Joshua 6:20; 10:20; 19:35

In Bible times most cities were surrounded by walls, often twenty to thirty feet thick. Sometimes a city even had two walls. The walls had gates that guards closed during the night. People farmed outside the city walls during the day and went into the city for protection at night.

Rahab Joshua 2; 6:16–25

Rahab lived in Jericho. Joshua sent men to spy on her city. She bravely hid the Israelite spies on the roof of her house. They rewarded her by saving her and her family when Jericho fell. She lived with the Israelites from then on and was even in Jesus' family line. Hebrews 11:31 names her as one of the heroes of faith.

Joshua 7:1–8:29 Ai and Bethel Fall

Right after the miracle of crossing the Jordan and defeating Jericho, Israel was badly beaten at the tiny town of Ai. The Israelites took only a few men to conquer it, because they thought God would help them in battle like he had at Jericho. But they lost! This was a terrible shock to Israel. It was all because of a man named Achan, who had stolen a robe, some silver, and some gold. Because of Achan's sin, God didn't go with the Israelites. Only after Achan had paid for his sin did God go with the army to overthrow Ai.

Joshua 8:30–35 Reading the Law

Before he died, Moses commanded that God's law be copied and then read to the Israelites after they entered Canaan (Deuteronomy 27). Joshua obeyed that command at Mount Ebal. He copied the law and then read it. Everyone listened.

Joshua 9–10 The Sun Stands Still

Imagine how people would react today if the sun stood still! It happened when the Israelites were fighting at Gibeon. The combined armies of five kings came into battle against them. Hailstones fell and killed many of Israel's enemies. Then the sun stood still for almost a whole day so that Joshua and his men could defeat them all. God can and will do the most amazing things so that his people can accomplish his plan.

Joshua 11 Kings of the North Defeated

Once the five kings at Gibeon had been defeated, Joshua broke the power of the people who lived in the south. Then he gained control over the whole land with the defeat of the kings of the north. The Israelites fought hard, yet it was God who gave them the land with his three amazing miracles—the crossing of the Jordan River on dry ground, the fall of Jericho, and the sun standing still.

Ruins at Gibeon

Joshua 12 Destroyed Kings

This chapter lists thirty-one kings defeated by Joshua and the Israelite armies. The whole land was then under Israelite power except for a few scattered groups of Canaanites. After Joshua died, these people made trouble for Israel.

Joshua 13–22 Dividing the Land

These chapters cover in great detail the boundaries for each tribe, the cities of refuge, and the cities for the Levites.

Tribal Territories

Tribal territories were designated lands given to each tribe of Israel. As the armies of Israel conquered the land of Canaan, each of the twelve tribes was given a specific piece on which to live.

Joshua 23–24 Joshua Says Good-Bye

After Canaan was conquered, the Israelites enjoyed peace. They built homes, harvested their fields, and enjoyed all that God had given them. Joshua was an old man now. But before he died, he wanted to make sure the Israelites understood how important it was for them to follow God. There were still Canaanites in the land. Joshua knew that it would take strength and determination to remain true to God.

Be Wise—Memorize!
Joshua 24:15 "Choose for yourselves right now whom you will serve. . . . But as for me and my family, we will serve the LORD."

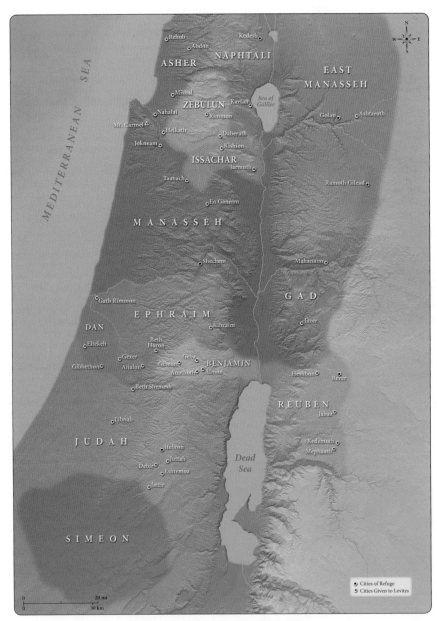

MEDITERRANEAN SEA

Rehob
Abdon
Kedesh
ASHER
NAPHTALI
EAST
MANASSEH
Mishal
ZEBULUN
Kartan
Sea of
Galilee
Nahalal
Rimmon
Golan
Ashtaroth
Mt. Carmel
Helkath
Daberath
Jokneam
Kishion
ISSACHAR
Jarmuth
Taanach
Ramoth Gilead
En Gannim
MANASSEH
Shechem
Mahanaim
Gath Rimmon
GAD
EPHRAIM
DAN
Kibzaim
Jazer
Eltekeh
Beth
Horon
Gezer
Geba
Gibbethon
Aijalon
Gibeon
BENJAMIN
Anathoth
Almon
Heshbon
Bezer
Beth Shemesh
REUBEN
Jahaz
Libnah
Kedemoth
JUDAH
Hebron
Mephaath
Juttah
Dead
Sea
Debir
Eshtemoa
Jattir
SIMEON

0   20 mi
0   30 km

Cities of Refuge
Cities Given to Levites

Map 2. Land Given to the Twelve Tribes

JUDGES

Three Hundred Years of Winning and Losing

After Joshua died, the twelve tribes of Israel had nothing to hold them together except their worship of God. Unfortunately, they continually turned to idol worship. God would punish them by sending an enemy to torment them. After a time, the people would turn from their idols back to God, begging him to save them from their enemy. God would then send a deliverer—a "judge." This sad cycle repeated itself many times throughout the history of the judges.

Writer:
Unknown

Place:
Canaan

People:
Gideon, Deborah, Samson, and Delilah

Why Is It Important?
Judges shows how serious God is when he tells his people to obey him, but that he's willing to forgive if they turn away from their sin and follow him.

Some Stories in Judges:
A Woman Warrior: Judges 4-5
Small Army Defeats Huge Army: Judges 7
The Strongest Man Who Ever Lived: Judges 13-16

Judges 1 Canaanites in the Land

When Joshua and the Israelites entered Canaan, they defeated most of the Canaanites. However, in some places, the Canaanites just wouldn't budge. Instead of making sure they were all gone as God had commanded (Deuteronomy 7:1–6), the Israelites let some remain. Some they took as slaves. Others were allowed to stay in their homes, keep their armies, and remain in power.

Gaza Judges 1:18; 6:3–4; 16:1, 2, 21

Gaza is one of the most southwestern cities in Israel. It was part of the land given to Judah, but it passed from Israelite hands back to the Philistines and back to Israel again. It was one of the five most important cities of the Philistines. Mighty Samson died there.

Judges 2 Idolatry Begins

First mistake. And a big one. The Israelites didn't teach their children about God as he had commanded (see Deuteronomy 6). The Israelites who defeated the Canaanites under powerful Joshua began to die. Their children knew nothing of God and what he had done to bring their fathers and mothers and grandparents out of Egypt and the desert. They settled on rich land and became selfish and careless. They stopped worshiping God and began to follow the ways of their idol-worshiping neighbors.

Judges Judges 2:16–19

Judges were leaders that God sent to deliver Israel from their enemies. They not only helped settle problems between the Israelites but also led Israel's armies into battle.

Judges 3 Othniel, Ehud, and Shamgar

Shamgar (in the north), Ehud (in the middle), and Othniel (in the south) are the first three judges in the book of Judges. Each defeated the enemies who attacked the people in their areas.

Baal and Asherah Judges 3:7

Baal was a Canaanite god. His followers thought he made the land produce crops and made people and animals have babies. Asherah was the main goddess (female god) of Canaan. Her role was similar to Baal's, and therefore many people worshiped them together.

Judges 4–5 Deborah and Barak

The enemies who fought against the armies of Barak and Deborah had one great advantage: nine hundred strong chariots made of iron. At that time, the Israelites had almost no iron. Most of their tools and weapons were made from wood or stone.

But Deborah and Barak defeated the enemies of Israel with God's help. A huge storm buried those chariot wheels in the mud. A woman named Jael struck the final blow by killing Sisera, the enemy general, with a tent peg.

Deborah Judges 4–5

Deborah was the only female to serve as a judge in Israel. When other women were at home caring for their children and grinding grain, Deborah sat under the palm tree that carried her name. The people of Israel came to have her decide their troubles. Amazing Deborah helped Barak lead the armies of Israel against their enemies.

Barak Judges 4:6–8

A leader of Israel's army. When Deborah told him that God wanted him to fight the Philistines, he was willing, but he was also scared. He would go only if Deborah went with him.

Jael Judges 4:17–22

Another brave woman in the book of Judges. She was not an Israelite, but she took a tent peg and killed Sisera, an enemy of Israel. While it may seem pretty gruesome and gross to us, Deborah and Barak praised her act as brave and good.

Mount Tabor Judges 4:6, 12, 14

A mountain in northern Israel where Barak gathered an army of ten thousand men and fought the armies of the Canaanite general, Sisera.

Judges 6–8 Gideon

For seven years, Israel's enemies swarmed into the land in huge numbers. The people lived in caves to get away from the Midianites and made deep pits to hide their grain. Gideon was hiding in a winepress in a place called Ophrah, threshing his wheat when God called him to lead his people. Gideon thought he was too weak, too little, and too unimportant to lead the people of Israel. God had to convince him to do his part.

Gideon led the armies of Israel in battle against their enemies. Following God's instructions, he cut the army down in size until only three hundred men were left. God wanted to be sure the people realized that *he*—not a strong Israelite army—had defeated the enemy. Gideon gave the enemy such a horrible beating that they never bothered Israel again as long as Gideon lived.

Judges 9 Abimelech

Abimelech was the son of a wonderful father—the judge Gideon—but he was a cruel man. He struggled to gain power, killing anyone who got in his way. When Gideon died, Abimelech killed his brothers to gain power. He ruled Shechem for three years and then destroyed it when its people rebelled against him. Finally, he was killed by a woman who hit him over the head with her millstone when he attacked the city of Thebez. When he came near the strong tower to set it on fire, she clunked him on the head.

> **Millstone** Judges 9:53
>
> A tool used to grind grain. A large lower stone had a stick coming up through its middle. A smaller upper stone had a hole in its center. The stick went through the hole. Grain was fed into the hole, and the upper stone was turned against the lower stone. The action of one stone against the other ground the grain for making bread.

Judges 10–12 More Judges

A number of Judges followed closely one after the other. God used them to save his people from different enemies.

Judges 13–16 Samson

Before Samson was even born, God chose him to be a judge. An angel appeared to Samson's parents to give them the news and instructions on rearing him. God gave Samson superhuman strength. His attraction to foreign and dangerous women led to his death. After Samson, Israel was organized under the priest Samuel (also known at times as a judge) and the kings Saul and David.

Samson Judges 13–16

Samson was a judge and a hero of Israel. He had mighty muscles in his arms and legs, but he was pretty weak in other ways. He let several wicked women sidetrack him from following God. Eventually, he suffered for his weaknesses. God answered his last request, however. When Samson appeared to be at his weakest, God's strength poured through him. Samson died that day and took a huge number of Philistines with him.

Lions Judges 14:5–6

Wild animals roamed the countryside during early Israelite times. Samson and David (1 Samuel 17:36) both killed lions with their bare hands. This act was not so much a sign of their strength as it was a sign of God's power in their lives.

Judges 17–18
The Tribe of Dan Moves

The tribe of Dan had been given land that included an area they couldn't defeat. Since they were cramped for room, part of the tribe moved north and settled near where the Jordan River starts.

Judges 19–21 The Sin of a Man of Benjamin

A terrible act by a man from the tribe of Benjamin led to civil war between Benjamin and all the other tribes of Israel. The tribe of Benjamin never regained its strength.

The Beauty of God's Work in the Lives of His People

After all the trouble, disobedience, and death in the book of Judges, the book of Ruth feels like a fresh breeze blowing through the Bible. A thousand years before, God had called Abraham to start a nation. God's purpose was to one day bring a Savior to the world through that nation. In the book of Ruth, the family line of Jesus is established in Israel. Ruth was the great-grandmother of King David. From the book of Ruth on, the Old Testament centers mainly on the family of David.

Writer:
Unknown

Place:
Moab and Bethlehem

People:
Ruth, Naomi, and Boaz

Why Is It Important?
Ruth continues the story of God's plan to bring a
Savior into the world.

Some Stories in Ruth:
Long-Lost Friend Returns Home: Ruth 1:22
A Beautiful Wedding: Ruth 4:13

Ruth 1 Living in Moab

A family from Bethlehem—Elimelech, Naomi, and their two sons—went to live in Moab during a famine in Israel. The Moabites were distant relatives of the Israelites, but they worshiped idols. Naomi's two sons married women from Moab. While in Moab, Naomi's husband and both of her sons died.

After ten years, Naomi heard that the famine in Israel was over. She decided to go home to Bethlehem. Both of her daughters-in-law, Orpah and Ruth, went with her until Naomi insisted that they go back to their homes in Moab. Orpah returned. Ruth refused. Ruth's statement of love for Naomi and her God is one of the most beautiful passages in the Bible.

The people of Bethlehem noticed what a wonderful woman Ruth was. Boaz was one of the people who noticed. Soon Ruth and Boaz got married and had a son. Their son, Obed, was the start of the family line of Jesus (see Matthew 1:5).

Moab Ruth 1:1

Moab was a country on the east side of the Dead Sea near its southern end. The land was rolling and grassy, great for raising animals. The people of Moab, the Moabites, came from Abraham's nephew Lot. He had a grandson named Moab. The Moabites worshiped idols instead of God.

Ruth 2 Ruth Cares for Naomi

It was harvesttime when Ruth and Naomi arrived in Bethlehem. Ruth immediately showed her love for Naomi by going into the fields and picking up the grain dropped or left behind by the harvesters. This is called "gleaning." While gleaning, Ruth met Boaz.

Boaz Ruth 2:1

Boaz was a wealthy and important man from Bethlehem. He noticed Ruth gathering grain in his field. He'd already heard about her and how she cared for her mother-in-law, Naomi. Boaz was related to Naomi. Israelite law said he or another close relative should take over Naomi's property, marry Ruth, and have sons for their family's line.

Kinsman-Redeemer Ruth 3:9

Boaz was Ruth's "kinsman-redeemer," or "family protector" in some translations of the Bible. He took care of her and saved her from living as a lonely and poor woman. In this role, Boaz was an example of Christ. Jesus saved us by his death and resurrection and made us part of his family.

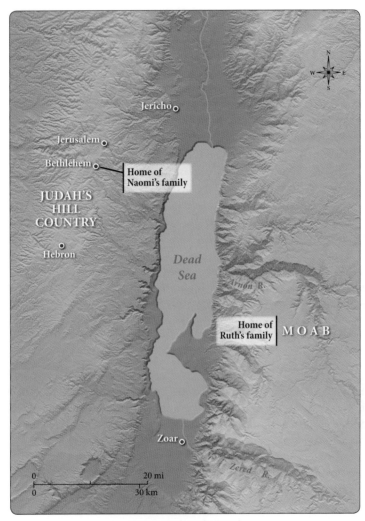

Map 3. Ruth and Naomi

Glean Ruth 2:3

Gleaners, usually women, followed the men who were harvesting a crop. They picked up what was left by the men, keeping it for their own use. Most often gleaners were poor people who had no other way to support themselves. Gleaning was one way God had commanded that the people take care of the poor (Leviticus 23:22).

Ruth 3–4 Ruth and Boaz Get Married

Carefully following God's laws, Boaz offered a man who was a close relative of Naomi the right to redeem (or buy back) her land. When that kinsman-redeemer refused, Boaz bought Naomi's land and married Ruth. They had a son together and named him Obed. He became the grandfather of King David.

Threshing Floor Ruth 3:3

A flat spot of earth where grain was separated from the chaff, the stalks, and weeds. It was usually a place that sat higher than the ground around it, where night winds came to blow the chaff away. An owner would often sleep at the threshing floor when his grain was being threshed to protect the new grain from thieves.

Sandals Ruth 4:7

The most common footwear in Israel. Sandals were usually made of tough leather and tied on the foot with thongs or strings of leather. In early Israelite times, one person would give his sandal to another to signify that the rights to a piece of property had been exchanged.

Ruth and Boaz's Family Line Ruth 4:16–22

When Ruth and Boaz had a son, Obed, their particular family line began. Obed was the father of Jesse, who was the father of David. David became the second king of Israel, and all of the rest of the kings were from his family line. David's family line finally fulfilled its purpose when Jesus, the Savior of the world, was born.

1 SAMUEL

The Last Judge and the First King

As the time of the judges was coming to an end, Israel's history began to make a huge turn in a new direction. Up until that time, the Israelites had been just a loosely united group of tribes who ruled over only parts of the land God had given them. The only thing that held them together was their worship of God. But a change was coming. The Israelite people were beginning to see themselves as one nation, needing one ruler. Samuel was their last judge. The people came to him begging for a king. With God's direction, Samuel anointed the first two kings of Israel—Saul and later David.

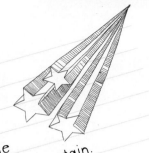

Writer:
Some scholars think Samuel wrote the books of 1 and 2 Samuel, but others are uncertain.

Place:
Israel

People:
Samuel, Saul, and David

Why Is It Important?
The book of 1 Samuel shows a new and important part of the history of Israel.

Some Stories in 1 Samuel:
Woman in Temple Begs God for a Son: 1 Samuel 1:1–20
Philistines Steal the Ark in Battle: 1 Samuel 4:2–11
Israel Has a King!: 1 Samuel 10:17–24
Youngest Son Chosen as New King: 1 Samuel 16:1–13
Young Boy Kills Giant with Only a Stone: 1 Samuel 17:22–51
The King and His Sons Die: 1 Samuel 31:1–6

1 Samuel 1–2 Samuel Is Born

A woman stood alone in the temple and prayed and cried so hard that a priest thought she was drunk. It was Hannah. She begged God for a son. Hannah told God that if he gave her a son she would give the boy back to God for his whole life. God blessed Hannah and her husband with a son, and she named him Samuel. Samuel was from the tribe of Levi—the tribe of priests. Samuel's life was one of the purest and most honorable in Bible history.

Shiloh 1 Samuel 1:3

Shiloh was a city in Canaan where Joshua set up the Tent of Meeting (Joshua 18:1). The people got together at Shiloh to worship God. It was the center for worship in Israel until Solomon built the temple in Jerusalem.

Eli 1 Samuel 1:3; 2:12; 3:1

Eli was the high priest in Israel. He was already an old man when the book of 1 Samuel begins. He served God, but he had two sons who didn't. When he heard that his sons had lost the Ark of the Covenant in a battle with the Philistines, Eli was so sick with grief that he fell over, broke his neck, and died.

Samuel 1 Samuel 2:18, 26; 3:1

Samuel's mother prayed for him a long time. When he was still very young, she brought him to Eli, the high priest, at the Tent of Meeting. Samuel lived and learned and served with Eli. Samuel was the last leader of Israel before they had kings. He anointed the first two kings of Israel—Saul and David.

Be Wise—Memorize!
1 Samuel 2:2 "There isn't anyone holy like the LORD. There isn't anyone except him. There isn't any Rock like our God."

1 Samuel 3 God Calls Samuel

"Samuel! Samuel!" It took a while for Samuel to realize God was calling him. God called Samuel while he was still a young child. Samuel became a priest and the last judge of Israel. He was also a prophet. God spoke to him and gave him messages for the people of Israel (1 Samuel 3:19).

1 Samuel 4–7 The Philistines Steal the Ark

Eli's sons brought the Ark of God into battle with the Philistines. They thought it would help them win. But the Philistines stole the ark and kept it for seven months. During that time, the Philistines suffered terrible plagues. Finally, the Philistines begged the Israelites to let them return the ark.

When the Israelites didn't return the ark to Shiloh, that town lost its importance as a center for worship. Instead, they took the ark first to Beth Shemesh and then to Kiriath Jearim. The ark stayed there for twenty years until David brought it to Jerusalem and built a tent for it (2 Samuel 6:12, 17). It stayed in that tent until Solomon built the temple. No one knows what happened to the ark after the Babylonians destroyed Jerusalem about 450 years later.

1 Samuel 8–9 The Kingdom of Israel

The Israelite people wanted desperately to be like the other nations around them (1 Samuel 8:5). That was not a good thing, especially since the nations around them did not follow or obey God. God wanted his people to depend only on him, not some human king. But God let the Israelites have their way. He knew they needed to be strong in order to survive the attacks of the nations around them. So he permitted them to unite under a king. The first king, Saul, was a failure. But the second king, David, was a brilliant success.

> **Anoint** 1 Samuel 9:16; 16:12
>
> To *anoint* means to pour oil on a person to signify that that person has been set apart in a special way to serve God. Samuel anointed Saul and David to be kings of Israel.

1 Samuel 10–15 Saul as King

Israel's first king was tall, handsome, and even a bit humble. He hid in the baggage when Samuel told all the Israelites that he was their new king (1 Samuel 10:20–22). Saul began his reign over Israel with a huge victory over the Ammonites. Then he made three big mistakes.

First, Saul's success quickly gave him a big head. Saul grew proud and arrogant. He offered sacrifices, something only priests were supposed to do (1 Samuel 13). This was the first sign of Saul's growing sense of self-importance.

Second, Saul gave a silly order for his army to go without food. Then, when his son Jonathan ate some honey, Saul sentenced him to die (1 Samuel 14). It didn't take long for the people to realize what a fool they had for a king.

Next, Saul made his biggest mistake. God had told him to completely destroy the Amalekites—people, animals, everything. Instead, Saul and his army destroyed only what was weak, keeping what was valuable. A huge mistake. God wanted complete obedience. And Saul didn't give it. God rejected him as king.

1 Samuel 16 David Secretly Anointed as King

David had to be anointed secretly. If Saul had known about it, he would have killed him. David was a handsome young man, strong and very brave. He was also a poet and a musician. Saul was as impressed with him as everyone else. He appointed David to be his armor-bearer, not knowing David had been anointed to be king in his place. David's position brought him into close association with Saul and his counselors. What a perfect place for David to be trained for his future duties as king!

David 1 Samuel 16:1–13

David was the second king of Israel—a shepherd, a warrior, a poet, and a harp player. God chose him to be king when King Saul refused to follow God. David was not a perfect man, but he loved God with his whole heart. He was known then and is still known today—thousands of years later—as the greatest king Israel ever had.

1 Samuel 17 David and Goliath

David's position as armor-bearer for King Saul must have been a temporary position because he returned home to Bethlehem. Sometime later he returned to the army's camp to bring food for his brothers, who were soldiers under Saul.

Be Wise—Memorize!
1 Samuel 16:7 "Man looks at how someone appears on the outside. But I look at what is in the heart."

Goliath, a Philistine warrior, mocked the Israelite soldiers every morning. He knew they shook in their sandals whenever they looked at him. Goliath was about nine feet tall, and his armor weighed about 120 pounds.

Then young David came along. No armor. No spear. No training. With only a sling and a few stones, David bravely took on the giant. He remembered what the soldiers had forgotten. The battle wouldn't go to the strongest person but to the one who trusted in God. Goliath fell flat on his face and died when a stone from David's sling hit him in the head. Overnight, David became a hero.

Philistines 1 Samuel 17:1–3

The Philistines were Israel's enemy for many years. They lived in the southern area of Canaan. They constantly bullied the Israelites, making life miserable for them and stealing their land. During his reign as king, David conquered the Philistines, and they never regained their power over Israel.

Goliath 1 Samuel 17

A big bruiser. A giant of a man. A hero of the Philistines, Israel's enemy. Goliath scared all the Israelite soldiers with his huge size and his booming voice. But he didn't scare young David. Goliath fell flat on his face and died when a stone from David's sling hit him in the head.

Armor 1 Samuel 17:4–5, 38–39

Clothes made of metal that soldiers wore into battle. The metal plates of the armor protected the soldier against the swords and spears of the enemy.

Bear 1 Samuel 17:34–37

A wild animal that roamed the woods of Israel. Bears are large and usually eat plants and berries. But they will sometimes attack animals and humans.

David killed one that was going to attack his father's sheep. In David's victories over bears and lions as a boy, God showed him that the power to overcome enemies was from God. This was important later when David fought Goliath.

1 Samuel 18–20
Saul Is Jealous of David

How would you feel? You come back from a war, and the people are cheering and shouting. But then you hear what they're saying: "Saul has killed a thousand men, but David has killed ten thousand men!" David was more popular with the people, and Saul hated him for it. David had to run from Saul.

That was a difficult time for David. But God gave him a special gift. He and Saul's son Jonathan became close friends. Jonathan was heir to the throne, meaning he should become king when Saul died. But God had chosen David. That's a recipe for rivalry rather than friendship. But Jonathan's unselfish devotion to David and David's love for Jonathan form one of history's noblest stories of friendship.

Jonathan 1 Samuel 20

Here's an amazing man. Jonathan was the son of King Saul and a brilliant warrior (1 Samuel 14). He was next in line to be king, and he would have been a good one. When he met David, they became good friends. That was rather odd since it looked like God wanted David to be king instead of Jonathan. But Jonathan loved David and wanted God's way more than he wanted to be king.

1 Samuel 21–27 David Runs from Saul

David ran from an angry King Saul. He stayed for a while with the Philistines, and then moved on to Moab and the southern parts of Israel. He had six hundred followers with him. Several times David could have killed Saul, but he was not about to gain the throne by murder.

While David was running, the prophet Samuel died. All Israel mourned for him. Also during this time, David met Abigail, a good woman in a bad marriage. David moved again to stay with the Philistines and remained there until Saul died.

Abigail 1 Samuel 25

If you like love stories, here's a good one. Abigail was a wise and beautiful woman, but she was married to a rude and mean man. She stopped David from making a big mistake. When she told her husband what she had done, he was so shocked that he died. When David heard that her husband had died, he married her.

1 Samuel 28–31 Saul and Jonathan Die

When the Philistines invaded Israel, Saul was afraid. Samuel was dead, but Saul wanted to talk to him. So he contacted a witch, who brought up Samuel's spirit from the dead. (No one is sure whether Samuel's spirit actually appeared or whether the witch somehow faked his appearance.) Either way, Samuel's news was not good. The Philistines would defeat the Israelites in the battle. Samuel's prophecy came true. And Saul killed himself when the battle was lost. He had reigned over Israel for forty years. It was now David's time to be king of Israel.

2 SAMUEL

David Rules over Israel

Saul, the first king of Israel, had died in battle. Now David, God's next choice for king, begins his reign. He ruled only Judah, the southern part of the Israelites' nation, for the first few years, and then later over all of Israel. Everyone wondered, *Will David be as big a disappointment as Saul?* The answer was a resounding *no!* David certainly wasn't perfect. But he was a man who loved God. Though he had problems with a woman named Bathsheba and with his sons, David followed God throughout his reign.

Writer:
Some scholars think Samuel wrote the books of 1 and 2 Samuel, but others are uncertain.

Place:
Israel

People:
King David

Why Is It Important?
The book of 2 Samuel shows how God continued to bless the nation of Israel, using David to make it one of the most powerful nations on earth.

Some Stories in 2 Samuel:
A City for David: 2 Samuel 5:6–10
The Ark Arrives in Jerusalem: 2 Samuel 6
A Prince of Israel Rebels: 2 Samuel 15, 18
The People Are Counted: 2 Samuel 24

2 Samuel 1–6 David Becomes King of Israel

After Saul and Jonathan died, David became king. But not right away. For the first seven years, David was king over only Judah. He lived in Hebron. David's men and Saul's men fought many battles during that time. Finally, David was crowned king over all of the tribes of Israel. He then defeated Jerusalem and made it the capital of Israel. He built himself a palace, and then built a tent and brought the ark there. He had planned to build a temple also, but God said David's son would have that job. David became king when he was thirty years old, and he was king for forty years.

Hebron 2 Samuel 2:3

Hebron is one of the oldest cities in the world. Abraham lived there. So did David. After Saul died, David moved his wife and family and soldiers to Hebron, and it served as David's capital for seven years while he was king over only Judah.

Abner 2 Samuel 2:8

Abner was King Saul's cousin and general of Saul's armies. He led the revolt against David after Saul died. Later Abner made plans to join David, but he never got the chance. Joab, David's general, killed him.

Jerusalem 2 Samuel 5:6–10

Jerusalem has been called the city of David and the city of God. Solomon built a temple there, where the Israelites came to worship God. Jerusalem is the most important city in biblical history (its name appears almost a thousand times in the Bible) because Jesus died there. In Revelation, you will learn about the new Jerusalem (see Revelation 21).

> **Be Wise—Memorize!**
> **2 Samuel 7:20** "Lord and King, you know all about me."

2 Samuel 7 God's Promises to David

The Old Testament is the story of God and the nation of Israel. God planned to use Israel to bless all the people of the world. The blessing would come through David's family. A great king would one day be born into the family, a king who would live forever and set up a kingdom that would never end. That king is Jesus.

2 Samuel 8–10 David's Victories

King David was a great warrior. With God's help, he defeated all the nations around Israel. Almost overnight the kingdom of Israel under David became one of the most powerful on earth at that time.

Joab 2 Samuel 8:16

Joab was King David's nephew and general of David's armies. He led them in war against Jerusalem as well as against Saul's supporters. Joab led a violent life. He killed not only during war but also during peace. He finally died a violent death himself (1 Kings 2:31–34).

Mephibosheth 2 Samuel 4:4; 9:1–7

Mephibosheth's name may have been hard to say, but he was a prince. His father was Jonathan, son of King Saul. When Mephibosheth was only five years old, he fell down and hurt both of his feet and was unable to walk for the rest of his life. When David became king, he took care of Mephibosheth because of his love and friendship for Jonathan.

2 Samuel 11–12 David and Bathsheba

This story is the darkest spot in David's life. His sin with Bathsheba and the murder of her husband affected the rest of his life. David's sorrow for his sin crushed him. God forgave David but pronounced a fearful future: "Time after time members of your own royal house will be killed with swords" (2 Samuel 12:10). David's sin brought punishment instead of blessing on his family. David's sons and daughters hurt each other, killed each other, and rebelled against their father. David's wonderful reign over Israel was clouded by

constant trouble. God forgave David, but David still suffered from the results of his sin.

David showed that he loved God with his whole heart and was sorry for what he had done. If you read Psalms 32 and 51, you'll get a clear picture of how David felt during this time.

Bathsheba 2 Samuel 11; 12:24

Bathsheba was the wife of Uriah, a soldier in King David's army. When Uriah was gone to war, David brought her to his room. She got pregnant, and David had her husband killed to cover up his sin. She later married David, and her son, Solomon, became king after him.

2 Samuel 13–21 David's Troubles

Big-time troubles now came to David. His son Amnon raped his sister Tamar. Another son, Absalom, killed Amnon. Absalom went unpunished and later gathered an army to rebel and try to gain his father's throne for himself. Absalom's army lost the battle, and Absalom lost his life. David then faced another rebellion, led by a man named Sheba. David's armies won again, and he held on to his throne.

Absalom 2 Samuel 15, 18

One of King David's sons, known for his good looks and lots of hair (2 Samuel 14:25–26). He got an army together and tried to make himself king instead of his father. When his army lost the battle, he ran away on his donkey and got his head caught in a tree. Joab, David's army general, killed him.

Modern-day Jerusalem

2 Samuel 22 A Praise Song

Still, David praised God. Like many of his other poems, this one thanks God for his constant love and care.

2 Samuel 23 David's Last Words

This is David's last psalm. At the end of his life, David didn't think about all that had gone wrong in his life. Instead, he focused on the good things God had done.

2 Samuel 24 Numbering the People

Why it was a sin to count the people isn't certain. God had commanded that they be counted earlier in Israel's history (see Numbers 1:2; 26:2). Maybe this counting showed that David was beginning to trust in the size and greatness of his kingdom rather than in God. There were about 1.3 million soldiers at this time, which would mean the total number of people was probably around 6 to 8 million.

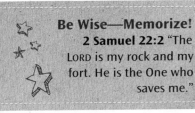

Be Wise—Memorize!
2 Samuel 22:2 "The LORD is my rock and my fort. He is the One who saves me."

Because of David's sin, God sent a plague to Israel. The angel that brought the plague was stopped by God near Jerusalem, at the threshing floor of a man named Araunah. David bought that piece of land and offered sacrifices to God there. God answered David's prayer for the plague to be stopped. David's son Solomon later built the temple on that same spot.

1 KINGS

A Kingdom United Then Divided

Wisdom. Riches. Long life. What more could anyone want? Solomon became king after his father, King David, died. When God came to him in a dream, Solomon asked God to give him wisdom to rule Israel. God answered Solomon beyond his wildest dreams. God made him not only the wisest man who ever lived but the richest as well. But the story isn't so pretty after Solomon died. His son wasn't as wise. His bad decisions caused the kingdom of Israel to divide into two parts—the northern kingdom and the southern kingdom. The rest of the book of 1 Kings records the stories of both of those kingdoms.

Writer:
Some scholars think the prophet Jeremiah wrote the books of 1 and 2 Kings. Others are unsure.

Place:
Israel

People:
King Solomon, Rehoboam, and Elijah

Why Is It Important?
The books of 1 and 2 Kings reveal how God could no longer continue to protect and bless the disobedient Israelites.

Some Stories in 1 Kings:
Solomon Asks God for Wisdom: 1 Kings 3:5–14
A Trial between Two Mothers: 1 Kings 3:16–28
King Builds a Magnificent Temple: 1 Kings 6
Sheba's Queen Visits Jerusalem: 1 Kings 10:1–13
Israel Divides: 1 Kings 12:1–24
Prophet Fed by Birds: 1 Kings 17:1–6
Challenge Won by God's Prophet: 1 Kings 18:16–39

1 Kings 1–2 Solomon Becomes King

Solomon wasn't the obvious choice to follow David as king. His brother Adonijah was David's oldest living son (Amnon, Absalom, and probably Chiliab were dead). While David was dying, and before Solomon was officially anointed as king, Adonijah plotted to seize the throne. When he was discovered, Solomon treated him generously. But as Adonijah continued to try to gain the throne, he eventually earned the death sentence for himself.

Adonijah 1 Kings 1:5–6

David's oldest living son. Many people probably thought Adonijah would be king after David, but Solomon had been chosen. Before David died, Adonijah set himself up as king. He eventually died for his actions.

Solomon 1 Kings 1:38–40

Solomon was the king of Israel after David. He was David and Bathsheba's son. Because of God's blessings on him, Solomon became one of the wisest and richest kings who ever lived. But was he perfect? No, far from it. Later in his life, Solomon's seven hundred wives and three hundred concubines (1 Kings 11:3) turned his heart away from God. A concubine lives with the king like a wife, but the woman is not married to the king in a marriage ceremony.

> **Be Wise—Memorize!**
> **1 Kings 2:3** "Do everything the LORD your God requires. Live the way he wants you to."

1 Kings 3 Solomon Chooses Wisdom

Solomon went to Gibeon to sacrifice to God. The Tent of Meeting was there at that time. While there, God came to Solomon in a dream and told him he would give him whatever he asked. Solomon asked for wisdom to rule God's people. God was so pleased that he also promised to give Solomon riches (1 Kings 10:14–29) and a long life.

High Places 1 Kings 3:2–4; 11:8; 12:31–32

Throughout the early history of the world, people often chose high places to worship their gods. They wanted to be sure their gods could see them. The Israelites also, at times, worshiped God in high places. Before the temple was built, they worshiped at a high place called Gibeon. But after the temple was built, the people were to worship there. However, they just couldn't completely let go of their high places. They continued to worship God—and idols too—at high places in Israel. God judged the righteousness of many of the kings of Judah and Israel based on whether or not they destroyed the high places.

1 Kings 4 Solomon's Power, Riches, Wisdom

Solomon gained the throne of the world's most powerful kingdom at that time. He took part in vast business dealings and became famous not only for his wisdom but also for his riches. Like his father, Solomon was a poet and a writer. He wrote a thousand songs and three thousand proverbs, or wise sayings, as well as works about plants and animals.

Horses 1 Kings 4:26–28

Solomon's twelve thousand horses were used as defensive weapons against Israel's enemies. He stationed them in cities throughout Israel (1 Kings 10:26). He also used them in trade with other countries (1 Kings 10:28–29). At that time in history, horses were used in battle rather than for pleasure riding or farmwork.

1 Kings 5–8 Solomon Builds the Temple

Solomon began to build the temple in his fourth year as king. He built it according to the specific plans God had given to David, Solomon's father. If you read 1 Kings 6, you'll be amazed at the description of the temple Solomon built with its huge rooms and gold walls and tall golden cherubim. Then look at 1 Kings 7:15–50, and you'll be even more amazed by the description of the furniture that went into the temple—most of it was made of pure gold!

Temple 1 Kings 6

The temple Solomon built in Jerusalem was one of the richest and most magnificent buildings in the world at that time.

Three temples were built on the same location in Jerusalem. Solomon's was first. The Babylonians destroyed it when they defeated Jerusalem. Zerubbabel built another smaller temple on the same site when the people returned from their captivity in Babylon. Later Herod built another larger temple on the same site. During his time on earth, Jesus taught in Herod's temple.

1 Kings 9–10 Solomon's Grand Kingdom

Take a look at some of the riches listed in 1 Kings 10:14–29. Gold shields, gold cups, a huge gold and ivory throne, robes, spices, horses, chariots—Solomon's riches amazed everyone. The Queen of Sheba said that people didn't even "begin to tell the whole story about" Solomon's riches and wisdom (1 Kings 10:7). Gold was as common in Jerusalem as stones (1 Kings 10:27)!

Sadly, that time of riches didn't last very long. Within five years after Solomon's death, Shishak, king of Egypt, came and took a lot of the gold away (1 Kings 14:25–26). In fact, Egyptian records show that Shishak and his son

Model of Herod's temple

gave more than 383 tons of gold (that's worth billions of dollars today) to their gods. Probably some of this was the very gold of Solomon listed in these verses.

The time of David and Solomon was the most powerful time in Israel's history. Jerusalem was one of the most glorious cities, and the temple one of the most splendid buildings. People came from all over the world to hear Solomon's wisdom and see his riches (1 Kings 10:23–25).

Camels 1 Kings 10:2

Camels were called the ships of the desert. Camels carried people as well as goods. Camels could carry loads as large as four hundred pounds and travel long distances without stopping for water. The Queen of Sheba came to Jerusalem followed by a huge caravan of camels. Each camel carried rich gifts for King Solomon.

Queen of Sheba 1 Kings 10:1–14

The Queen of Sheba was the ruler of a wealthy kingdom south of Israel. She had heard about Solomon's amazing riches and wisdom and wanted to see them for herself.

Gold, Silver, Apes, and Baboons 1 Kings 10:22

Isn't that wild? You would expect Solomon's ships to bring gold and silver. But apes and baboons? What Solomon did with these apes and baboons isn't certain. Perhaps they were part of his animal studies (1 Kings 4:33) or were put in a zoo or used as entertainment.

Chariot 1 Kings 10:26–29

A chariot is a cart with two wheels drawn by two horses. Chariots were used for battle. Usually a chariot carried two men—a driver and a warrior. Sometimes a man carrying a shield also rode along.

1 Kings 11 Solomon's Wives

King Solomon had seven hundred wives and three hundred concubines (women he lived with but didn't marry), which makes this wise man seem sort of foolish. Many of these marriages were for political reasons, but the idols the women brought with them tempted Solomon. He built altars and high places for them. And he worshiped the false gods. God said Solomon would pay for his sin. And it wasn't long in coming.

1 Kings 12–14 The Kingdom of Israel Divides

The kingdom of Israel had lasted 120 years—40 under King Saul, 40 under King David, and 40 under King Solomon. Solomon's heart turned away from God, and God warned that punishment was near. Foolish Rehoboam, Solomon's son, refused to listen when the people asked for lighter taxes and easier work on royal projects. So the kingdom split in two.

Judah and Israel 1 Kings 12:16–17

When Solomon died, his son Rehoboam became the next king. His unwise leadership caused a split in the kingdom. Rehoboam remained king of the southern kingdom—the tribes of Judah and Benjamin. Jeroboam became the first king of the northern kingdom—the remaining ten tribes of Israel. The northern kingdom of Israel lasted a little more than two hundred years. Assyria destroyed it in 722 BC. The southern kingdom lasted a little more than three hundred years. Babylon destroyed it in 586 BC.

1 Kings 15–16 Kings of Israel and Judah

(For more information on Abijah, Asa, Nadab, Baasha, Elah, Zimri, Omri, and Ahab, see "The Kings of Israel and Judah" beginning on page 103.)

Samaria 1 Kings 16:23–24

Samaria was the capital of the northern kingdom of Israel from King Omri on.

1 Kings 17–18 The Drought

In an attempt to get the people's attention and turn them away from idol worship, God gave his prophet Elijah the power to turn off the rain for three and a half years. No crops grew, and there was little food to eat. Many people suffered. During this time, Elijah was fed by ravens that carried food to him. Elijah was later fed by a widow, whose little jar of flour and jug of oil never ran out, no matter how much bread she made for Elijah and herself.

Elijah 1 Kings 18:6–40

A prophet of God during the reign of Israel's most wicked king, Ahab, and his equally wicked wife, Jezebel. Elijah bravely confronted the priests of Baal, who were supported by Ahab and Jezebel, and challenged them to a contest between God and Baal. What faith that took! Elijah waited all through the

day for the priests of Baal to fail. Then he poured jug after jug of water on his altar and with only a few words called down fire from God. Wow! Elijah proved the reality and power of God with his act of faith. But it had no effect on Ahab or Jezebel.

Elijah was one of only two men that the Bible says went to heaven without dying (see 2 Kings 2). Some people think that because of this, Elijah might be one of the prophets (or witnesses) that God sends to earth in Revelation 11.

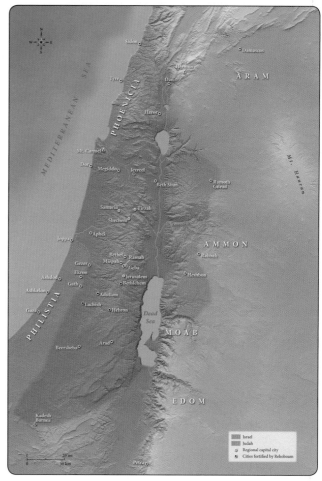

Map 4. Divided Kingdom

Mount Carmel

1 Kings 18:19

Mount Carmel is a mountain that juts out into the Mediterranean Sea. Elijah challenged the priests of Baal to a contest there—and won.

Jezebel

1 Kings 18:4; 19:2; 2 Kings 9:30–37

Jezebel was the wife of wicked King Ahab, and she was terribly wicked herself. She worshiped Baal and tried to get the people of Israel to do so also. She killed many of the prophets of God and threatened to kill Elijah also. She died a horrible death for her wickedness.

1 Kings 19 A Gentle Whisper

Elijah's success on Mount Carmel made Jezebel furious. She said she'd kill Elijah within the next twenty-four hours. Elijah, who had bravely faced all the priests of Baal, now ran for his life. He was tired, drained, and discouraged—so discouraged he asked God to just let him die (1 Kings 19:4).

Instead, God taught Elijah a wonderful lesson. God was not in the wind or in the earthquake or in the fire but in a "gentle whisper" (1 Kings 19:12). It seems that God wanted Elijah to know that sometimes he would work through spectacular events, like those Elijah had just been part of. But most of the time, God would work gently and quietly in people's hearts, urging them to follow him.

1 Kings 20–22 Kings of Israel and Judah

(For information on Jehoshaphat and Ahaziah, see "The Kings of Israel and Judah" beginning on page 103.)

Naboth 1 Kings 21:1–19; 22:37–38

Naboth owned a vineyard that King Ahab wanted. When he wouldn't sell it to the king, Jezebel had Naboth killed and took the vineyard. Elijah brought a gruesome message from God to Ahab. It said that just as dogs had licked up dead Naboth's blood, so dogs would lick up dead Ahab's blood.

Vineyard 1 Kings 21:1–16

A place where fruits, especially grapes, were grown. A stone wall usually surrounded vineyards to keep out animals and thieves. Many vineyards also had a tower, where the owner could stand watch when the grapes were ripe. Some grapes from vineyards were dried and pressed into cakes. Other grapes were crushed to make fresh grape juice and wine.

2 KINGS

The End of Israel and Judah

There were twelve more kings for the northern kingdom of Israel and sixteen more kings for the southern kingdom of Judah. All of the kings of Israel led their people further and further away from God. As always, God wanted his people to worship and obey only him. God even gave them a bunch of warnings, but they continued to turn their backs on him. Finally, as a result of their disobedience, God punished them by sending the Assyrians. The Assyrians destroyed the capital city of Samaria and took the people as captives to other lands. The people of Judah wavered between following God and following idols. But they also slipped further and further away from God. After another 130 years, God sent the Babylonians to punish them. The Babylonians demolished Jerusalem and sent the people of Judah off to Babylon as captives.

Writer:
Some scholars think the prophet Jeremiah wrote the books of 1 and 2 Kings. Others are unsure.

Place:
Israel and Judah

People:
The prophet Elisha and kings Joash, Hezekiah, and Josiah

Why Is It Important?
The books of 1 and 2 Kings reveal how God could no longer continue to protect and bless the disobedient Israelites.

Some Stories in 2 Kings:
Swing Low Fiery Chariot: 2 Kings 2:11–12
Young Boy Revived by Prophet: 2 Kings 4:8–37
Assyrians Defeat Israel: 2 Kings 18:10–12
Angel Kills 185,000 Soldiers: 2 Kings 19:35–36
Babylonians Defeat Judah: 2 Kings 25:1–21

2 Kings 1 Ahaziah, King of Israel

(For information on Ahaziah, see "The Kings of Israel and Judah" beginning on page 103.)

2 Kings 2 A Chariot of Fire

God's prophet Elijah went to heaven like no other person. He was walking down the road with the prophet Elisha, who would take his place. Suddenly, a chariot of fire whipped down from heaven and rushed between the two men. Then a strong wind blew and took Elijah up to heaven. Several signs made it clear that Elisha was God's next prophet. The waters of the Jordan River divided for Elisha, just as they had for Elijah (2 Kings 2:8, 14). Elisha made the water of Jericho drinkable (2 Kings 2:21), and then bears attacked some young men who mocked Elisha's bald head (2 Kings 2:23–24).

2 Kings 3 Joram, King of Israel

(For information on Joram, see "The Kings of Israel and Judah" beginning on page 103.)

2 Kings 4:1–8:6 Elisha's Miracles

Just like Elijah, Elisha's ministry was powerful. A widow's oil supply increased miraculously, so she and her sons had money to live on (2 Kings 4:1–7). The son of a woman who was kind to Elisha was raised from the dead (2 Kings 4:8–37). Elisha threw some flour into a poison stew and made it safe to eat (2 Kings 4:38–41). Elisha fed one hundred men with only twenty loaves of bread (2 Kings 4:42–44). He told a man named Naaman to dunk himself seven times in the Jordan River, and when he obeyed, he was healed of leprosy (2 Kings 5:1–14). Elisha threw a stick in the water and made an ax head float to the surface (2 Kings 6:1–7). Almost every story about Elisha has a miracle in it. And most of his miracles were acts of kindness to other people.

Aram 2 Kings 5:1

Aram was the kingdom north of Israel. David defeated Aram, but it later regained its strength and became a constant enemy of the northern kingdom.

Naaman's Servant 2 Kings 5:2

This young Israelite girl had been captured and made a slave to Naaman's wife. She bravely told her master about God's prophet Elisha, who could heal Naaman of his leprosy. Naaman followed her suggestion and went to see Elisha, who told him how he could be healed.

2 Kings 8:7–15 Elisha Meets Hazael

What a strange scene this was. Elisha told Hazael that he would be the next king of Aram. God allowed Aram to rule over Israel and Judah because of their disobedience. As Elisha met with Hazael, he had a glimpse of the terrible things Hazael would do to Elisha's people (2 Kings 8:12).

2 Kings 8:16–17:6 Kings of Israel and Judah

(For information on all of these kings of Israel and Judah, see "The Kings of Israel and Judah" beginning on page 103.)

Assyria 2 Kings 17:5–6; 19:35–36

Assyria was an enemy of Israel and Judah. It conquered Israel and its capital, Samaria. The people of Israel were sent into captivity in Assyria, and the Assyrian army almost defeated Jerusalem. The only thing that saved Jerusalem was an angel that went through Assyria's camp and killed 185,000 soldiers.

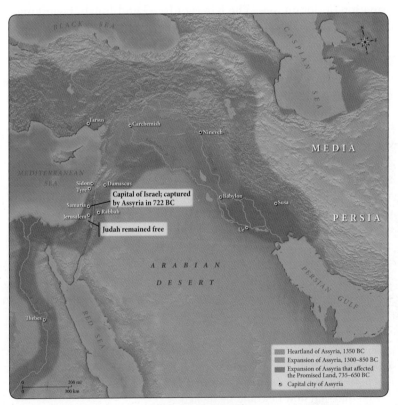

Map 5. Assyrian Empire

2 Kings 17:7–41 Israel Is Destroyed

Finally, God could not ignore the sins of Israel any longer. He allowed the Assyrians to destroy the capital city of Samaria. They took the people as captives back to Assyria. People from other defeated countries were settled in Samaria.

2 Kings 18–24 Kings of Israel and Judah

(For information on these kings of Israel and Judah, see "The Kings of Israel and Judah" beginning on page 103.)

Babylon 2 Kings 24:15–16; 25:7–13

Babylon was the enemy of Judah. When Babylon came into power, Judah was defeated. The Babylonian army destroyed Jerusalem, killed many, and took the rest as captives back to Babylon.

Hezekiah's Tunnel 2 Kings 20:20

King Hezekiah built a tunnel from a spring of water outside of Jerusalem to a pool inside the city. He wanted to be sure that the people had plenty of water if an enemy attacked them. Workers cut the tunnel through solid rock. That tunnel can still be seen in Jerusalem today.

Hezekiah's Tunnel

2 Kings 25 Judah Is Destroyed

As a result of Judah's disobedience, the armies of Babylon arrived and destroyed the city of Jerusalem. They took the people of Judah as captives back to Babylon. Jerusalem remained in ruins for many years.

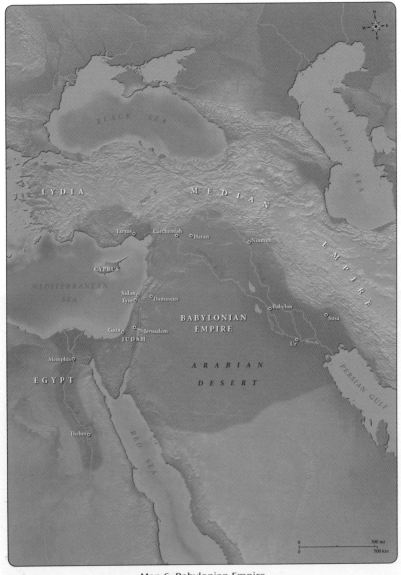

Map 6. Babylonian Empire

The Kings of Israel and Judah

THE UNITED KINGDOM

KING	TIME	BIBLE	GOOD/BAD
Saul	40 years	1 Samuel 9–31	Good, then bad

The longer Saul was king, the more he acted like he didn't need or want God in his life.

KING	TIME	BIBLE	GOOD/BAD
David	40 years	2 Samuel	Good

David loved God with his whole heart. He defeated many of Israel's enemies.

KING	TIME	BIBLE	GOOD/BAD
Solomon	40 years	1 Kings 1–14	Good, then bad

Solomon was the wisest and richest man who ever lived. He built the first temple in Jerusalem. He followed God early in his reign, but then he married many women who drew him away from God.

THE KINGDOM OF JUDAH

KING	TIME	BIBLE	GOOD/BAD
Rehoboam	17 years	1 Kings 12:1–24; 14:21–31; 2 Chronicles 10–12	Bad

He wasn't as wise as his father Solomon had been. His foolish actions caused the kingdom to divide into two nations.

KING	TIME	BIBLE	GOOD/BAD
Abijah	3 years	1 Kings 15:1–8; 2 Chronicles 13	Bad

He was at war with Israel all through his reign.

KING	TIME	BIBLE	GOOD/BAD
Asa	41 years	1 Kings 15:9–24; 2 Chronicles 14–16	Good

He loved and served God.

KING	TIME	BIBLE	GOOD/BAD
Jehoshaphat	25 years	1 Kings 22:1–50; 2 Chronicles 17:1–21:3	Good

He went into battle with the king of Israel against Aram and was almost killed.

KING	TIME	BIBLE	GOOD/BAD
Jehoram	8 years	2 Kings 8:16–24; 2 Chronicles 21:4–20	Bad

He married a daughter of wicked Ahab, king of Israel.

KING	TIME	BIBLE	GOOD/BAD
Ahaziah	1 year	2 Kings 8:25–29; 2 Chronicles 22:1–9	Bad

Jehu, the next king of Israel, killed both Ahaziah and Joram, king of Israel.

THE KINGDOM OF JUDAH (continued)

KING	TIME	BIBLE	GOOD/BAD
Athaliah	7 years	2 Kings 11; 2 Chronicles 22:10–23:21	Bad

The only woman who ruled Judah. She was a horrible woman who killed her own sons and grandsons in order to gain the throne.

| Joash | 40 years | 2 Kings 11–12; 2 Chronicles 22–24 | |

Joash was only seven years old when he began to reign over Judah.

| Amaziah | 29 years | 2 Kings 14:1–22; 2 Chronicles 25 | Good and bad |

Some evil people in Judah killed Amaziah.

| Uzziah | 52 years | 2 Chronicles 26 | Mainly good |

Uzziah got leprosy late in life, after he pridefully tried to do the priest's job.

| Jotham | 16 years | 2 Kings 15:32–38; 2 Chronicles 27 | Good |

He ruled when his father, Uzziah, was sick with leprosy.

| Ahaz | 16 years | 2 Kings 16; 2 Chronicles 28 | Bad |

He worshiped idols and even sacrificed his own son to an idol.

| Hezekiah | 29 years | 2 Kings 18–20; 2 Chronicles 29–32 | Good |

He built a tunnel to bring water into Jerusalem.

| Manasseh | 55 years | 2 Kings 21:1–18; 2 Chronicles 33:1–20 | Bad |

He reigned the longest of any king of Judah.

| Amon | 2 years | 2 Kings 21:19–26; 2 Chronicles 33:21–25 | Bad |

His own officials killed him in his palace.

| Josiah | 31 years | 2 Kings 22:1–23:30; 2 Chronicles 34–35 | Good |

He led the people of Judah back to God when some priests discovered the Book of God's Law in the temple.

| Jehoahaz | 3 months | 2 Kings 23:31–35; 2 Chronicles 36:1–4 | Bad |

He reigned only three months before Pharaoh Neco from Egypt took him captive.

| Jehoiakim | 11 years | 2 Kings 23:36–24:7; 2 Chronicles 36:5–8 | Bad |

He ruled Judah but was under the control of Egypt and Babylon during his reign.

| Jehoiachin | 3 months | 2 Kings 24:8–17; 2 Chronicles 36:9–10 | Bad |

During his reign Judah was defeated by Nebuchadnezzar. Jehoiachin went as a captive to Babylon.

| Zedekiah | 11 years | 2 Kings 24:18–25:7; 2 Chronicles 36:11–14 | Bad |

He rebelled against Nebuchadnezzar, and his kingdom was completely destroyed as a result. He went to Babylon as a captive after soldiers poked out his eyes.

The powerful and beautiful city of Jerusalem was completely destroyed by the Babylonians in 586 BC.

THE KINGDOM OF ISRAEL

KING	TIME	BIBLE	GOOD/BAD
Jeroboam	22 years	1 Kings 11:26–14:20; 2 Chronicles 10:1–11:15	Bad

God gave him ten northern tribes away from Rehoboam. He set up calf worship in the north so his people wouldn't go to Jerusalem to worship God.

| Nadab | 2 years | 1 Kings 15:25–32 | Bad |

One of his own soldiers killed him.

| Baasha | 24 years | 1 Kings 15:27–16:7 | Bad |

He killed all of Jeroboam's family.

| Elah | 2 years | 1 Kings 16:8–14 | Bad |

One of his officials killed him while he was drunk.

| Zimri | 7 days | 1 Kings 16:9–20 | Bad |

He set his palace on fire and died there.

| Tibni | 5 years | 1 Kings 16:21–22 | Bad |

He ruled part of Israel during part of Omri's reign.

| Omri | 12 years | 1 Kings 16:21–28 | Bad |

He made Samaria the capital of Israel.

| Ahab | 22 years | 1 Kings 16:29–34; 18; 20:1–22:40 | Bad |

He married wicked Jezebel and hated God's prophet Elijah.

| Ahaziah | 2 years | 1 Kings 22:51–53; 2 Kings 1 | Bad |

He fell through a window in his palace and died from his injuries.

THE KINGDOM OF ISRAEL (continued)

KING	TIME	BIBLE	GOOD/BAD
Joram	12 years	2 Kings 3; 8:28–29; 9:14–24	Bad

One of his generals, Jehu, led a rebellion against him and killed him.

Jehu	28 years	2 Kings 9–10	Good and bad

He killed Joram and the entire family of Ahab. He killed the priests of Baal and destroyed their altar. But he didn't follow God with all his heart.

Jehoahaz	17 years	2 Kings 13:1–9	Bad

During his reign the king of Aram defeated Israel.

Jehoash	16 years	2 Kings 13:10–24; 14:8–16	Bad

He went to war against Judah and defeated them. He broke down part of Jerusalem's wall and stole gold and silver from the temple.

Jeroboam II	41 years	2 Kings 14:23–29	Bad

He defeated many of Israel's enemies.

Zechariah	6 months	2 Kings 15:8–12	Bad

Shallum killed him right in front of the people of Israel.

Shallum	1 month	2 Kings 15:13–16	Bad

Menahem killed him after only one month.

Menahem	10 years	2 Kings 15:17–22	Bad

He gave the king of Assyria 37 tons of silver to keep him from attacking Israel.

Pekahiah	2 years	2 Kings 15:23–26	Bad

One of his own officials killed him.

Pekah	20 years	2 Kings 15:27–31	Bad

Assyria attacked Israel and took some of the people captive during his reign. One of Pekah's own men killed him.

Hoshea	9 years	2 Kings 17:1–6	Bad

Assyria conquered Israel completely during his reign. All the people of Israel were sent away, and people from other countries were settled in the land.

The city of Samaria was defeated by the Assyrians in 722 BC.

1 CHRONICLES

David Unites Israel into a Powerful Nation

Second verse, same as the first. Well, not quite. The books of 1 and 2 Chronicles retell the stories of the kings—but with a little different focus. The writer wants to be sure the people understand that they are still part of God's plan. They have sinned and been punished, but God has not forgotten them. The book of 1 Chronicles covers Israel's history from Adam to King David. It highlights what is good about the nation of Judah. And it shows the people how God has been with them all through their history.

Writer:
Possibly Ezra

Place:
Judah

People:
David

Why Is It Important?
God wants to be sure his people know that even
though they have sinned, he still loves them and has
a plan for their nation.

Some Stories in 1 Chronicles:
A New King for Israel: 1 Chronicles 11:1-3
A New Capital for Israel: 1 Chronicles 11:4-9
David Brings the Ark to Jerusalem: 1 Chronicles 13, 15
David Makes Plans for the Temple: 1 Chronicles 28

1 Chronicles 1–9 The Genealogies

These long lists of names may seem sort of boring today. But each of these people was important to God and to the Israelites. The Israelites were returning from being captives in Babylon. Since the land in Israel had been divided up by families, the returning captives needed to know what family they were from and the location of their family's land. Those from the tribe of Levi also needed to be identified before they would be allowed to serve in God's house.

Genealogy 1 Chronicles 1–9
A genealogy is a list of a family's members going back through as many generations as possible. It's like a family tree.

Priest 1 Chronicles 9:13; 23:13
God chose all the men who were from Aaron's family in the tribe of Levi to be priests. They worked in the Tent of Meeting and offered sacrifices in the temple, serving both God and his people.

Levites 1 Chronicles 9:14, 19, 29–33
The men from other families in the tribe of Levi had other duties in the Tent of Meeting and the temple. They did things like guard the gates, mix the spices for special holy incense, make the special bread for the table in God's house, and provide music for worship.

1 Chronicles 10–12 David Is King

After Saul died, David became king. David had been a warrior for many years by this time. He had hundreds of strong warriors who were willing to fight with him. The first place he went to fight was Jerusalem. He defeated that city and made it his capital.

Fort/Fortress 1 Chronicles 11:5–8
A fortress is a strong building or tower that can be easily defended in times of war. It was often part of the wall of a city.

1 Chronicles 13–16 David Brings the Ark to Jerusalem

The Philistines had captured the Ark of the Covenant in a battle. It stayed with them for seven months, until the plagues God sent forced them to return it to Israel. The ark then stayed at a city called Kiriath Jearim for twenty years. Kiriath Jearim was about eight miles from Jerusalem.

After David made Jerusalem his capital, he called for a great celebration. He wanted to bring the ark to Jerusalem, but his celebration didn't go as planned. He and the people forgot to follow the rules. They put the ark on a cart rather than having the Levites carry it. First bad move. Then Uzzah put his hand on the ark when it started to tip. Second bad move. The ark was holy—it couldn't be treated like any other old box made of gold. Uzzah died when he touched the ark.

David's great celebration stopped right there. Three months later, after being sure they knew what they were doing, the Levites carried the ark into Jerusalem.

> **Be Wise—Memorize!**
> **1 Chronicles 16:34**
> Give thanks to the LORD, because he is good. His faithful love continues forever.

1 Chronicles 17 David Plans to Build the Temple

David made plans to build a temple for God. After all, he was living in a palace, and God's ark was in a tent! That didn't seem right to David.

God said it was okay to build a temple, but David couldn't do it. David was a warrior, and God wanted a man of peace to build the temple. So Solomon, David's son, was chosen to do the job.

Jesus in the Old Testament 1 Chronicles 17:14

God promised David that someone from his family line would always rule over God's people. That promise was fulfilled when Jesus came. Jesus is from David's family line (Matthew 1:1) and is the king forever over all God's people (Luke 1:31–33).

1 Chronicles 18–20 David's Victories

David, the warrior, fought and defeated many of the nations around Israel. He gained lots of land and made Israel one of the most powerful nations in the world at that time.

1 Chronicles 21 Numbering the People

The first verse in this chapter makes it clear that numbering the people was Satan's idea: "Satan rose up against Israel. He stirred up David to count the men of Israel" (1 Chronicles 21:1). Problem was, David listened. He counted the soldiers when he knew he shouldn't. Because of David's sin, God allowed a plague to be sent to Israel. The plague was stopped when David offered sacrifices to God. He offered those sacrifices on a threshing floor that he bought from a man named Araunah. Solomon later built the temple on that site.

1 Chronicles 22 David's Plans for the Temple

David wasn't supposed to build the temple, but that didn't mean he couldn't make plans for it. He spent a lot of time drawing up plans and gathering materials. The gold and silver that he collected were probably worth several billion dollars. David wanted God's temple to be like a beautiful jewel that sat in the middle of the beautiful city of Jerusalem.

1 Chronicles 23–25 The Jobs of the Priests and Levites

Since the Levites would no longer need to carry the Tent of Meeting and the ark from place to place, they received new assignments. Some of them would watch over building the temple and guard the doors, others would provide music (1 Chronicles 23:4–5). Some Levites would become the officials and judges who worked for David in the government (1 Chronicles 23:4).

The priests were divided into twenty-four divisions, and each division had a certain time when they would serve in the temple (1 Chronicles 24:7–19). The Levites from the family of Asaph must have been especially musical, since they were to provide music for temple worship (1 Chronicles 25:1).

1 Chronicles 27 Other Leaders

David also divided the people in the military and government into groups with leaders over them. Specific people were assigned to manage the jobs that provided the food for the royal household.

1 Chronicles 28–29 David's Last Words

David's final words and prayer concerned the temple. His whole heart and soul had gone into the plans for building it, and he wanted to be sure those plans were carried out by the people and by his son Solomon.

2 CHRONICLES

Judah Continues to Sin

King Solomon's reign provided a time of peace and riches for Israel. The nation was one of the most powerful in the world. Then Solomon died, and his son Rehoboam became king. Rehoboam was not as wise as his father. Not by a long shot. Under Rehoboam's rule, the nation divided. The sad story of the nation of Judah, as it wavered between following God and ignoring him, continues in 2 Chronicles. The people just couldn't seem to stop worshiping their neighbors' idols. And God couldn't bear to see them wandering so far from him. God sent the Babylonians to defeat the Israelites and take them captive. But God didn't forget them. While living in Babylon as captives, the people began turning back to God. The last verses of 2 Chronicles tell about King Cyrus and his order that the Jews could go home.

Writer:
Possibly Ezra

Place:
Judah

People:
Solomon, Joash, Hezekiah, and Josiah

Why Is It Important?
It illustrates how God's promise of obedience leads to blessing while disobedience leads to disaster.

Some Stories in 2 Chronicles:
Solomon Asks God for Wisdom: 2 Chronicles 1
Dazzling Temple Is Completed: 2 Chronicles 4–7
New King Divides Nation: 2 Chronicles 10
Judah's Only Woman Ruler: 2 Chronicles 22–23
Hezekiah Celebrates Passover: 2 Chronicles 30
Defeat in Jerusalem: 2 Chronicles 36:15–21

2 Chronicles 1 Solomon's Wisdom

Before anyone got the wrong idea, the writer of Chronicles wanted his readers to know that all of Solomon's wisdom, riches, and glory came from one source: God. In himself, Solomon would probably have been a great king. But he would never have been as great as God was able to make him—the wisest and richest king who ever lived.

2 Chronicles 2–7 Solomon Builds the Temple

Solomon carefully followed the plans his father, David, had made for building the temple. He built the temple of huge stones, cedar beams and boards, all covered inside with gold. The gold and silver and other materials used to build the temple weighed about 370 tons. All that gold and grandness was intended to honor God. But the kings around Judah wanted that gold for themselves and went to war to get it.

Cherubim 2 Chronicles 3:7–14

Cherubim are angels with wings. Solomon used representations of them all through the temple. Cherubim were a symbol of God's presence with his people, so it was only natural for them to appear in the temple decorations.

2 Chronicles 8–9 Other Things about Solomon

These chapters describe many of Solomon's accomplishments. He built beautiful palaces, sent out ships to bring back the riches of other nations, and built a magnificent throne for himself. He made so many things out of pure gold that people thought plain old silver wasn't worth much.

2 Chronicles 10–16 Kings of Judah

(For information on Rehoboam, Abijah, and Asa, see "The Kings of Israel and Judah" beginning on page 103.)

Shishak 2 Chronicles 12:1–19

Shishak was a king of Egypt. He attacked Jerusalem while Rehoboam was king. He brought more soldiers than anyone could count and defeated many of Judah's other cities before coming to Jerusalem. When the people saw him coming, they prayed to God. Shishak attacked Jerusalem and went back to Egypt with all the gold and silver from the temple and the palace, but the people were spared.

2 Chronicles 17–23 Kings of Judah

(For information on Jehoshaphat, Jehoram, Ahaziah, and Athaliah, see "The Kings of Israel and Judah" beginning on page 103.)

2 Chronicles 24–26 Kings of Judah

(For information on Joash, Amaziah, and Uzziah, see "The Kings of Israel and Judah" beginning on page 103.)

2 Chronicles 27–28 Kings of Judah

(For information on Jotham and Ahaz, see "The Kings of Israel and Judah" beginning on page 103.)

Be Wise—Memorize!
2 Chronicles 29:36
God had provided for his people in a wonderful way.

2 Chronicles 29–32 Hezekiah

Hezekiah didn't have an easy job. His kingdom was a mess, and he had to pay money to keep Assyria from invading. But Hezekiah took care of those things that were important. He destroyed the idols his father, Ahaz, had set up. He reopened and cleaned up the temple. He helped the people begin to worship God again. (For more information on Hezekiah, see "The Kings of Israel and Judah" beginning on page 103.)

Sennacherib 2 Chronicles 32:1–23

Sennacherib was a king of Assyria who attacked Jerusalem. King Hezekiah and the prophet Isaiah prayed to God for help. God sent an angel who put to death all the soldiers in Sennacherib's camp—all 185,000 of them (2 Kings 19:35)!

2 Chronicles 33–35 Kings of Judah

(For information on Manasseh, Amon, and Josiah, see "The Kings of Israel and Judah" beginning on page 103.)

2 Chronicles 36:1–14 Kings of Judah

(For information on Jehoahaz, Jehoiakim, Jehoiachin, and Zedekiah, see "The Kings of Israel and Judah" beginning on page 103.)

2 Chronicles 36:15–23 Jerusalem Falls

The armies of Nebuchadnezzar, king of Babylon, destroyed Jerusalem, and the people of Judah were taken to Babylon as captives. Some of the people who were left behind, including the prophet Jeremiah, ran for safety to Egypt (Jeremiah 42–43).

Sounds like a horrible ending, doesn't it? But it's not. A horrible *time* maybe, but not the *end*. There's good news! Judah's people survived captivity in Babylon. Almost fifty years later Cyrus, the new king, allowed the Jews to return home and even helped them to rebuild Jerusalem.

The People Return to Judah

King Cyrus and the Persians defeated the Babylonians, and Cyrus decided the Israelite captives in Babylon could return home. The people of Judah left and took some of the things that had been stolen from the temple with them. When they got to Jerusalem, their first order of business was to rebuild the temple.

Writer:
Ezra may have written some, and the writer of the
rest is unknown

Place:
Babylon and Israel

People:
Ezra and King Cyrus

Why Is It Important?
God had promised the people of Judah that they would
one day return home, and he kept his promise!

Some Stories in Ezra:
Jews Leave for Judah: Ezra 1–2
Rebuilding the Temple Begins: Ezra 3:7–13
The Temple Is Finished: Ezra 6:13–18
Sin Is Discovered and Punished: Ezra 9–10

Ezra 1 Cyrus Helps the Jews

The first three verses of Ezra are the same as the last two verses of 2 Chronicles. Ezra and Chronicles probably started out as one book.

King Cyrus's announcement that the Jews were free to go home was likely given shortly after the scene in Daniel 5:25–31. A hand wrote on the wall that Babylon would fall to Persia—and it happened that same night!

Persia Ezra 1:1

Persia is a country east of Babylon. Persia gained power and defeated Babylon less than fifty years after the Babylonians destroyed Jerusalem.

Cyrus Ezra 1:1

Cyrus was king of the Persians and led them to victory over the Babylonians. Cyrus had a different idea about how to treat captive people. He let them live in their own lands. Right after he defeated Babylon, he sent out a letter urging the Jews to return to Judah.

Ezra 2 Lists of Those Who Returned

In Ezra 2:64–65, it states that 42,360 Jews returned to Judah, along with 7,337 servants. That makes a total of 49,697 people, plus all their animals and goods. That many people hiking nine hundred miles from Babylon to Jerusalem must have been quite a sight!

Ezra 3 Rebuilding Begins

After seven months of settling back in their homeland, the Jews built an altar for burnt offerings. Then they got together in Jerusalem and celebrated the Feast of Tabernacles. Can you imagine what a great celebration that must have been? They were all together again to praise God for what he had done.

Several months later, they gathered again to celebrate the completion of the temple's foundation. The temple had not been built yet, but the people were excited that the building had begun. At least most of them were excited. Others had seen Solomon's temple before it was destroyed.

> **Be Wise—Memorize!**
> **Ezra 3:11** "The LORD is good. His faithful love to Israel continues forever."

They were pretty sad because this new temple would be so small compared with it. Those who cheered and cried made so much noise they could be heard miles away!

Zerubbabel Ezra 3:8

Zerubbabel was the leader of those who rebuilt the temple in Jerusalem. This second temple is known as Zerubbabel's temple. He was a grandson of King Jehoiachin, the king who was taken captive to Babylon (2 Kings 24:8–16). Zerubbabel would have been king if Judah hadn't been defeated.

Ezra 4 The Work Is Stopped

Work on the temple stopped for fifteen years because the people from other lands, who had been settled in Jerusalem and Samaria after the Israelites left, complained to the king of Persia about the rebuilding.

Darius Ezra 4:5

Darius was another Persian king. Many people around Judah had opposed the rebuilding of the temple, as well as the houses and cities. The kings between Cyrus and Darius did little to help the Jews. Darius, however, took the Jews' side and allowed the rebuilding to begin again.

Letter Ezra 4:7–8

Not the licked, sealed, stamped, and mailed sort of letter that's common today. These letters were probably written in soft clay that was allowed to harden, or on animal skins. Then they were hand carried from one person to another. A series of letters passed between the kings of Persia and the people of Samaria, who didn't want the Jews to rebuild the temple.

Ezra 5–6 The Temple Is Finished

When Darius became king, he allowed work on the temple to go forward. He even gave permission for money to be taken from the royal funds to pay for the work. Within four years, the temple was completed. The Jews again gathered in Jerusalem to celebrate. They offered burnt offerings to God and celebrated the Passover.

Ezra 7–8 Ezra Goes to Jerusalem

There is a gap of about sixty years between Ezra 6 and 7. The temple had been rebuilt. But then Ezra somehow got news that the people's passion for God was decreasing. He went to Jerusalem to teach them God's law and to beautify the temple.

Ezra 9–10 Mixed Marriages

When Ezra got to Jerusalem, he found that some of the men—even the priests and Levites—had married women who worshiped idols instead of God. This was something God had told them again and again that they should not do. The solution (sending the women away) may seem harsh and unfair. But it was effective. Nothing could be allowed to draw God's people away from him again!

NEHEMIAH

Rebuilding Jerusalem's Wall

When Nehemiah arrived in Jerusalem, Ezra had already been there for fourteen years. The Jews had been back home for almost a hundred years, but the wall around the city still hadn't been rebuilt. Whenever the rebuilding would begin, their neighbors would oppose them and they would stop. Nehemiah arrived with the king's permission to rebuild. His excitement and encouragement were enough to fire up the people and get them started again. Ezra taught them God's laws, while Nehemiah supervised the rebuilding.

Writer:
Unknown. Some scholars think Ezra wrote it.

Place:
Susa, the capital of Persia, and Jerusalem

People:
Nehemiah

Why Is It Important?
Because God wanted his people in Jerusalem to finish what they had started, he sent Nehemiah, a good and brave leader, to encourage them.

Some Stories in Nehemiah:
Nehemiah Prays: Nehemiah 1:1–2:5
The Wall Is Rebuilt: Nehemiah 2:11–3:32; 6:15
Ezra Reads the Law: Nehemiah 8

Nehemiah 1–2 Nehemiah Goes to Jerusalem

Pray! That was Nehemiah's first reaction to the news that the people of Jerusalem were suffering. In fact, before he brought the matter up to the king, Nehemiah prayed for four months—from the month of Kislev (Nehemiah 1:1), the third month, to the month of Nisan (Nehemiah 2:1), the seventh month.

Susa Nehemiah 1:1

Susa was the capital of the kingdom of Persia. Nehemiah and Esther both lived there.

Artaxerxes Nehemiah 1:1

Artaxerxes was the king of Persia. Nehemiah was his cupbearer. He gave Nehemiah permission as well as money to rebuild the wall around Jerusalem.

Jewish Calendar Nehemiah 1:1

The book of Nehemiah begins in the month of Kislev, the third month of the Jewish calendar, which falls during our November/December. The months of the Jewish calendar and their equals in our calendar are as follows:

Nisan (Aviv) . . . . Month 1—March/April

Ziv (Iyyar) . . . . Month 2—April/May

Sivan . . . . Month 3—May/June

Tammuz . . . . Month 4—June/July

Ab . . . . Month 5—July/August

Elul . . . . Month 6—August/September

Ethanim (Tishri) . . . . . . Month 7—September/October

Bul (Heshvan) . . . . Month 8—October/November

Kislev. . . . . Month 9—November/December

Tebeth . . . . Month 10—December/January

Shebat . . . . Month 11—January/February

Adar. . . . . Month 12—February/March

The months of Tammuz and Ab are not mentioned in the Bible.

Wine Taster Nehemiah 1:11

A wine taster, called a "cupbearer" in some Bible translations, was an important position in a king's household. This person tasted the king's wine and food to be sure they hadn't been poisoned.

Nehemiah's Jerusalem Nehemiah 2:11

You may be picturing a big city. But Jerusalem at this time was probably more like a small town. It was quite a bit smaller now than when the Babylonians destroyed it almost a hundred years earlier. Nehemiah's Jerusalem included only the eastern hill where the original City of David had stood.

Nehemiah 3 The Walls Are Repaired

This chapter gives a detailed list of all the people who repaired the wall.

Gates of Jerusalem Nehemiah 3

Nine of the gates in the city wall are named here. The wall was smaller than the one that had circled Solomon's Jerusalem, but some of the gates were the same.

Nehemiah 4–6 The Wall Is Built

Old enemies of the Jews as well as the Samaritans (people from other defeated lands, who had been settled in Samaria when the northern kingdom was defeated; 2 Kings 17:24) didn't want the Jews to rebuild the wall. They came to fight and stop the building. But Nehemiah was smarter than they were. He carefully arranged and armed the builders so the work could continue. They worked day and night, holding their tools in one hand and their weapons in the other. They finished building the wall in only fifty-two days! Almost 150 years after it was destroyed, Jerusalem was once again a city with a wall to protect it.

Nehemiah 7–8 Reading the Law

The Jews had church for seven days in a row! All morning long! But the people didn't seem to mind. They were eager to hear God's law and understand it. Ezra and his helpers read the law and explained it to the people. When they understood, the people were sad. They realized how sinful they had been and how much they now wanted to live for God.

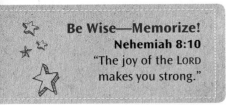

Be Wise—Memorize!
Nehemiah 8:10
"The joy of the LORD makes you strong."

While they were sobbing and moaning out loud, Nehemiah got their attention. He told them something amazing—stop crying and remember that the joy of the Lord is what makes you strong.

Nehemiah 9–10 Dedicating the People

The people got together in Jerusalem to review their history, including their tendency to sin and God's willingness to forgive. Then they agreed together to obey God from then on. They were so serious about it that they signed their names to a written agreement.

Jeshua, Bebai, Adin, Bezai, and Mijamin signed the agreement along with eighty-one others. You don't know who these people are? Neither does anyone else. The only thing we know about most of them is that they signed an obedience agreement. That's really quite astonishing! Today we still have the names of eighty-four people who agreed to follow God more than twenty-five hundred years ago.

After signing the agreement, the people dedicated the wall. Then they assigned one person out of every ten to live inside the city. With Nehemiah's help, they organized their government and the temple services.

Be Wise—Memorize!
Nehemiah 9:17 "You are a God who forgives. You are gracious. You are tender and kind. You are slow to get angry. You are full of love."

Nehemiah 11–12 Dedicating the Wall

Finally, Jerusalem was a nice city with a new wall. But not too many people wanted to live there. The people knew their neighbors had been opposed to their rebuilding project and many probably thought that it wasn't a safe place to live. But Jerusalem was an important city just the same—important enough that God said one out of every ten people should live there. They threw lots to decide who those people would be. Then they dedicated the wall.

Nehemiah 13 Final Warnings and Charges

Nehemiah reminded the people how important it is to obey God's laws. He reminded them to give one-tenth of their income to God and to obey the rules of the Sabbath. He also reminded them of the dangers of marrying women who worshiped idols.

ESTHER

Saved by the Queen

Y ou've heard of "saved by the bell"? The Jews living in Susa during this time were saved by the queen. Xerxes had chosen Esther, a Jewish woman, as his queen. When she realized that Haman, one of Xerxes' officials, planned to kill all the Jews, she risked her life to save her people. She went to the king, even though he could kill her for doing it, and revealed Haman's horrible plan. Her people were saved because of her brave actions.

God's name is not mentioned in the book of Esther. But that doesn't mean he isn't there. His care of his people is clear throughout the story.

Writer:
Unknown

Place:
Susa, the capital of Persia

People:
Mordecai, Esther, Xerxes, and Haman

Why Is It Important?
The book of Esther is important because it shows God's work to save his people. If Esther hadn't been willing to go to the king, the Jews in Persia all would have been killed. If they all had been killed, there would have been no Jesus. If Jesus hadn't been born, there would be no salvation.

Some Stories in Esther:
Queen Vashti Dethroned: Esther 1
A New Queen Named Esther: Esther 2:1–18
A Plot to Kill the Jews: Esther 3
Queen Esther Saves Her People: Esther 5:1–8; 7

Esther 1 Queen Vashti Removed

Xerxes gave a great banquet and asked his queen to show herself to all the men who had gathered there. It is not known why Vashti refused. But she did. And Xerxes removed her as his queen.

Xerxes Esther 1:1

Xerxes was the king over the huge kingdom of Persia. He took beautiful young Esther as his queen, not knowing that she was Jewish. During his reign, an official named Haman planned to kill all the Jews. But the Jews were saved when Xerxes' queen, Esther, bravely revealed the plot and the fact that she was a Jew.

Esther 2 Esther Becomes Queen

Perfumes, oils, baths—each young woman had to go through twelve full months of beauty treatments before she could go to the king. Many beautiful young women were brought to Susa in the search for a new queen. Esther was one of those young women. The women probably didn't have a choice in the matter, but Esther made the best of the situation. She was soon a favorite with the man in charge—and she proved to be Xerxes' favorite too. When Esther went to the king, his search was over. He was so pleased with her that he made her his queen.

Mordecai Esther 2:5–7

Mordecai was a Jew who had been taken as a captive to Babylon when Jerusalem was defeated. He served God faithfully, even in this foreign country. He also reared his cousin Hadassah (Esther) as his own daughter. Both of her parents were dead.

Esther Esther 2:7

Esther was this young woman's Persian name. Her Hebrew name was Hadassah. She kept her Jewish background a secret until Haman plotted to kill all of her people. Then she had to tell the king that she was a Jew in order to save them.

> **Be Wise—Memorize!**
> **Esther 4:16** "I'll go to the king. I'll do it even though it's against the law. And if I have to die, I'll die."

Esther 3–7 Haman's Plot

Haman was a high official in the court of Xerxes of Persia. He hated Mordecai, who was Esther's cousin and an official in Xerxes' kingdom. Haman hated Mordecai so much that he plotted not only to kill him but also to kill all of the Jews. This was in Xerxes' twelfth year as king and probably Esther's fifth year as queen. Esther knew Xerxes could have her killed for coming to him without being called. But she went anyway in order to save her people.

The king was obviously still pleased with Esther. He not only didn't have her killed, but he said he'd give her anything she wanted. When Xerxes and Haman had dinner with Esther, Haman's plot was uncovered, he was hanged, and his place of honor was given to Mordecai.

Haman Esther 6:6

Haman was an important official in King Xerxes' government—but it seems he thought a little too highly of himself. One time, Xerxes asked Haman how to honor a man who had served the king well. Haman assumed *he* was the man the king had in mind, so he suggested showy honors including fancy clothing and a parade with the king's own horse. It turns out the king wanted to honor Mordecai, who Haman hated. And Haman got the job of leading Mordecai's parade!

Seal Esther 3:10; 8:2

A seal was a tool that could be pressed into soft clay or wax in order to leave an impression or picture. The king's seal was a sign of his approval and authority. Some seals were carried on a cord around the neck, but most were finger rings.

Esther 8–9 The Jews Are Saved

Since an order given by a Persian king could not be changed (Esther 8:8), the order to kill all the Jews could not be taken back. However, the king sent out another order that the Jews could resist and even kill those who attacked them. Esther's actions saved the Jews from being wiped out. She was not only a beautiful woman, but also a wise and brave queen. The Feast of Purim celebrates the Jews' escape from death during Esther's time.

Purim Esther 9:26

Purim is a Jewish holiday celebrated to this day. It recalls the day when the Jews were saved from Haman's murderous plot. The word comes from the Persian word for "lot"—*pur.*

Esther 10 Mordecai's Greatness

Mordecai became more and more powerful in Persia. He was second only to King Xerxes. His acts were written down in the records of the kings of Persia. Mordecai and Esther set the stage for the work of Ezra and Nehemiah. Their relationship with Xerxes caused him to be kind to the Jews in Persia as well as in Israel.

JOB

Why We Suffer

Suffering. It's a problem not just because it hurts but also because it makes people wonder why a loving God would allow people to suffer. Few people suffered as greatly as Job. All his wealth, his family, and even his health were stripped away from him, leaving him to search for answers. He had loved and served God his whole life. Why would God let him suffer so horribly? Job looked at the problem of suffering with fierce honesty. The answers were not always clear, but God was with Job through it all. He loved Job. And Job remained faithful to God.

Writer:

Unknown

Place:

Uz

People:

Job

Why Is It Important?

At one time or another, everyone suffers. And everyone asks the same question: Why? Why does a good God allow people who love him to suffer? Though Job gets no clear answer to his question, he does get God's promise that he is with him even in his suffering.

Some Stories in Job:

Job Loses His Family, Wealth, and Health: Job 1:1–2:10

Job's Friends Arrive: Job 2:11–13

God Speaks to Job: Job 38–41

Job Gets Back What He Has Lost: Job 42

Job 1:1–2:10 Job Is Tested

Job was a prince in his land—a rich man with plenty of power. He was famous for his honesty and his faith in God. When he suddenly lost all his wealth, as well as his family and his health, Job was stunned as were all those around him.

Satan said Job followed God only because God had given him good things. God said Job would be faithful no matter what. The test began. Would Job remain faithful even when everything was taken from him? Who would be right about Job? Satan or God?

We know, of course, that God won this contest. Job remained faithful, just as God said he would.

Uz Job 1:1

No one knows for sure where Uz was. It may have been near the Sea of Galilee or in the desert of Arabia, about two hundred miles east of Petra.

Oxen Job 1:3; 42:12

Oxen are animals similar to cattle that were used for food as well as for plowing the fields. Oxen are large and strong and can pull heavy loads. Two are usually yoked together for plowing. Job had five hundred pairs of oxen before his suffering and a thousand pairs after.

Job 2:11–13 Job's Friends

Three of Job's friends came quickly when they heard of his troubles. At first they sat with him and didn't say a word. They realized that Job's suffering was so great that words would not help. When Job began to speak, however, his friends responded. That's when the trouble started. Their words showed their lack of compassion as well as their lack of understanding.

Job's Wife Job 2:9–10

Job's wife urged him to curse God and die. That doesn't make her look very good next to Job, who answered her quickly by saying, "We accept good things from God. So we should also accept trouble when he sends it."

Eliphaz Job 2:11

Eliphaz was the first of Job's friends who came to comfort him but then argued with him. Eliphaz was from Teman, a place famous for its wise men. Teman was part of the country of Edom, located south of the Dead Sea.

Bildad Job 2:11

Bildad was the second of Job's friends. He also came to comfort Job. Bildad was from the family of Shuah, a son of Abraham by his second wife, Keturah (Genesis 25:2).

Zophar Job 2:11

Zophar was the third of Job's friends who came to comfort him. He ended up arguing as much as comforting.

Job 3 Job Complains

Job's suffering was so horrible that he wished he had never been born. He simply wanted to die.

Job 4–14 The First Group of Speeches

Job 4–5
Eliphaz told Job to turn to God. He said that if Job would repent of his sins, his troubles would disappear.

Job 6–7
Job answered by saying he was disappointed in his friends. He needed help— not arguments or disapproval. Job felt like he was in a daze. He knew he was not a wicked man. He couldn't understand why all those bad things had happened. Even if he had sinned, certainly he hadn't done something that deserved such a harsh punishment! He prayed to die.

Job 8
Bildad insisted that God is just. Job must have been suffering because of some sin. If he would turn to God, all would be well again.

Job 9–10
Again Job answered, "Not guilty!" He knew God allowed hardship in the lives of the faithful and the wicked. Again he complained and wished he had never been born.

138

Job 11
Zophar entered the argument with cruel words: Job was being punished even less than he actually deserved. If Job would just ask for God's forgiveness, the good life would return.

Job 12–14
Now Job began to sound sarcastic. What did these men know anyway? Did they really think they were so wise? Nothing they said helped to answer his questions. Job then called on God to speak and tell him what he had done to deserve so much suffering.

Job 15–21 The Second Group of Speeches

Job 15
Eliphaz spoke again. The argument became more heated, but the accusation remained the same—Job was being punished for his sins.

Job 16–17
Job told his friends that if they were suffering, he would not be so unkind to them. He would comfort them instead. He knew that only those who have suffered can truly help those who are suffering.

Job 18
Bildad spoke again. He was angry with Job and tried to frighten him into repenting of his sin by picturing the terrible future of the wicked.

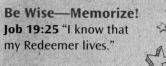

Be Wise—Memorize!
Job 19:25 "I know that my Redeemer lives."

Job 19
Job reached the bottom. His friends didn't understand. His wife didn't understand. But right when Job was at his lowest, he turned a corner. He looked to his future instead of his past. He knew he could still trust God. He burst out with one of the most beautiful expressions of faith in the Bible: "I know that my Redeemer lives!"

Job 20
Zophar was still angry and worried that Job would die in his wickedness. He followed the pattern of the other friends and pictured the horrible fate in store for the wicked.

Job 21
Job agreed that the wicked would suffer in the end. But in the meantime, they seemed to be doing pretty well. If God sent suffering in order to punish sin—as Job's friends claimed—why were the wicked enjoying life and growing richer? Job didn't feel that their arguments held up.

Jesus, Redeemer Job 19:25

Job's hopelessness suddenly gave way to hope. He expressed his faith with words that looked to the future rather than the past. He knew he had a Redeemer, one who would save him. Job's words gave us a glimpse of the Savior of the world, who would come and be the Redeemer, the Savior, of all who believed in him.

Job 22–27 The Third Group of Speeches

Job 22
Eliphaz came down even harder on Job—still insisting that he was a wicked man. He claimed that Job had mistreated the poor around him.

Job 23–24
Job again defended himself. He loved God's words and had obeyed them all his life.

Job 25
Bildad gave another short speech but added little to the argument. Neither side would give in, and the debate fizzled out. Zophar didn't even bother to speak again.

Job 26–27
Job stated his problem as bluntly as he could. It might have looked like he was being punished for sin. But, he said, "I'll never admit you people are right. Until I die, I'll say I'm telling the truth" (Job 27:5).

Job 28 A Question on Wisdom

Job continued to speak, but his tone changed. Job 28 is much like the book of Proverbs—a question about where wisdom can be found.

Job 29–31 Job Winds Down

Job doesn't sound quite as angry in these chapters as in earlier ones. He sounded sad. He contrasted his past riches, happiness, kindness, and usefulness with his present sufferings. Then he tiredly asked God to *please* tell him if he was actually guilty of any of the things his friends said he was. Job was finally out of things to say—that was exactly when he could begin to listen to God.

Job 32–37 Elihu's Speech

Job had argued his three friends into silence. Then a fourth friend, Elihu, spoke. Elihu was angry with Job's other three friends because they had wrongly accused Job of sin. And he was angry with Job because he said Job was close to claiming that God was treating him unfairly. Elihu paved the way for God's speech to Job.

> **Elihu** Job 32:1–6
> Elihu was a younger friend who arrived later than the other three (Job 2:11). He was from the family of Buz, a nephew of Abraham (Genesis 22:20–21).

Job 38–41 God Speaks

These are some of the most awesome chapters in the Bible. God spoke to Job. But he didn't answer Job's questions. Instead, *he* asked the questions and told Job to answer *him*. God reminded Job of his power and majesty. And he asked if Job was anything compared with God's greatness.

> **Leviathan** Job 41:1, 9, 12, 18, 25, 33
> Leviathan was a large, fierce animal. Some think perhaps a leviathan was a hippopotamus or an elephant. Others think it might have been a large crocodile. No one knows for sure.

Job 42:1–6 Job Answers God

In the end, Job received something better than answers—comfort from God. Job realized that his understanding of God was very limited. He now experienced the life-changing greatness, majesty, and power of God. He also experienced God's love, since God came to Job in a personal way, responding to his suffering. That experience came only when Job ran out of words—when he was quiet and listening to what God was saying to him.

Job 42:7–17 The End

Job deserved a medal for how faithful he was to God during his suffering. But God gave him a lot more than a medal! God gave Job another ten children and doubled all of the stuff Satan had taken away—sheep and camels and oxen and donkeys.

The Israelites' Songbook

The book of Psalms is a book of poems. But Hebrew poetry is not like the poetry we have today. The lines of the psalms don't rhyme. Instead of words that repeat *sounds*, the lines of psalms repeat *ideas*. The psalms were written to show God's people—that includes you!—how to talk to God. The writers of the psalms were incredibly honest with God. They could say anything to him, knowing he would still listen and continue to love them.

Writer:
David wrote seventy-three psalms,
Asaph wrote twelve, the sons of
Korah wrote eleven, Solomon wrote two,
Moses wrote one, Ethan wrote one, and fifty psalms
have unknown writers.

Place:
Israel, but probably many were written in Jerusalem

People:
God

Why Is It Important?
Psalms expresses how people feel about God and
teaches us that it's okay to be very honest with him.

Some Favorite Psalms:
The Shepherd Psalm: Psalm 23
A Psalm for When You're Afraid: Psalm 27
A Psalm for When You're Sad: Psalm 42
A Psalm That Praises God for Who He Is: Psalm 66
A Psalm That Praises God for What He's Done: Psalm 103
A Psalm of Thanks: Psalm 107

Six Kinds of Psalms

Most of the psalms easily fall into six basic types:

1   **Praise psalms**—These praise God for who he is or what he has done (see Psalms 66 and 103).

2   **Psalms of complaint**—These complain to God about troubles in the writer's life and often ask God to punish the writer's enemies (see Psalms 35 and 83).

3   **Worship psalms**—While all the psalms could be used in worship, these were written specifically for different worship occasions (see Psalms 120 to 134 . . . they are called "songs of ascents" or psalms for those who go up to Jerusalem to worship God.)

4   **Jesus psalms**—A number of psalms described the coming of the Messiah (see Psalms 69 and 72).

5   **Forgiveness psalms**—These ask God to forgive the writer for sinning (see Psalms 32 and 51).

6   **Wisdom psalms**—These express the differences between the wise and foolish person (see Psalms 92 and 107).

BOOK 1 Psalms 1 to 41

These psalms declare the beauty and value of God's Word in a believer's life.

Psalm 1 Enjoy God's Word

Psalm 1 says that those who get their view of life from the Bible—rather than from their sinful neighbors and surroundings—will be blessed.

Psalm 2 A King Is Coming

This psalm looks ahead to Jesus, who will one day rule over the whole earth (Psalm 2:8).

Psalm 3 David Trusts in God

David wrote this psalm when his son Absalom rebelled against him. It gives a wonderful picture of trusting God even when you are going through hard times.

Psalm 4 An Evening Prayer

This is another psalm of David about trusting God. Psalm 4:4 talks about getting into bed and being quiet before God, letting him help you look deep inside yourself.

Psalm 5 A Morning Prayer

David must have had a ton of enemies. This psalm shows that he knew he could trust God to protect him. He knew God would hear him when he prayed.

Psalm 6 Cry of a Broken Heart

David's emotions came out loud and clear in this psalm. He groaned in misery because of his sin and the sinful people around him. But he knew God was there—listening and willing to heal.

Psalm 7 Prayer for Protection

In this psalm, David was in danger again and asked God to protect him.

Psalm 8 Praise for Creation

This psalm says that God created everything. And people are the crown of creation—the best of all he created.

Psalm 9 Thanks for Victory

This psalm shows that David, the brave and strong warrior, knew his victories against his enemies weren't the result of his own strength and bravery. He thanks God for his victories.

Psalm 10 A Prayer for Help

This psalm indicates that David needed God's protection not only from his enemies on the battlefield but also from the wicked people around him.

Psalm 11–13 Evil All Around

These psalms tell us that David was almost overcome by the wicked who surrounded him—almost, but not quite. Instead, he trusted in God and sang for joy.

Psalm 14 Sin

This psalm talks about sin. It's everywhere! Only a fool says there is no God.

Psalm 15 Those Who Live with God

This psalm gives a clear description of what God wants his people to be like—kind, truthful, and honest.

Psalm 16 Safety with God

This psalm shows that David knew where his true safety came from—God!

Psalm 17 A Prayer for Help

This psalm indicates that when David was overcome by the power of his enemies, he went to God for help and protection.

Psalm 18 Thanks to God

David wrote this psalm after years of running away from King Saul. He became king and gave all the thanks to God for his place as ruler of Israel.

Psalm 19 The Glory of Creation

God's hand can be seen in his creation. But he is known best through his Word.

Psalm 20 Trusting God

This psalm appears to be a battle song that was sung while preparing for war.

Be Wise—Memorize!
Psalm 18:2
My God is my rock.

Psalm 21 Thanks for Victory

In this psalm, David thanked God for giving the victory in battle.

Psalm 22 A Preview of Jesus on the Cross

Though David appears to be talking about himself in this psalm, many of these things never happened to him. Instead, the psalm is a picture of what would happen to Jesus a thousand years later.

Pierced Hands and Feet Psalm 22:16

We don't know that David had his hands and feet pierced. Perhaps he means that the dogs nipped and bit them. But this verse foretells what will happen to Jesus. He had his hands and feet nailed to the cross for our sins.

King Psalm 22:28

All through the Bible, the word *king* usually refers to a ruler over a nation on earth. But in the Psalms, it also refers to God, who is king even over the kings of the world.

Psalm 23 The Shepherd Psalm

This is one of the best-loved chapters in the Bible. David may have written this psalm when he was still a boy, taking care of his father's sheep.

Shepherd Psalm 23:1

A shepherd is someone who guards and cares for a flock of sheep. A shepherd usually carried a bag with food, a staff for walking and reaching out to sheep, a sling for protection, and a flute or harp for entertainment and for calming the sheep.

Psalm 24 The King of Glory

In Bible times when a king won in battle, the gates of the city would be thrown open and the people would gather and shout as the king entered the city. David may have been speaking about his return to Jerusalem after victory in a battle. But he also pictures a time in the future when Jesus would enter Jerusalem as the King of glory (Matthew 21:1–11).

Be Wise—Memorize!
Psalm 23:1 The LORD is my shepherd. He gives me everything I need.

Psalm 25 Prayer of Repentance

Several of David's psalms reveal how he was overcome at times by his sinfulness. He wanted and needed God's forgiveness.

Psalm 26 Trusting God

In a real switch from Psalm 25, this psalm expressed how David lived a good life and how different he was from the wicked people around him.

Psalm 27 God's House

God was the strength of David's life. David trusted God completely.

Psalm 28 A Prayer

This psalm demonstrates that David's only hope was God. When he prayed to God, God answered, and David was thankful.

Psalm 29 The Voice of God

This psalm expresses the vast strength and might and glory of God.

Psalm 30 Victory

David may have written this psalm shortly after taking the city of Jerusalem and making it his capital.

Psalm 31 A Song of Trust

David was in constant danger, but he never forgot to trust in God—even when he felt like God had abandoned him. Jesus used the words of Psalm 31:5 as he died on the cross (Luke 23:46).

Psalm 32 A Psalm of Forgiveness

David is overcome with thanks to God for his forgiveness. He may have written this psalm (as well as Psalm 51) after his sin with Bathsheba. David was a righteous man but not a perfect one. He went to God in sorrow and received forgiveness.

Psalm 33 A Psalm of Praise

There's no better way to praise God than by singing. David talks about a "new song," meaning that he has new experiences and love for God with each step he takes in life.

Psalm 34 Thanks for Rescue

Whenever David was in trouble, he asked God for help. This psalm shows that when God rescued him, David responded with thanksgiving and praise.

Psalm 35 An Angry Psalm

In this psalm, David didn't hesitate to be honest with God. His enemies were bothering him, God seemed far away, and David needed God to act. Right away!

Psalms 36–37 Trust in God

These psalms conclude that even when the wicked people around him seemed to do well, David knew that he had to trust in God's faithfulness and focus on his relationship with God.

Psalm 38 A Psalm of Misery

David's sin made him sick. He was miserable. In this psalm, he says that he needs God's forgiveness in order to get well again.

Psalm 39 The Shortness of Life

Our lives may seem long and important. But if we look at all of history, they're short and not terribly important. In this psalm, David speaks about the importance of making the most of every day, rather than wasting time in sinful activities.

Psalms 40–41 Songs about Rescue

David thanks God for saving him in the past, and asks for another rescue.

> **Hymn** Psalm 40:3
> A hymn is a song of praise to God. It can be sung in worship alone or in a group.

BOOK 2 Psalms 42 to 72

Psalms 42–43 Thirst for God

David was so thirsty for God, that in these psalms he said he looked like a deer panting for water.

Sons of Korah Psalm 42

The sons of Korah were a family of Levites. David organized them into a musical group (1 Chronicles 6:31–47).

Psalm 44 Crying Out to God

This psalm seems to have been written during a time of national disaster. The Israelite armies had been defeated.

Psalm 45 A King's Wedding Song

This psalm was originally written to celebrate the marriage of a king, perhaps David or Solomon. But it also pictures Jesus coming to take the church as his bride (see Revelation 19:7).

Psalm 46 A Battle Song

No matter what happens, this psalm urges God's people not to fear. He is with them even in the most terrible times.

Psalms 47–48 God Reigns

God is king. God is on the throne. He is our God forever. These psalms praise God for this.

Psalms 49–50 Don't Trust Riches

God is the owner of the earth and everything in and on it. When people give to God, they are just giving back to him what is already his. Even those who get rich will die and leave their riches behind. These psalms remind us that the only thing worth trusting is God.

Psalm 51 Asking Forgiveness

David wrote this psalm after his sin with Bathsheba. He was broken, and he let God see it. Then he asked God to give him a clean heart (Psalm 51:10).

Psalm 52 Trusting in God

This psalm speaks of David's trust in God when his enemy Doeg came against him.

Psalm 53 All Are Sinful

This psalm stresses the sinfulness of every human being (see Romans 3:10–12) and points out the foolishness of the person who says there is no God.

Psalm 54 David's Cry

This is another psalm written when David was running from Saul. He asked God to rescue him.

Psalm 55 Betrayed by Friends

David may have written this psalm during Absalom's rebellion. At that time Ahithophel, David's friend and adviser, betrayed him (2 Samuel 15:12–13). Even when his friends had left him and life seemed dark, David trusted in God.

Psalm 56 Prayer for Rescue

In this psalm, David again prayed for God to rescue him, this time from the Philistines (1 Samuel 21:10–15).

Psalm 57 David's Prayer

In this psalm, David prayed even when hiding from Saul in a cave (1 Samuel 22:1).

Psalm 58 The Wicked Punished

David complained about the success of wicked people in this psalm. But he knew that in the end, wickedness would be punished.

Psalm 59 Another Prayer of David

David prayed when Saul sent soldiers to trap him (1 Samuel 19:10–17). In this psalm, we see again that he trusted God and was saved.

Psalm 60 Rejected by God

In this psalm, David felt as though God had rejected Israel when the war with Syria and Edom (2 Samuel 8:3–14) was not going well. As at other times, God heard David's prayer and rescued him.

Be Wise—Memorize!
Psalm 62:11–12 God, I have heard you say two things. One is that you, God, are strong. The other is that you, Lord, are loving.

Psalm 61 A Psalm of Confidence

David must have been far from home when he wrote this psalm, but he knew that even so far away God would hear his prayers.

Psalm 62 Devotion to God

By looking through the psalms, we can see that David had a lot of trouble. But he never stopped trusting in God.

Psalm 63 In the Desert

David wrote this psalm while he was in the desert. He used pictures of desert life to show his thirst for God.

Psalm 64 A Prayer for Protection

David prayed for protection from his enemies in this psalm. He was sure that God would help him win over his enemies.

Psalm 65 A Song of Harvest

It was a year for huge crops and plenty of food to eat. David wrote a song about God's goodness in caring for the land.

Psalm 66 Everyone Praise God

This psalm encouraged the people to praise God, to fear him, to sing to him, and to trust that he would keep his eye on them.

Psalm 67 Looking Ahead

This psalm looked forward to the time when the whole world would hear the Good News of God and his Son, Jesus.

Psalm 68 A Battle March

Armies sang this psalm after a victory. It has also been a favorite of many in times of mistreatment.

Psalm 69 A Psalm of Suffering

Again, David described to God the terrible state of his life in this psalm. His enemies were closing in around him, and he needed God's help to survive.

Psalm 70 Hurry!

In this psalm, David wanted God to hurry up and save him. God acts in his own time—but he does understand when we call for help and ask him to hurry.

Psalm 71 A Psalm of Old Age

In this psalm, David looked back on a life of troubles and suffering and trusting in God anyway. He saw that throughout his life, God proved that he could be trusted.

Psalm 72 An Amazing Kingdom

Solomon wrote this psalm. It may seem like he's bragging about his wonderful kingdom. But he is drawing a picture for us of Jesus, the Messiah, and the majesty of his kingdom.

Everyone Will Bow Down Psalm 72:11

Lots of kings and queens bowed down to Solomon as one of the greatest kings who ever lived. But this verse is also describing Jesus, the King of Kings. Everyone will at some point bow down before him (Philippians 2:10).

BOOK 3 Psalms 73 to 89

Psalm 73 The Success of the Wicked

The success of the wicked is hard to take. It seems so unfair for them to have it so good when the righteous are suffering—unless you look at their end. This psalm is a reminder that the wicked may succeed for a time, but that judgment is coming.

Psalm 74 Disaster

This psalm was written when the Babylonians destroyed Jerusalem and left it in ruins.

Psalm 75 God Is Judge

God is the judge over all. He will decide when judgment will take place, and he will judge with total fairness. Eventually, the wicked will be punished and the righteous will triumph, according to this psalm.

Psalm 76 Thanks for Victory

This psalm may have been written when the angel of God destroyed Sennacherib's army outside of Jerusalem.

Psalms 77–82 Psalms of History

So many times Israel had wandered away from God and worshiped idols. Time after time, as a result of their disobedience, God allowed an enemy to defeat them. When those hard times came, the people would seek God. These psalms recall those times of disaster in Israel.

text

Psalm 83 Prayer for Protection

Israel had many enemies. This psalm asked God for protection for all of them.

Psalms 84–85 God's House

It appears that the writer of Psalm 84 longed for God's house because he or she could not be there. It may have been written while the writer was being held captive in a foreign land. Now that worship in the temple was no longer available, the psalmist longed for it. In Psalm 85, the writer thanked God for bringing the people back to their homeland.

Psalm 86 David Prays for Mercy

In this psalm, David knew he needed God's forgiveness. He also knew he needed God's help to lead a life that pleased God.

Psalm 87 Zion

God loved Zion and the people of Zion. This psalm could be sung by Israelites who were born in Israel. But those born into God's family through Jesus can also sing it. Believers in Jesus are citizens of God's city of Zion.

> **Zion** Psalm 87
> Zion was one of the hills on which the city of Jerusalem stood. It was the original fortress defeated by David. He called it the City of David. Zion later came to mean the hill on which the temple stood as well.

Psalm 88 A Sad Psalm

The person who wrote this psalm, sick and close to dying, had been ill for a long time and felt abandoned by God. This is one of the saddest songs in the book of Psalms.

Psalm 89 God's Promise

God promised that David's throne would last forever. At first, the psalmist was happy. Then, possibly when David's throne fell, and Judah with it, the writer seemed negative. The writer doesn't see what we can see—that Jesus sits on David's throne forever.

Forever Psalm 89:4

God promised that David's family line would continue and rule forever. Jesus fulfilled that promise to King David. He was born into David's family line, and he lived and died and rose again. He lives forever as the greatest king of all (Revelation 19:6).

BOOK 4 Psalms 90 to 106

Psalms 90–97 Psalms about God

These psalms describe God. He is powerful (Psalm 90). He is a fortress, a strong place (Psalm 91). He deserves praise (Psalm 92). He is holy (Psalms 93–94). He will reign forever (Psalms 95–97).

Psalms 98–100 Psalms of Praise

These psalms praise God for the good things he has done (Psalm 98), for his justice (Psalm 99), and for his love and faithfulness (Psalm 100).

Psalm 101 A Psalm for Rulers

This psalm may have been written when David became king of Israel. It states how David planned to live and rule as the king of Israel.

Psalm 102 A Prayer for Forgiveness

The psalmist here poured out his heart to God, recognizing his own failures and asking God to forgive.

Psalm 103 A Psalm of God's Goodness

Many think that David wrote this psalm when he was old. He describes in it how God dealt with him throughout his life.

Psalm 104 A Nature Psalm

This psalm declares that God is the creator and caretaker of the world.

Psalms 105–106 Historical Psalms

These psalms recall the Israelites' history, especially when God freed them from slavery in Egypt.

BOOK 5 Psalms 107 to 150

Psalms 107–109 God's Love and Justice
The wonders of God's love and his justice when dealing with the wicked are themes of these psalms.

Psalm 110 The Coming King
Though it was written a thousand years before Christ, this psalm can only refer to him. God inspired these psalmists to write of things that would happen in the future.

Psalms 111–118 Songs of Praise
These psalms were written to praise God for his righteousness and goodness to those who followed him. These psalms also praised God for delivering Israel from Egypt and their enemies in the past.

The Most Important Stone Psalm 118:22
The most important stone in a building is the cornerstone—the stone that the whole building begins with. This psalm refers to Jesus as "the stone the builders didn't accept." The leaders of the Jews rejected Jesus, even though he was the Messiah. Jesus was the most important stone, the most important person in God's plan to save the world. Jesus used this verse to describe himself (Matthew 21:42).

Psalm 119 The Glory of God's Word

Be Wise—Memorize!
Psalm 119:105 Your word is like a lamp that shows me the way. It is like a light that guides me.

With 176 verses, this is the longest chapter in the Bible. Every verse mentions God's Word, using one name or another. This psalm is an acrostic poem, which means each of its twenty-two stanzas begins with a letter of the Hebrew alphabet, in its proper order. Each stanza has eight lines, and each of those lines begins with the same letter.

Psalms 120–134 Songs of Ascents
These psalms were written specifically for those going up to Jerusalem to worship. Perhaps they were sung as the people traveled toward Jerusalem for religious feasts. Every road that led to Jerusalem from every direction actually went uphill. Or these songs may have been sung going up the fifteen steps to the men's court in the temple.

Psalms 135–139 Psalms of Thanksgiving

Each of these five psalms thanks God for something specific: for his work in nature, for answered prayer, for his presence.

Psalms 140–143 Prayers for Protection

David's many enemies only drove him closer to God. In these psalms, he prayed for protection from those enemies (Psalms 140, 142, 143) and for protection from sin (Psalm 141).

> **Selah** Psalm 140:3, 5, 8
>
> This word appears in the middle and at the end of psalms in the book of Psalms as well as in Habakkuk 3. No one knows for sure what the word means, but many think it's a musical term that signals a break in the music.

Psalms 144–145 Songs of Praise

David's armies may have sung these psalms as they marched into battle or after gaining victory.

Psalms 146–150 Praise the Lord Psalms

Each of these five psalms begins and ends with the words "Praise the LORD." This grand burst of praise that ends the psalms is also one of the last great images in the Bible. Revelation 19 pictures great crowds of people shouting "Hallelujah," which means "Praise the Lord!"

> **Dancing** Psalm 149:3
>
> The Israelites often danced as part of their worship and celebration. They whirled and twirled and played the drums and tambourine to thank God for his goodness to them. Men and women didn't dance with each other. They danced alone.

PROVERBS

A Book of Wise Sayings

Do you need some good advice? Start here! The book of Proverbs has great advice on just about every topic you can think of: friendship, laziness, marriage, parents, children, money, work, and worry—you name it! These proverbs, or wise sayings, are not promises. They are truths about how things happen most of the time. The book of Proverbs is an excellent tool for anyone who needs advice or is looking for help in making a decision.

Writer:
Solomon

Place:
Israel

People:
People of all ages and times

Why Is It Important?
Proverbs teaches us how to live wisely.

Some Favorite Proverbs:
Listen to Mom and Dad: Proverbs 1:8
More Important Than Being Rich: Proverbs 8:10–11
Only the Foolish Tell Lies: Proverbs 10:18
Honesty: Proverbs 16:17
Like Honey: Proverbs 16:24
Good Training: Proverbs 22:6
Controlling Anger: Proverbs 29:11
Worth More Than Rubies: Proverbs 31:10

BOOK 1 Proverbs 1 to 9
Solomon's Proverbs

Proverbs 1

Wisdom is more than just being smart. Wisdom is good sense, understanding, and the ability to live a godly life. Your relationship with God is the most important part of being wise. The second most important thing is your relationship with your parents, and then your relationship with your friends. (Many of the proverbs encourage you to stay away from people who aren't good for you.)

Proverbs 2

If you were certain there was a treasure hidden somewhere, how hard would you look for it? That's how hard God wants you to look for wisdom. The only place to find wisdom is through God and the study of the Bible.

Proverbs 3

Proverbs provides a lot of advice about a lot of different things. You should honor God by giving him the best of yourself and what you earn. Being wise is better than being rich. Be good to those who live near you.

Proverbs 4

What happens when you try to walk in the dark? Do you sometimes stub your toe? Or fall down? Well, wisdom is like a light that keeps you from doing that. The way of wisdom (righteousness) grows brighter and brighter, better and better. But the way of foolishness (sin) grows darker and darker, worse and worse.

Proverbs 5

This chapter gives advice on the joys of being married. Men should stay away from wicked women—those who want to steal them from their wives. Married couples should be faithful to each other. Why would a man want to "hug the wife of another man" (Proverbs 5:20)? God sees it and says it's wrong.

Proverbs 6

In this chapter, you'll find warnings against crooked business dealings, laziness, and lying.

Proverbs 7

In this chapter, you will find another warning against going near wicked women. When their husbands are away from home, they tempt men away from their wives.

Proverbs 8–9

Wisdom is described in this chapter as a woman who invites everyone to a beautiful banquet. Those who come and eat with her get knowledge and respect for God.

BOOK 2 Proverbs 10 to 24

More Proverbs of Solomon

Proverbs 10

This chapter spells out the differences between people who are wise and those who are foolish, the righteous and the wicked, hardworking people and lazy people, rich people and poor people.

Proverbs 11

God hates dishonest businesses. He loves it when businesspeople are honest. Proverbs 11:22 compares a beautiful but empty-headed woman with a pig with a gold ring in its nose. Not very flattering, is it? But that is just what this whole book is about! Nothing—not money, good looks, or fame—*nothing* is more important than being wise and loving and serving God.

Proverbs 12

This chapter compares what will happen to those who are good and wise with what will happen to those who are evil and foolish.

Proverbs 13

When you say something bad about someone, you hurt that person as well as yourself. But saying nice things is good for the one who speaks and the one who hears.

Proverbs 14

According to Solomon, anger hurts everyone, most of all the person who is angry. He also says, "jealousy rots the bones" (Proverbs 14:30). Being jealous of what others have only makes you sick on the inside!

Proverbs 15

Have you ever shouted at someone when you were angry? Did it help? Or did it just make things worse? Usually if you shout at someone who's angry with you, you only make that person angrier. But if you answer quietly and carefully, you make him or her less angry.

Proverbs 16

What's better—to be poor and truthful or rich and dishonest? Read this chapter to find out.

Proverbs 17

Feeling sick? Feeling a bit down? Take a happy pill! Proverbs 17:22 says that "a cheerful heart makes you healthy." Being cheerful isn't always easy, but it's good for you!

Be Wise—Memorize!
Proverbs 15:13 A happy heart makes a face look cheerful. But a sad heart produces a broken spirit.

Proverbs 18

You probably aren't thinking much yet about getting married. But when you do, you'll know that if you find a good husband or a good wife, you are blessed!

Proverbs 19

The person in Proverbs 19:24 is so lazy! How lazy? Even when he's hungry, he's too lazy to lift his hand from the dish of food to his mouth to eat. Talk about lazy!

Proverbs 20

How about a mouthful of sand? Sound good? No? Well, that's what people get to eat if they cheat in order to earn money for food (Proverbs 20:17). Also, did you know that God knows you better than anyone else (Proverbs 20:27)? He knows all about you—the good and the bad. What's even more amazing, he loves you.

Proverbs 21

Picture yourself on the very edge, squeezed into the corner of the roof of a house (houses at that time were flat on top). Would you rather live there or live inside the house with someone who's always fighting and arguing? You'll see what Solomon thought if you read Proverbs 21:9.

Proverbs 22

Turn to Proverbs 22:1 to find out what you should want more than you want to be rich. Then look at Proverbs 22:6 to see why your parents are so serious about teaching you to live a life that pleases God.

Proverbs 23

Proverbs 23:20–21 warns you not to spend too much time with those who drink too much or eat too much. Neither is good for you! Friends like those only cause you trouble. And in the end, drinking too much bites you like a snake (Proverbs 23:32).

Proverbs 24

An honest and clear answer is so sweet that the writer says it's like getting kissed on the lips (Proverbs 24:26).

BOOK 3 Proverbs 25 to 29
More of Solomon's Proverbs

According to Proverbs 25:1, these wise sayings of Solomon were gathered together when Hezekiah was king. Hezekiah was king more than two hundred years after Solomon. People probably spoke these proverbs to each other before then. But not until this time did someone add these to the original written collection of proverbs.

Be Wise—Memorize!
Proverbs 25:21 If your enemy is hungry, give him food to eat. If he is thirsty, give him water to drink.

Proverbs 25

Proverbs 25:11 says that a good word is like an apple made out of gold. Pretty nice, huh? That means that good words spoken at the right time are beautiful and valuable.

Proverbs 26

A lot of the advice in this chapter is about the dangers of speech. You can hurt others with your words. Quarreling doesn't do anyone any good. So, watch your tongue!

Proverbs 27

Don't forget: You don't know what will happen tomorrow! Also, if you want to know what you are really like, do what Proverbs 27:19 tells you.

Proverbs 28–29

You have two choices. You can choose to be wise, or you can choose to be foolish. These two chapters will tell you many things about wise people—and about foolish people. Then you can decide which you want to be.

Proverbs 30 Agur's Proverbs

No one knows who Agur was. Maybe he was one of Solomon's friends. Solomon liked his proverbs so much that he included them in his own book.

Proverbs 31 King Lemuel's Proverbs

This chapter is a mother's advice to her son, the king. King Lemuel may have been another name for Solomon. If so, Bathsheba was the mother who taught him.

The book of Proverbs ends with an outstanding poem that praises wise wives. They are "worth far more than rubies" (Proverbs 31:10).

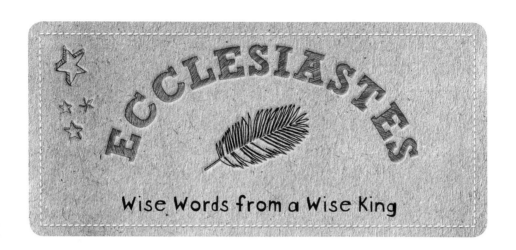

ECCLESIASTES

Wise Words from a Wise King

Without God, life isn't worth living. It's "meaningless"! The great King Solomon discovered that riches and opportunities didn't satisfy. He discovered that life is pretty empty without a solid foundation to build it on. And no foundation is solid except God. Only a relationship with God can give true meaning to life.

Writer:
King Solomon

Place:
Jerusalem

People:
God

Why Is It Important?
Ecclesiastes reveals that a satisfying, meaningful life
can be found only in God.

Some Lessons in Ecclesiastes:
Everything Is Meaningless: Ecclesiastes 1–2
There Is a Time for Everything: Ecclesiastes 3
Remember God When You're Young: Ecclesiastes 11:7–12:7

Ecclesiastes 1–4 Nothing Is Worth Anything

These verses may seem like a real downer. But they have a point other than making you feel terrible. The Teacher wants you to know that nothing in life is worth anything if God isn't in it. Solomon studied everything, tried everything, learned everything—and still he wasn't satisfied. Then to top it off, people around him were wicked and cruel.

Teacher Ecclesiastes 1:1

The writer of Ecclesiastes is called "the Teacher." The Teacher has learned a lot about life and now wants to teach what he has learned to anyone who will listen. Solomon, David's son and the king of Israel, is the Teacher.

Meaningless Ecclesiastes 1:2

Already in the second verse of the book, the writer uses this word "meaning-less" three times. He's upset because it seems to him that nothing in life has any meaning or purpose. Nothing is worth the bother. Everything is pointless. Everything is "meaningless"!

Ecclesiastes 5–10 Proverbs and Sayings

Solomon wrote thousands of proverbs (1 Kings 4:32). Some of them are in these chapters. Between the proverbs, you'll find Solomon's notes about life in general. If you read some of them, you'll be surprised at how true they are even today!

Ecclesiastes 11–12 The Answer

Solomon answers his own questions about what makes life meaningless and what can give it meaning. Only God can make life worth living. Solomon ends his thoughts by encouraging readers to remember, love, and respect God.

> **Be Wise—Memorize!**
> **Ecclesiastes 3:1** There is a time for everything. There's a time for everything that is done on earth.

SONG OF SONGS

A Love Song

God's love is perfect. He loves you, and he loves grown-ups too. God wants married people, especially, to understand his love and know that he is with them in their love for each other. The Song of Songs is a love song that expresses how a husband and wife feel for each other when God is in their lives.

Writer:
King Solomon

Place:
Jerusalem

People:
The king and bride

Why Is It Important?
Song of Songs praises the beauty and joy of married love between one man and one woman, which was God's idea. This book can also be seen as a picture of God's love for his people or of Jesus' love for the church, which is sometimes called his bride.

Some Lessons in Song of Songs:
The Beauty of Spring: Song of Songs 2:11–13
The Strength of Love: Song of Songs 8:6–7

Song of Songs 1 The King and His Bride

Kisses and perfume and love words. In this first chapter, the king and his bride expressed their love for each other. Their words were intimate and very descriptive.

Shulammite Song of Songs 1:1, 8; 6:13

This could be a form of the word "Shunammite," which is a person from the town of Shunem. Or the word could be the female form for "Solomon." It would then mean "Solomon's girl."

Song of Songs 2–3 More in Love

The bride was so in love with the king that she felt weak (Song of Songs 2:5). Spring has always been known as a time for love. The bride saw that spring was on the way, and she was ready for her lover to come to her.

Antelope Song of Songs 2:9

A graceful animal that is beautiful to look at. The woman thought her lover was as beautiful as a young antelope or deer.

Foxes Song of Songs 2:15

Small wild animals that look something like a small dog. They raid vineyards and destroy the vines. The lovers didn't want anything (any "little foxes") to get in and destroy their love for each other.

Beds Song of Songs 3:1

During Bible times most people slept on mats or animal skins on the floor. They used their long robes as blankets. Rich people sometimes had beds made of wood or metal with soft sheets and blankets.

Song of Songs 4 The King's Speech of Love

The king described his bride's beauty in ways we may think rather weird, but they were understood by the people of that time. Her teeth were like a flock of sheep, each with its "twin" (Song of Songs 4:2), meaning that she was not missing any of her teeth! Her neck was "like the tower of David" (Song of Songs 4:4), meaning it was long and slender. The king was so crazy for his bride that he said she had "stolen" his heart (Song of Songs 4:9).

Perfume Song of Songs 4:10

Plants and spices were added to oil to make perfumes for personal use as well as for anointing. The oil was spread over the hair and body to make the person smell good to other people.

Song of Songs 5 The Bride's Speech of Love

Now it's the bride's turn to describe her king. His eyes are "washed in milk" with "jewels" (Song of Songs 5:12), meaning they are clear and white with irises like gems. His legs must have been powerful and strong since she described them as "pillars of marble" (Song of Songs 5:15).

Song of Songs 6–8 Vowing to Love

The king and his bride again spoke of their love for each other. Their love was as "powerful as death" (Song of Songs 8:6). Nothing can hold back death—and nothing could hold back their love.

Pomegranate Song of Songs 7:12

Pomegranates grow on small bushes. The fruit is sweet and juicy and shaped something like an orange.

Pomegranates on a fruit stand

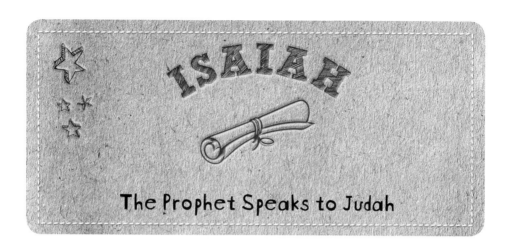

ISAIAH

The Prophet Speaks to Judah

The people of Judah are saying one thing and doing another. Isaiah hates that! They pretend they love God and want to worship only him, but then they live like they don't care what God says. Isaiah wants the people of Judah and of Israel to turn back to God and follow him with all their hearts. He tells the people that punishment is coming if they don't ask forgiveness for their sins. But he also tells them that God will forgive their sins if they will only turn to him and ask.

Writer:
Isaiah

Place:
Judah

People:
Isaiah

Why Is It Important?
God wants the hearts of his people to turn to him and love him. The book of Isaiah is also important because it contains almost twenty direct prophecies about Jesus Christ called "messianic" prophecies.

Some Stories in Isaiah:
Isaiah Is Called: Isaiah 6
Entire Assyrian Army Dies: Isaiah 36:1–37:20; 37:36–38
Hezekiah Gets Fifteen More Years: Isaiah 38:1–8

Isaiah 1 Unbelievably Wicked

Isaiah warned the people of Judah that their sins would bring punishment. They listened at first but then turned away and went back to their sins.

> **Isaiah** Isaiah 1:1
>
> Isaiah was a prophet or messenger from God who lived in Judah. Isaiah was the son of Amoz. He willingly took on the hard job of passing along the words that God wanted Judah (and sometimes Israel) to hear.

Isaiah 2–4 A Bright Future

These three chapters turn from punishment to a bright future for Judah. At some point in the future, the land will enjoy a time of peace and glory. The amazing thing is that Isaiah wrote this message when Jerusalem was a terribly sinful place. Whenever this time comes, the people of God will enjoy it, but the wicked will be left out.

Be Wise—Memorize!
Isaiah 2:4 "They will hammer their swords into plows. They'll hammer their spears into pruning tools. Nations will not go to war against one another. They won't even train to fight anymore."

Isaiah 5 A Vineyard Song

God cared for his "vineyard" (his people Israel) for hundreds of years. He loved them and gave them good things. But they sinned and didn't follow his ways. Now punishment was coming. Isaiah was especially talking to those who were greedy or drunk, and who mistreated the poor. The rich had gotten richer by stealing from the poor, but their wealth would soon be gone.

Isaiah 6 Isaiah's Call

What Isaiah saw in the temple must have been pretty awesome and scary, because it terrified him. He saw God on his throne, with a long flowing robe that filled the whole temple. Creatures called seraphs guarded God's throne and worshiped him. The temple shook, and smoke billowed all around. All of this showed Isaiah how holy God was and how wicked Isaiah and the people of Judah were. But when God called Isaiah to be his messenger, Isaiah didn't hesitate for even a second. Like students in a class who know the right answer and raise their hands high, shouting, "Pick me! Pick me!" Isaiah said, "Pick me, Lord! I'll go!"

Seraphs Isaiah 6:2, 6

Seraphs are creatures from heaven. The word means "burning ones." These beings guard God's throne and praise him. The ones that Isaiah saw had six wings each.

Isaiah 7 Immanuel

Judah had been attacked by Syria and by the northern kingdom of Israel. Isaiah assured King Ahaz that Judah would not be defeated. He also pictured a time far into the future when Immanuel would be born.

Immanuel Isaiah 7:14

Immanuel is a name for Jesus that means "God is with us." Almost seven hundred years before it happened, Isaiah told the people that a baby would be born who would become their Savior.

Isaiah 8 Maher-Shalal-Hash-Baz

Isaiah's first son was called Shear-Jashub (Isaiah 7:3). His name meant "a part will return." Isaiah saw the people of Judah being carried away as captives to Babylon one hundred years before it happened. And he also saw that some of them would eventually return to Judah. So he gave his son this special name.

Isaiah's other son was called Maher-Shalal-Hash-Baz. It means "quick to the plunder, swift to the spoil." It showed that Syria and Israel would both be destroyed. The Assyrians came, conquered those nations, and then moved toward Judah. Only a miracle from God stopped the Assyrians from destroying Jerusalem (see Isaiah 37:36).

Isaiah 9:1–10:4 The Wonderful Child

Israel was about to fall to the Assyrians, just as Isaiah predicted in Isaiah 7–8. Isaiah interrupted that picture of destruction with another picture, one of the Messiah that would come. His mother would be a virgin, and he would reign forever. Isaiah then jumped back to the destruction of Israel and how Samaria would be destroyed.

Jesus in the Old Testament Isaiah 9:6–7

These verses of Isaiah look into the future. Jesus would come as a baby, so he would be a person like we are. But he would also be God, so Isaiah called him "Mighty God." He would be the one to rule on David's throne, but he wouldn't die like all the other kings on earth. He would live and reign forever.

Isaiah 10:5–34 The Assyrians Are Coming!

After the Assyrians defeated Samaria, they marched south into Judah, right to the gates of Jerusalem. The cities mentioned in Isaiah 10:28–32 were just north of Jerusalem. Through Isaiah, God told the Assyrians not to be so proud of their power. They would not always be strong. As the Assyrian army gathered outside Jerusalem, God made good on his promise. The Assyrians were so badly defeated there (see Isaiah 37:36) that they never again had the power to march against Jerusalem.

Isaiah 11–12 A Wonderful World

Isaiah again looked far into the future. He saw a world without war, without fighting, without violence. Those who love God will live in peace. Lions and lambs will sleep together, and snakes won't bite. This is a world that is still in the future, of course, when Jesus comes back to reign.

Isaiah 13:1–14:27 Babylon Falls

During Isaiah's time, Assyria was the leading power in the world. Babylon was under Assyria's control. Later Babylon would rise to power, and then it would be defeated by the Persians. Isaiah wrote about Babylon's fall one hundred years before it had even come into power!

Dogs Isaiah 13:21–22

In Bible times, dogs were *not* man's best friend. They ran wild through towns eating the scraps of food that people threw away. Kids probably played with dogs, but they weren't pets.

Isaiah 14:28–32 The Philistines

The Philistines were glad when the king of Assyria died ("the rod of Assyria" mentioned in Isaiah 14:29). But they didn't have long to party. Assyria's new king came to power and defeated the Philistines.

Isaiah 15–16 Moab

Moab was a land of rich farms and grasses for raising animals. Isaiah said Moab was going to be destroyed by the Assyrians.

Isaiah 17 Damascus

Damascus was the capital of Syria. In Bible times, all the most important trade routes went through Damascus. It would be destroyed, too, according to Isaiah.

Isaiah 18 Cush

Cush was southern Egypt. During the time of Isaiah, its powerful king ruled over all of Egypt. But, unlike the others, this message isn't about destruction. The people of Cush prepared for war when the Assyrian army marched against Jerusalem. They knew they had been saved when God defeated the Assyrians outside of Jerusalem.

Isaiah 19 Egypt

Isaiah predicted that Egypt would not always be a world power. He also predicted that many in Egypt would follow the true God. When Judah was destroyed, many people ran to Egypt and settled there. Alexandria, the second most important city in the world during Jesus' time, had a large population of Jews.

Isaiah 20 Egypt and Cush

Isaiah warned that Egypt and Cush would be defeated. He didn't want the people of Judah to look to them for help against Assyria.

Isaiah 21 Babylon, Edom, Arabia

The Assyrians would defeat all three of these nations.

Isaiah 22 Jerusalem

With the Assyrian army coming down on them, the people of Jerusalem did everything to defend themselves—except turn to God.

Isaiah 23 Tyre

For hundreds of years, Tyre was the center of trade by ship. Isaiah said it would be completely destroyed by the Assyrians.

Tyre Isaiah 23:1

A port city on the Mediterranean Sea. Hiram, King David's friend, made it a major trading place in the world at that time. Although Tyre resisted a thirteen-year battle (yes, that's right! *thirteen years!*) with Babylon, the strain ruined her for many years. She was under the rule of Egypt for a time, then under Babylon, and then under Persia.

Isaiah 24 The Earth Is Destroyed

This vision of Isaiah was focused on the whole earth instead of on a specific city or country. At some point in the future, he saw that the entire earth will be destroyed because of the sin of human beings. The descriptions are a lot like those found in Revelation 19 and Matthew 24.

Isaiah 25–26 Praising God

Isaiah turned quickly away from scenes of destruction to a song that praised God. The scene he pictured seems to be one yet in the future, when Jesus returns again. Isaiah said this new king would wipe away all tears (Isaiah 25:8), a promise that is repeated in Revelation 7:17; 21:4.

Isaiah 27 Israel Is Saved

Isaiah used a picture of a vineyard to show how Israel would be restored. It will blossom again and be fruitful. Meanwhile, God will kill Leviathan and the sea monster. This is Isaiah's way of saying that God will defeat evil for sure!

Isaiah 28 Watch Out, Samaria

Isaiah now turned to the people of his own day to warn them that danger was coming. And soon! The beautiful city of Samaria would be destroyed.

Isaiah 29 Watch Out, Jerusalem

The Assyrian army would come to Jerusalem very soon, Isaiah warned. He said that the army would not defeat Jerusalem, however. It would be defeated "all of a sudden, in an instant" (Isaiah 29:5). God himself would come and defeat the Assyrians.

Isaiah 30 Judah's Dependence on Egypt

A long line of camels carrying gifts to Egypt made its way across the desert. The people of Judah sent gifts to Egypt, hoping to gain help in their battle for survival. They should have looked to God. He was the only one who could save them. Babylon destroyed them one hundred years after Isaiah spoke these words.

Isaiah 31 God Promises to Deliver

Isaiah remained confident that Assyria would not defeat Judah. The events of Isaiah 37:36 proved that he was right.

Isaiah 32 Messiah's Reign

Isaiah began by picturing the joy of Judah's deliverance from the Assyrian army (Isaiah 37:36). King Hezekiah regained some of his power when Jerusalem was saved. Then Isaiah's vision moved into the future, when the Messiah would reign. All the history of the Old Testament moves toward that Messiah, the King of Kings.

Isaiah 33 Before Battle

Isaiah 28–33 pointed to the terrifying days when the Assyrian army ran through Judah, destroying cities, killing people. Everyone was panicking (Isaiah 33:13–14). Everyone, that is, except Isaiah. He calmly assured the people that God would cut Assyria's armies down with one swoop and that the Assyrian soldiers would flee, leaving all their belongings behind.

Isaiah 34 Judging the Nations

Barely stopping to take a breath, Isaiah revealed God's plan to punish all nations who oppose him, whether Israel or elsewhere.

Isaiah 35 Great Joy

This is one of the Bible's most beautiful poems. Isaiah presented a picture of the last times when those God had saved, after suffering, would finally gain peace and joy. The earth would respond with the same joy. Flowers bloom in the desert (Isaiah 35:2), burning sand becomes cool water (Isaiah 35:7). "The Way of Holiness" would be cleared of wild animals and would be safe for God's people (Isaiah 35:8–9).

> **Papyrus** Isaiah 35:7
>
> Papyrus was a tall plant that grew mostly along the banks of rivers, especially the Nile River in Egypt. The tall stalks of the plant were sliced open and laid out next to each other to form large sheets of paper. The juice of the plant formed a glue that held the pieces together. Many of the books of the Bible were originally written on long sheets of papyrus. Instead of putting many sheets together into a book, one long sheet was rolled up into a scroll.

Isaiah 36–37 Time for Victory!

The king of Assyria came with his huge army. He invaded Judah and captured many of its cities. Then he camped outside Jerusalem. No one could go in or out. The situation looked hopeless until God came, and in one quick action, killed all 185,000 Assyrian soldiers. This miracle of God was so fantastic that the Old Testament writers recorded it three times: here, and in 2 Kings 18–19 and 2 Chronicles 32. Isaiah told the people over and over again that God would save them from the Assyrians—and he did!

Isaiah 38–39 Hezekiah's Sickness

King Hezekiah was so sick, he was sure he was going to die. Then God said he would give him a few more years to live. God performed a miracle as a sign to Hezekiah that what he had said would happen *would* happen!

Isaiah 40 God's Comfort

Isaiah's words in this chapter give all God's people a wonderful assurance of comfort and peace. The God who is able to do anything will do everything to save his people. Isaiah 40:3–5 is quoted in all four books that tell of Jesus' birth (Matthew 3:3; Mark 1:3; Luke 3:4–6; John 1:23). Just as Isaiah said he would, John the Baptist came as a "messenger" to tell the people Jesus was coming.

Isaiah 41 King Cyrus

Isaiah predicted the rise of King Cyrus to power in Persia 150 years before it happened. Cyrus would conquer the Babylonians and send all those who were captives in Babylon home to their own lands—including the Jews.

Be Wise—Memorize!
Isaiah 40:31 Those who trust in the LORD will receive new strength. They will fly as high as eagles. They will run and not get tired. They will walk and not grow weak.

Isaiah 42 The Lord's Servant

This is another prophecy about the coming Messiah. Here Isaiah told the people that the Messiah would be a servant of God. He would willingly do whatever God wanted in order to save the Jews, and all the other people of the world, from their sins.

Isaiah 43 God's Care for Israel

God had formed the nation of Israel for himself. The people of Israel, however, had never stopped being disobedient. Still, they belonged to God, and through their sins and sufferings, God would show to all the world that he, and he alone, is God.

Isaiah 44–45 Cyrus

These two chapters predicted Israel's return from captivity under King Cyrus of Persia. Cyrus let the Jews return to Jerusalem and gave them permission to rebuild the temple. Now, remember—Isaiah spoke these words before Cyrus was even born and before the temple had even been destroyed!

Blacksmith Isaiah 44:12

Bam, bam, bam! That's the sound heard most often in a blacksmith's shop. Blacksmiths work with metal that must be heated and then beaten with a hammer to form the shape needed.

Isaiah 46–48 The Fall of Babylon

God is the only God, and he wants his people to know that. Isaiah talked about the gods of Babylon and how they wouldn't be able to help the people of Babylon against the armies of Cyrus. Instead, these false gods would be hauled away as loot.

Isaiah 49–50 The Lord's Servant

In some of these verses, the servant seems to be the nation of Israel. In others, the servant seems to be the Messiah. The meaning is mainly that the servant's work (whether Israel or the Messiah) is to bring people to God.

Isaiah 51–52 Zion Saved

Just as certain as what God had done in the past is what God would do in the future. Israel's sufferings in Babylon would be temporary. Everything that has happened and that will happen is part of God's plan to save the world.

Isaiah 53 A Man of Sorrow

This chapter gives a clear picture of the suffering that Jesus would face. Isaiah wrote about it so clearly that it's almost as if he stood beneath the cross, watching Jesus die. But he wrote almost seven hundred years before Jesus' death.

Jesus in the Old Testament Isaiah 53

This chapter is one of the clearest prophecies about Jesus in the Bible. Isaiah pictured how Jesus would suffer and how his suffering would not be for his sins but for ours.

Isaiah 54–55 Glorious Jerusalem

Trouble was on the way, but so was blessing. Isaiah compared the destruction of Jerusalem to a woman who had sinned and was a widow (Isaiah 54:4) or who was sent away by her husband (Isaiah 54:6). But Isaiah also said that this situation would be temporary. This woman (Jerusalem) would be restored. God would be her husband again and would bring her joy and children.

Isaiah 56–59 Sins of Isaiah's Day

The people of Isaiah's day sinned by not keeping the Sabbath, by overeating, by not giving to the poor, by worshiping idols instead of God, and by being unkind to those who were weaker. All of these sins would be punished.

Isaiah 60–62 Zion's Redeemer

Zion would receive "a new name" (Isaiah 62:2), and God's servants would be called by "new names" (Isaiah 65:15).

Isaiah 63–64 God's People Saved

Most of these two chapters were a prayer to God to free the Jews who were in exile in Babylon. Only God could save them. There was no one else to help (Isaiah 63:5).

Isaiah 65–66 New Heaven and Earth

These two chapters were God's answer to the prayer in Isaiah 63–64. The people's prayer would be answered. They would be restored to their homeland. These chapters also looked to the end of the world when those who have loved and served God would be given a place in a new heaven and earth (see Revelation 21–22.) When Adam and Eve sinned, even creation was affected. Now people, as well as creation, would be saved and renewed.

Prophecies about Jesus in Isaiah
He is coming (Isaiah 40:3–5).
He will be born of a virgin girl (Isaiah 7:14).
He will work in Galilee (Isaiah 9:1–2).
He is God and will rule forever (Isaiah 9:6–7).
He will suffer (Isaiah 53).
He will die (Isaiah 53:9).
He will be buried (Isaiah 53:9).
He will rule with power (Isaiah 40:10–11).
His rule will be fair (Isaiah 32:1–8; 61:1–3).
He will be faithful and kind (Isaiah 42:3–4, 7).
He will rule over all people, not just Jews (Isaiah 2:2–3; 42:1, 6; 49:6; 55:4–5; 56:6; 60:3–5).
Even other kings and queens will bow down to him (Isaiah 49:7, 23).

Isaiah

Isaiah's Prophecies about the End of Time

Idols will disappear (Isaiah 2:18).

People will finally know true peace (Isaiah 2:4; 65:25).

The earth will be destroyed (Isaiah 24; 26:21; 34:1–4).

Death will be destroyed (Isaiah 25:8; 26:19).

God's people will be called by a new name (Isaiah 62:2; 65:15).

A new heaven and a new earth will be created (Isaiah 65:17; 66:22).

Those who love and follow God and those who don't will be separated (Isaiah 66:15, 22–24).

JEREMIAH

God's Final Effort to Save Jerusalem

Jeremiah lived about one hundred years after the prophet Isaiah. Isaiah had been around when God saved Jerusalem from Assyria. Now Jeremiah was trying to save Jerusalem from Babylon. But he failed. Jeremiah lived through forty horrible years. Little by little, the Babylonian armies destroyed Jerusalem. They finally burned it to the ground. Jeremiah saw the end of the kings and the nation of Judah. He watched as the Babylonians took his people away from their homes. He was God's messenger to a people who were still attached to their idols instead of their God. Jeremiah cried out to the people. If only they would turn to God, he would save them from Babylon. But they wouldn't listen.

Writer:
Jeremiah

Place:
Judah

People:
Jeremiah

Why Is It Important?
People who disobey God will eventually be punished because a holy God can't ignore sin forever. But if they will only turn back to God, he will forgive and bless them.

Some Stories in Jeremiah:
God Calls Jeremiah: Jeremiah 1:4–19
A Linen Belt: Jeremiah 13:1–11
The Potter's Work: Jeremiah 18:1–6
Jeremiah's Enemies: Jeremiah 26:1–15
Jeremiah Buys a Field: Jeremiah 32:1–15
Jeremiah's Friends Save Him: Jeremiah 38:1–13
Jerusalem Is Destroyed: Jeremiah 39:1–14

Jeremiah 1 God Calls Jeremiah

Jeremiah was only about twenty years old when God called him to be his messenger. He didn't have an easy job. His first message was that Babylon would destroy Jerusalem (Jeremiah 1:14–15)—not something the king or the people wanted to hear.

> **Jeremiah Jeremiah 1:1**
>
> Jeremiah was a great prophet of God. He told the people that punishment was coming if they didn't turn back to God. Jeremiah is often called the crying prophet. He saw many people hurt and killed. He saw his homeland destroyed, and he saw his people taken away. No wonder he was sad.

Jeremiah 2 Israel Worships Idols

Jeremiah scolded Israel for worshiping idols instead of God. He compared Israel to a wife who had run away from her husband to chase after other men.

Jeremiah 3 Judah Is Worse Than Israel

Jeremiah told the people of Judah that they were worse than the people of Israel. Almost one hundred years before, Assyria had destroyed Israel and had taken her people away. Judah watched as all that happened. But they still didn't turn away from their idols. In fact, they went deeper and deeper into idol worship. It's amazing, but God still said he'd forgive them if they would turn to him. But they didn't.

Jeremiah 4 Trouble from the North

The Babylonian armies came from the north and invaded Judah and Jerusalem. They came with their chariots (Jeremiah 4:13) and attacked the cities of Judah (Jeremiah 4:16).

Jeremiah 5 No Honesty in Judah

If even one righteous person could be found in Jerusalem, God would not have destroyed it (Jeremiah 5:1). But even that one righteous person couldn't be found.

Jeremiah 6 Babylon Will Attack Jerusalem

Jeremiah described the horrors of Babylon's destruction of Jerusalem. All this happened during Jeremiah's lifetime. Over and over again, Jeremiah told the people that being sorry for their sins was their only way out.

Jeremiah 7 Judah's Only Hope

Jeremiah begged the people to ask God to forgive their sins. That's the only hope they had, the only way they would be saved. The people had put idols in God's temple and worshiped them there. But they still seemed to think that God wouldn't destroy Jerusalem because his temple was there.

Jeremiah 8 God Punishes His Sinful People

Jeremiah was so overcome with sadness for what would happen to Jerusalem that he talked as if it had already happened. The false prophets said Jeremiah was crazy. The people would rather listen to their lies than to the truth that Jeremiah spoke.

Jeremiah 9 The Sad Prophet

Jeremiah cried day and night at the thought of the horrible events that were coming to Judah. He walked among the people and begged them to turn from their wickedness. But the people refused.

Be Wise—Memorize!
Jeremiah 10:6 LORD, no one is like you. You are great. You are mighty and powerful.

Jeremiah 10 The True God

The threat of attack by Babylon made the people of Judah more and more active in their worship and building of idols—as if those idols could save them! In fact, their sinful activity only made their destruction more certain.

Jeremiah 11 A Broken Promise

Jeremiah reminded the people of God's promise to bless them if they obeyed and to punish them if they did not. Instead of listening, the people plotted to kill Jeremiah (Jeremiah 11:21).

Jeremiah 12 Jeremiah Argues with God

While Jeremiah obeyed God and suffered, those who didn't obey God were living the good life. Jeremiah complained to God about that. But God showed him that there was no safety in the good life. All Jeremiah's enemies would be pulled up by their roots (Jeremiah 12:14). That was God's way of saying that they would be taken away from their homes and land. Even then, God included his plan to bring his people back after they had been punished.

Jeremiah 13 A Ruined Belt

Jeremiah's linen belt was probably beautiful, carefully sewn and richly decorated. It was an obvious part of Jeremiah's clothing. Of course, it was even more noticeable after it had spent time in the dirt. Jeremiah used that ruined, filthy belt to explain that Judah had once been beautiful, but it would soon be ruined—worth nothing except to be thrown away.

Jeremiah 14–15 Jeremiah's Prayer

A long time without rain had stripped the land of food. Jeremiah's heart ached for his people as he watched them go hungry. Even though the people cared nothing for Jeremiah, he continued to pray for them.

> **Be Wise—Memorize!**
> **Jeremiah 17:7** "I will bless any man who trusts in me. I will show my favor to the one who depends on me."

Jeremiah 16 No Marriage

Isaiah and Hosea were both prophets of God who got married. They gave their children names with a message for God's people. Jeremiah, however, was not allowed to marry. It was a part of his horrifying message to the people. What was the use of marrying and having children just so they could be killed when the Babylonian armies attacked?

Jeremiah 17 Judah's Sin

Judah's sin had to be punished. Its sin was carved deep into its heart; not a little sin here, a little sin there, though that's bad enough. Judah's sin went deep. Yet, through Jeremiah, God declared again and again that even though the people would be punished because of their sins, he would not forget them.

Jeremiah 18 The Potter

Jeremiah used a visit to a potter's house to show how God has power to make and destroy nations. Jeremiah used this event to ask the people again to turn to God and change. But they ignored his words.

Potter Jeremiah 18:3–4

A potter is a person who makes pots and jars out of clay. Potters put a lump of clay on a wheel and then turn the wheel with their feet. As the wheel turns faster and faster, the potter forms the lump of clay into the desired shape. Clay pots and jars were used to store liquids as well as household goods.

Jeremiah 19 The Clay Jar

Jeremiah took a clay jar, as God told him, and smashed it to the ground. It broke into hundreds of little pieces. It was a sign from God that he would "smash" or break Judah for her sins.

Jeremiah 20 Jeremiah's Enemies

An official from the temple heard that Jeremiah was saying God would destroy Jerusalem. The man had Jeremiah beaten and put into prison. When Jeremiah was let out, he told the official that soon the official and his family would be carried off to Babylon as a punishment for their sins. Jeremiah again complained to God about how mean his enemies were being to him.

Jeremiah 21 The Attack Begins

Babylon's army camped at the gates of Jerusalem. The king begged Jeremiah to ask God to deliver them. But Jeremiah had bad news—it was too late. The opportunity to repent had been lost. Babylon's armies would enter Jerusalem and destroy it.

Jeremiah 22 Against Jehoiachin

Through Jeremiah, God sent a message to the last kings of Judah. The words of this message to King Jehoiachin—the second-to-last king—were terrible and scary. And it all happened just as Jeremiah had described it. Babylon's armies destroyed Jehoiachin's beautiful palace. He was taken as a captive to Babylon and died there. You can read all about it in 2 Kings 24:8–15.

Jeremiah 23 A True Branch

The religious leaders of Judah had been leading the nation away from rather than toward God. They would be punished. But God would also bring a better, purer leader to them. That "true and rightful Branch" (Jeremiah 23:5) is Jesus.

Jeremiah 24 The Defeat Begins

The king of Babylon, Nebuchadnezzar, took the king of Judah, Jehoiachin, captive to Babylon. After he left, Jeremiah saw a vision about a basket of figs. Some of the figs were good; some were bad. God told Jeremiah that the bad figs were the leaders of Judah who led the people away from God. He said the good figs were the people of Judah, who would be punished in Babylon—but not forgotten. God would watch over them and bring them back to Jerusalem.

Fig Jeremiah 24:2
A fig is a fruit that grows on tall, bushy trees all over the Middle East. Figs taste good and are healthy to eat.

Jeremiah 25 Seventy Years

God told Jeremiah the amount of time that the people of Judah would be punished in Babylon: seventy years.

Jeremiah 26 Jeremiah in Danger

Jeremiah stood in the temple and told those listening that the temple was going to be destroyed. He made the religious leaders so angry that they captured him and put him in prison. But they didn't kill him as they had planned, because officials of the government stood up for Jeremiah.

Jeremiah 27 A Yoke

God told Jeremiah to put a heavy yoke around his neck. Jeremiah walked along, bowed over by the weight of the yoke. He told the people that just as that yoke weighed him down, so Nebuchadnezzar would weigh down Judah.

Yoke Jeremiah 27:2
A yoke is a large, heavy wooden bar with ropes used to hold two animals together. This allowed the animals to work together to plow the ground or pull a cart.

Jeremiah 28 Another Prophet Comes Along

Another prophet came on the scene. His message was exactly the opposite of Jeremiah's. While Jeremiah said that Judah and Jerusalem would be destroyed, Hananiah said that the armies of Babylon would be defeated. The articles Nebuchadnezzar had taken from the temple would be returned. King Jehoiachin would also return to Jerusalem. Hananiah took the yoke from Jeremiah's neck and broke it. He said God would break the power of Nebuchadnezzar just as he had broken the yoke. But Hananiah's message was not from God.

Jeremiah 29 A Letter from Jeremiah

Jeremiah sent a letter to the people who were already living as captives in Babylon. Each time Nebuchadnezzar attacked Jerusalem, he destroyed more of it and took more people captive. Jeremiah told the captives to live well in Babylon, to obey the laws there, and to worship God there. God hadn't forgotten them, and he had some good plans in store for them.

Jeremiah 30 A New Day

Jeremiah wrote on a scroll that God would punish his people, but he wouldn't forget them. After a time away in Babylon, God would bring his people back to Judah and bless them there.

Scroll Jeremiah 30:2

In Bible times, books were usually in the form of scrolls. They were long pieces of paper rolled up on each end. The reader would unroll one end and roll up the other as the words of the scroll were read. The paper used in scrolls was often made of papyrus or animal skins.

Jeremiah 31 Sad Times Turn to Joy

Jeremiah shared God's words to encourage the people. Hard times were coming. But God would help them through those times, and he would bring joy to them again. That joy came when the people returned to Jerusalem after being captives in Babylon (Ezra 1:2–3). Jeremiah's words were also a picture of the happiness that will belong to those who love and worship God at the end of the world.

Jesus in the Old Testament Jeremiah 31:31–34

Jeremiah talked here about a "new covenant." This new covenant, or promise, would replace the one God gave Moses at Mount Sinai. It would come through Jesus. The old covenant worked from the outside (God's laws) to the inside (people's hearts). The new covenant would work just the opposite—from the inside (people's hearts) to the outside (obeying God).

Jeremiah 32 Buying a Field

Who would ever want to buy a field in a land that was going to be destroyed? Seems a bit pointless, doesn't it? But God told Jeremiah to buy a field. He wanted Jeremiah—and all those who were watching him—to see that their situation was not hopeless. The people would be punished, just as Jeremiah said. But one day, they would be allowed to return to Judah. Buying a field was an act of trust for Jeremiah—trust that God would do what he had promised to do.

Baruch Jeremiah 32:12

Baruch was Jeremiah's secretary and good friend. He wrote down the words of Jeremiah's messages (Jeremiah 36:4) and sometimes read them to the people (Jeremiah 36:8). He even rewrote all the words of the scroll that King Jehoiakim had burned (Jeremiah 36:32).

Jeremiah 33 God, the Promise Keeper

God promised the people of Judah that he would punish them. And he did. But he also promised that he wouldn't forget them and that they would return to Judah one day. And they did. God is the great keeper of promises. He kept his promises back then, and he still keeps them today.

Jeremiah 34 A Warning

God sent a warning to Judah and to King Zedekiah through Jeremiah. Their punishment was coming. They had turned away from God. The armies of Babylon were right outside Jerusalem, ready to destroy it. To try to gain God's favor, King Zedekiah said that all the slaves in Jerusalem should be freed. The slave owners agreed and set their slaves free. But then they changed their minds and took their slaves back.

Be Wise—Memorize!
Jeremiah 33:2–3 "I made the earth. I formed it. And I set it in place. The LORD is my name. Call out to me. I will answer you. I will tell you great things you do not know."

Jeremiah 35 Recab's Family

Many years before, the family of Recab had promised that they would never drink wine. Now Jeremiah put big bowls of fresh wine in front of Recab's family members. "Drink up!" he said. But they refused. God used this family as a lesson to Judah. The family of Recab had been obedient. Why couldn't the people of Judah just obey God?

Jeremiah 36 A Burning Scroll

King Jehoiakim didn't much like the words of Jeremiah's message. As it was read to him, he cut the scroll up bit by bit and burned it in the fire in his room. Did Jeremiah and his secretary, Baruch, give up? Not a chance. They simply started over, writing everything down again on a new scroll.

Jeremiah 37–38 In Prison

Jeremiah was put in prison. Again. He was later moved to an empty well or cistern. There was no water in this cistern, only mud. So much mud that Jeremiah sank down into it. After a short time, some friends of Jeremiah came and carefully lifted him out of that dark, wet place.

Cistern Jeremiah 38:6

A cistern is a large storage place for water. Usually it was dug into the rock. Water collected in a cistern when it rained. It was stored there for use when the rains stopped.

Jeremiah 39 Destruction Comes

After years of warnings, the day finally came. There would be no more opportunities to repent. The armies of Nebuchadnezzar broke through Jerusalem's walls. They overran the city, killing many of its people and burning all of its buildings, including the palace and the temple that Solomon had built.

Jeremiah 40 To Babylon or Not?

Jeremiah stood in a long line of prisoners—all chained together, all being sent to Babylon. They were hungry, dirty, tired, and hurt. An official from Babylon walked along the line looking for one person. Finally, he found him. It was Jeremiah! Jeremiah was freed from the chains, given food and drink and gifts and told he could either stay in Judah or go with the rest of the people to Babylon. Jeremiah decided to stay in Judah.

Jeremiah 41 A Murder

King Nebuchadnezzar appointed Gedaliah to govern the few poor people left in Judah. Everyone else had been taken to Babylon. But when Gedaliah was murdered, the people left in Judah were afraid. Would the king of Babylon come and punish them? Maybe it would be best if they ran away.

Jeremiah 42–43 Asking for Advice

Before leaving Judah, the people asked Jeremiah for his advice. Should they leave or stay? Jeremiah told them that God wanted them to stay in Judah. Foolish people. They still had trouble believing and obeying God! Instead of listening to Jeremiah, they ignored the very advice they had asked for and left for Egypt. They took Jeremiah with them.

Jeremiah 44 A Message in Egypt

In Egypt, Jeremiah continued to bring God's messages to the people of Judah who had settled there. They had begun to worship the gods of Egypt. He warned them that they would pay for those sins. The people who heard the message only turned away. They didn't believe Jeremiah, even after all that had happened. They had run to Egypt to get away from war and danger. But now war and danger would find them in Egypt.

Jeremiah 45 A Message for Baruch

Baruch, Jeremiah's secretary, had high ambitions. God reminded him that high position wasn't as important as following God faithfully.

Jeremiah 46–49 Babylon Defeats Others

These chapters describe how Nebuchadnezzar and his armies defeated Egypt, the Philistines, Moab, Ammon, Edom, Syria, Hazor, and Elam.

Jeremiah 50–51 Babylon Defeated

Jeremiah described the defeat and destruction of Babylon. The Medes would be the ones to defeat Babylon. Jeremiah copied the words of these two chapters and sent them to Babylon to be read there. After reading them aloud, Seraiah, the official who read the words, was supposed to tie a stone to the scroll and throw it into the river. Then he would say, "In the same way, Babylon will sink down. It will never rise again" (Jeremiah 51:64).

Jeremiah 52 Jerusalem Falls

In King Zedekiah's ninth year, the armies of Babylon camped outside of Jerusalem. No person and no food could go in or out. The army camped there for two years. The people were starving. That's when the army of Babylon broke down the walls of Jerusalem and entered the city. They took many people captive and completely destroyed Jerusalem, just as Jeremiah had said would happen.

LAMENTATIONS

Crying over Jerusalem

Jeremiah prophesied that the city of Jerusalem would be destroyed. Then he watched as one by one his predictions came true. The book of Lamentations expresses Jeremiah's sadness over what happened to Jerusalem and its people. Jeremiah wrote the sad song of Lamentations soon after Jerusalem fell to the Babylonian armies.

Writer:
Jeremiah

Place:
Jerusalem

People:
The people of Judah

Why Is It Important?
The people of Jerusalem refused to follow God and brought destruction on themselves because of their sins. Even today, this book is read in Jewish congregations all over the world when they remember the temple being destroyed.

Some Lessons from Lamentations:
God's Amazing Faithfulness: Lamentations 3:21-24
God Reigns Forever: Lamentations 5:19

Lamentations 1 Jerusalem Empty

It's not easy to know the exact subject of each chapter. The same ideas, in different wording, run through all the chapters. The horrors of the Babylonian army surrounding Jerusalem, the fighting and destruction of Jerusalem—these are all events that make the author, Jeremiah, terribly sad. And he makes it clear in this first chapter that the people of Judah brought all this trouble on themselves by refusing to obey God.

> ### Lamentations Book Title
> A lamentation was a way of expressing deep sadness over something. A person would sob and cry because something awful had happened and then write down those awful feelings in a lament.

Lamentations 2 God's Anger

God's anger with the people of Judah brought about the destruction of Jerusalem. Jerusalem was set on a mountain, surrounded by even higher mountains. Because of its location, many thought it was the most beautiful city in the world at that time. On top of that, it was the city of God's special care, chosen by him as the place where he would live with his people. Because of its location and defenses, most people thought it couldn't be defeated. But this city had become more sinful than Sodom (Lamentations 4:6). So God destroyed it.

> **Be Wise—Memorize!**
> **Lamentations 3:23–24**
> His great love is new every morning. LORD, how faithful you are! I say to myself, "The LORD is everything I will ever need. So I will put my hope in him."

Lamentations 3 Jeremiah's Sadness

Jeremiah seemed to be complaining that God had ignored his prayers (Lamentations 3:8). But, even though he complained, he said that he knew the people of Judah deserved an even worse punishment than they got (Lamentations 3:22).

Lamentations 4–5 Suffering

Jeremiah could not forget the horrible time when the Babylonians surrounded Jerusalem. Children cried with thirst and hunger (Lamentations 4:4). Everyone was starving because there was no food. Jeremiah ends with a call to God to restore the people of Judah—to take them back and give them their city.

EZEKIEL

A Messenger's Visions

If you're interested in reading about dreams that have a touch of the unreal, a bit of the colorful, a lot of the hard to understand—Ezekiel is your book. Ezekiel was a prophet in Babylon. He had been taken there during one of the first battles between Judah and Babylon, eleven years before Babylon defeated Judah and destroyed Jerusalem. He was speaking to the people of Judah living in Babylon at the same time Jeremiah was speaking to the people of Judah who were left in Jerusalem.

Writer:
Ezekiel

Place:
Babylon

People:
Ezekiel and the captives in Babylon

Why Is It Important?
Ezekiel explains to the people of Judah that God has allowed them to be taken captive to Babylon because of their terrible sins against him and their unwillingness to turn back to God.

Some Stories in Ezekiel:
Fantastic Visions: Ezekiel 1
Ezekiel Is Called: Ezekiel 2
Ezekiel Eats a Scroll: Ezekiel 3:1-15
Dry Bones Live: Ezekiel 37:1-14
A New Temple: Ezekiel 40-43

Ezekiel 1 A Vision of God

The "living creatures" (Ezekiel 1:5) were cherubim (Ezekiel 10:20). These creatures stood, one in the middle of each side of a square. Their wings touched at the corners of the square. Each creature had four faces: the face of a man, a lion, an ox, and an eagle. The creatures had huge wheels beside them. The wheels were bright and shining and moved wherever the creatures moved. The sound of their wings, when they moved, was like a roaring waterfall or a huge army marching.

Above the creatures was a clear platform that looked like ice. On the platform sat a throne of blue jewels. A person that looked sort of human—but wasn't—sat on the throne. Ezekiel used words like "glowing metal" and "fire" and "bright light" and "rainbow in the clouds" to try to describe this person. When the person spoke, Ezekiel seemed to realize what he was seeing. He was seeing the glory of God!

Vision Ezekiel 1:1

A vision is sort of like a dream, but much more. A vision is a message from God. The person sees some event or thing that God uses to give a message to his people. Ezekiel had many visions, and he scolded the false prophets who said they had visions (Ezekiel 13:6–7).

Ezekiel Ezekiel 1:3

Ezekiel was God's messenger to the exiles in Babylon. Ezekiel lived with the other Jews in Babylon near the Kebar River, which connected to the Euphrates River. He was a married man (Ezekiel 24:18) and a priest (Ezekiel 1:3), and he lived in Babylon at the same time Daniel lived there (Daniel 1:3–6).

Ezekiel 2–3 Ezekiel's Calling

From the beginning, Ezekiel was told that he would have a difficult life. His message was a sad one. The people would not like hearing it. God gave Ezekiel his message in the form of a scroll and told him to eat it. The scroll tasted "sweet as honey" (Ezekiel 3:3), which probably meant that Ezekiel was happy to be God's messenger, even if the message was not a pleasant one. God also warned Ezekiel that at times he would need to be silent instead of preaching to the people (Ezekiel 3:26). This was probably a warning to Ezekiel that he should never speak his own thoughts and ideas, but only what God commanded.

Ezekiel 4–7 A Picture of Jerusalem

This was Ezekiel's first message to the Jews in exile. They were hoping they'd be able to return to Jerusalem before long. But Ezekiel told them that Jerusalem was about to be destroyed and that many more Jews would be coming to Babylon.

For a time, Ezekiel ate only bread and lay on his side, either all the time or almost all the time. This uncomfortable position and the small amount of food he ate each day made Ezekiel miserable. Ezekiel's actions were a sign to the people in Babylon that their sins were terrible before God and that their punishment was not yet over.

In Ezekiel 5, God told Ezekiel to shave his hair with a sword, tuck a few hairs into his clothing, and divide the rest into three equal piles. Ezekiel's hair was symbolic of the people of Judah. He would burn one pile of hair and smash another pile with the sword—this showed that two thirds of Jerusalem's people would be killed. The last pile of hair would be thrown to the wind, showing that one third of Jerusalem's people would be scattered to other places. But those few hairs tucked into Ezekiel's clothes stood for some of God's people who would one day be allowed to return to Jerusalem.

Ezekiel 6–7 mourned the destruction and desolation of the land of Israel. Through this terrible punishment, the Jews would finally come to know that God is God.

Ezekiel 8–11 A Trip to Jerusalem

In Ezekiel's next vision, he was being led by the hair (Ezekiel 8:3) on a trip to Jerusalem. God showed him the awful things the people were doing in the temple—worshiping idols. Even though they had been warned again and again and had been punished again and again, the people of Judah were still sinking deeper and deeper into idol worship. God couldn't stand it any longer.

In Ezekiel 9, the prophet saw in a vision the death of the idol worshipers in Jerusalem. Those faithful to God were spared. Ezekiel 10 pictured the reappearance of the living creatures from Ezekiel 1. They oversaw the destruction of Jerusalem. The future, when the exiles returned to Judah, was pictured in Ezekiel 11. The visions were now complete, and Ezekiel was brought back to his home in Babylon.

Ezekiel 12 Ezekiel Moves

This is an amazingly detailed prophecy of King Zedekiah's fate. Five years later it happened just as Ezekiel said it would: Zedekiah tried to escape and was captured. His eyes were put out, and he was taken to prison in Babylon (Jeremiah 52:7–11).

Ezekiel 13 False Prophets

There were many false prophets! And they were about to be punished.

Ezekiel 14 Here Comes Punishment

The time had come for Jerusalem to be destroyed. The punishment would only get worse. There would be war, hunger, wild animals, and plagues.

Ezekiel 15 A Useless Vine

A vine that does not grow fruit is useless. Its wood has no use except to be burned for fuel. In the same way, Jerusalem was no longer fit for anything but burning.

Ezekiel 16 An Unfaithful Wife

Ezekiel pictured Israel as an unfaithful wife whose husband was God. Her husband had loved her, had made her a queen, and had given her every beautiful thing. But she still would not be faithful to him. She was worse than Sodom and Samaria.

> **Be Wise—Memorize!**
> **Ezekiel 11:19** "I will give my people hearts that are completely committed to me. I will give them a new spirit that is faithful to me. I will remove their stubborn hearts from them. And I will give them hearts that obey me."

Ezekiel 17 Two Eagles

The first eagle (Ezekiel 17:3) was the king of Babylon. The other eagle (Ezekiel 17:7) was the king of Egypt. Judah looked to Egypt for help against Babylon instead of looking to God.

Jesus in the Old Testament Ezekiel 17:22–24

The "highest twig" that God would plant was a picture of a future king who would restore the glory of Israel and David's line of kings. That future king was Jesus, the Messiah.

Cedar Trees Ezekiel 17:22

A cedar tree is a strong evergreen that can grow both high (120 feet) and wide (40 feet). The wood from a cedar tree is a warm red color and doesn't decay easily. That's why it was used in the most important building projects in the ancient world: David's palace (2 Samuel 5:11) and the temple in Jerusalem (1 Kings 6:9–18).

Ezekiel 18 People Will Die Because of Their Sins

The people who were held captive in Babylon tried to blame their fathers for their troubles. Their fathers had sinned, so now they were being punished. They totally overlooked the fact that they were as bad or worse. The truth in this chapter is that God judges every person on the basis of his or her own heart. It was one of Ezekiel's most passionate calls to the people to turn back to God.

Ezekiel 19 The Fall of David's Throne

David's family—once great and powerful—had now been overthrown.

Ezekiel 20 Israel's Idolatries

Year after year, the people of Judah and Israel worshiped idols. Their love for idols grew greater and their love for God less. All hope was not lost, however. They would be judged and punished, but they would not be forgotten.

Ezekiel 21 The Sword of Babylon

God now used the sword of Babylon—its armies and its military might—to punish his people for their sins.

Ezekiel 22 The Sins of Jerusalem

Over and over, Ezekiel named the sins of Jerusalem. She worshiped idols. She killed innocent people. She didn't keep the Sabbath holy. She robbed others. She committed sexual sins. And her leaders were greedy and dishonest.

Ezekiel 23 Oholah and Oholibah

The story of these two sisters was used to illustrate Israel's idol worship. Oholah was Samaria; Oholibah was Jerusalem. Both had grown old in their evil ways. Many of the prophets used the relationship between a husband and wife to show the relationship between God and his people.

Ezekiel 24 The Cooking Pot

The cooking pot is a picture of the destruction of Jerusalem. The fire (the Babylonian army) will burn hotter and hotter. Ezekiel's wife died on the day the Babylonian army surrounded Jerusalem for the last time. Ezekiel lost the wife he loved, and the exiles were going to lose the city they loved—Jerusalem.

Ezekiel 25 Ammon, Moab, Edom, Philistia

These four nations were Judah's closest neighbors. They were glad when the Babylonians destroyed Judah. But Ezekiel told them that they would suffer the same fate.

Ezekiel 26–28 Tyre

These visions of the doom of Tyre came to Ezekiel in the same year that Jerusalem fell. Nebuchadnezzar surrounded Tyre, but it took him thirteen years to defeat it.

Ezekiel 29–32 Egypt

Six visions predicted Egypt's decline to a place of minor importance in the world. In the first vision, Egypt was pictured as a crocodile, king of the Nile, a powerful nation. In the second vision, Nebuchadnezzar turned his armies on Egypt. In the third vision, Pharaoh's army was defeated. In the fourth vision, Egypt was reminded to remember the fate of Assyria, which was more powerful than Egypt, yet had fallen to Babylon. The fifth vision was a lament over Egypt, which would be crushed by the Babylonians. The sixth vision pictured the death of Egypt.

Ezekiel 33 The Fall of Jerusalem

After getting the news that Jerusalem had fallen, Ezekiel told the people that those left in Judah would die.

Ezekiel 34 The Shepherds of Israel

The kings and priests—the leaders of Judah—were to blame for its destruction. They had been greedy and had led God's people astray. Ezekiel then saw a vision of another shepherd of God's people who would never lead his people astray.

> **Jesus in the Old Testament** Ezekiel 34:23–24
>
> While Ezekiel gave a warning of punishment to Israel's present leaders, he also gave a picture of a future shepherd who would lead with love and bring "showers of blessing" (Ezekiel 34:26). That future shepherd is Jesus.

Ezekiel 35 Edom

Now that the people of Judah had been taken away, Edom saw a chance to take their land. But three years later, the same punishment fell on Edom.

Ezekiel 36 The Land of Israel

The land of Israel was now deserted. But one day it would become like a garden (Ezekiel 36:35). The forgiven people of Judah and Israel would live there. This restoration of Israel would happen not for the people's sake but in order to glorify God (Ezekiel 36:22, 32).

Ezekiel 37 Dry Bones

A dance of dry bones. They clattered and clicked as they rose and joined to make human beings. Flesh and blood and breath came into them. This vision predicted the return and reunion of the Jewish people who had been separated into two nations (Judah and Israel) since the death of Solomon (1 Kings 12) and scattered into many foreign countries.

Ezekiel 38–39 Gog and Magog

Gog may be the name of a king. Bible scholars have not been able to identify him, however. Perhaps the name stood for a future enemy of God's people. In the book of Revelation, Gog and Magog were used to picture all the nations in Satan's final and furious attack on the people of God (Revelation 20:7–10).

Ezekiel 40–48 A New Temple

Ezekiel made another trip to Jerusalem in a vision. This second vision gave instructions for rebuilding the city. It dealt mostly with details concerning the new temple. This vision was not fulfilled when the captives returned from Babylon and rebuilt the temple at that time. Therefore, many think it is a prediction of what will happen in the last days when Jesus, our Messiah, returns.

DANIEL

A Young Leader in Babylon

Dens of hungry lions, tall golden idols, fiery furnaces, huge hands writing on walls, brave young men. Those are the things that make up the events in the book of Daniel. One exciting adventure after another fills its pages. Daniel is a young Hebrew man who is brought as a captive to Babylon. King Nebuchadnezzar picks a number of the young, strong, smart Hebrews to be trained to serve in the palace. Daniel is one of those men. Right from the start, he proves his faith in God. Along with his friends, Daniel's faith in God is never shaken, even when he's faced with death by hungry lions.

Writer:
Daniel

Place:
Babylon

People:
Daniel, Shadrach, Meshach, Abednego, and King
Nebuchadnezzar

Why Is It Important?
If you want to see a mighty God show his power in
thrilling ways, this is your book!

Some Stories in Daniel:
Not Eating Royal Food: Daniel 1:3-20
The Meaning of Nebuchadnezzar's: Dream: Daniel 2:24-45
Thrown into a Fiery Furnace: Daniel 3
The Handwriting on the Wall: Daniel 5
Thrown into a Den of Lions: Daniel 6

Daniel 1 Daniel

Daniel was in the first group of captives brought to Babylon from Jerusalem. He was from the royal family—handsome, brilliant, and under God's special care. The royal food and wine (Daniel 1:8) that he and his friends refused to eat may have been food that had been offered to idols or may have been food considered unclean under Hebrew law. Daniel rose to worldwide fame while still a young man. He was unswerving in his faithfulness to God and so loyal to the king that he was trusted with important affairs of the empire.

Daniel Daniel 1:6–7

Daniel is the hero of the book of Daniel and one of history's greatest heroes. His Babylonian name was Belteshazzar, which meant "may Bel [a god of Babylon] protect his life." He wrote the book of Daniel. He was an adviser to King Nebuchadnezzar. He interpreted the king's dreams when no one else could.

Shadrach, Meshach, Abednego Daniel 1:6–7

Shadrach, Meshach, and Abednego were also heroes of the book of Daniel. These were their Babylonian names. Their Hebrew names were Hananiah, Mishael, and Azariah. They refused to bow down to the king's golden idol. As punishment, they were thrown into a huge furnace of fire. But God saved them.

Babylon, the City Daniel 1:21

Babylon was the great capital city of the country of Babylonia. King Nebuchadnezzar worked on it throughout his reign of about forty-four years, building it up and making it beautiful. He is best known for building the hanging gardens in his palace there. His wife was from a country with mountains and trees and flowers, very different from the flat plains of Babylonia. So Nebuchadnezzar built up terraces and planted trees and bushes and flowers—all right within his palace grounds. The water to keep the plants alive came from the nearby Euphrates River. Twenty-four hours a day, slaves ran on treadmills to keep bucket after bucket of water running up to the hanging gardens.

Daniel 2 Nebuchadnezzar's Dream of a Statue

The king dreamed of a giant statue of a man, and its parts were made of different kinds of metal. Each metal stood for a world empire, starting with Nebuchadnezzar's own:

Babylon—head of gold
Persia—chest and arms of silver

Greece—belly and thighs of brass
Rome—legs of iron and feet and toes of iron and clay

From the days of Daniel to the coming of Christ, these four empires ruled the world.

Daniel 3 The Fiery Furnace

Thousands gathered around a huge golden idol. Thousands fell to their faces as soon as the worship music sounded. But not three brave Hebrew men. They remained standing. How obvious they must have been—three brave men, standing tall in a sea of bowed bodies. Because they wouldn't bow down, they were thrown into a fiery furnace, but God went with them into the fire. Nebuchadnezzar saw him as "a son of the gods" (Daniel 3:25). God showed the Babylonians that his power was greater than all of them or their gods. The king was so amazed by God's power that he declared him to be the true God.

Daniel 4 The King Is Insane

Nebuchadnezzar had another dream that came true just as Daniel predicted. Daniel knew the dream meant the king would be insane for a time. At first he was scared to tell the king the dream's meaning.

Daniel 5 Belshazzar's Big Party

Nebuchadnezzar had died, and now Belshazzar was king of Babylon. He gave

a huge party. The people drank wine from golden cups that had been taken from God's temple in Jerusalem. While the party went on, a huge hand showed up and wrote on the wall. Daniel had been in Babylon for about seventy years by this time and was quite old. He was called to tell what the writing meant. The news was not good. Before the party could break up, the Medes and Persians invaded and defeated Babylon.

Daniel 6 In a Den of Lions

Daniel must have been close to ninety years old by the time Darius, king of the Medes, defeated the Babylonians. He put

Daniel in charge of the Babylonian government. This was probably because Daniel had predicted the victory of the Medes. Faithful to God throughout his captivity in Babylon, Daniel continued to be a great example of courage and faith in the face of danger.

Gentle Lions Daniel 6

These lions weren't usually gentle. But God closed their mouths so that they wouldn't hurt his servant Daniel. Daniel was thrown into a den of lions for disobeying the king and obeying God. It looked like Daniel would be supper for the ferocious felines. But God protected Daniel just as he had protected Shadrach, Meshach, and Abednego in the fiery furnace.

Daniel 7 The Four Beasts

Daniel had a vision about four beasts. The meaning of his vision was a lot like Nebuchadnezzar's dream in Daniel 2. The lion was Babylon, the bear was Persia, the leopard was Greece, and the beast was Rome.

Daniel 8 A Ram and a Goat

Daniel also had a vision about a ram and a goat. The ram was the same as the bear in his other vision. It was the empire of the Medes and Persians (that's probably why the ram had two horns). The ram was defeated by a goat, which represented the empire of Greece. The Greek emperor, Alexander the Great, defeated the Persian Empire two hundred years after Daniel saw this happen in his vision.

Gabriel Daniel 8:15–17; 9:21

Gabriel is God's angel messenger. He came to Daniel to help him understand some of the visions God had given. Gabriel also appeared to Zechariah to tell him that John the Baptist would be born (Luke 1:19) and to Jesus' mother, Mary, to tell her that Jesus would be born (Luke 1:26).

Daniel 9 Seventy Weeks

Many scholars think the seventy weeks of Daniel's next vision are seventy periods of seven years, which equals 490 years (70 x 7). It was about that amount of time between the rebuilding of the temple in Jerusalem and Jesus' time on earth. Others think that the seventieth week has a future fulfillment in the end times, a seven-year period of trouble on the earth. They believe that this seventieth week will begin with Christ's return to earth. This seven-year period is called the Great Tribulation. (See Revelation 7:14 for more on the tribulation period.)

Be Wise—Memorize!
Daniel 9:9 "You are the Lord our God. You show us your tender love. You forgive us."

Daniel 10 What Will Happen to Israel

God now let Daniel see what would happen to Israel in the future. It appeared that God was showing Daniel some of his secret agents (angels) working behind the scenes to bring about the return of Israel.

> **Michael** Daniel 10:13, 21; 12:1
>
> Michael is a leader of the angels of God. Some translations of the Bible call him an "archangel." He is also mentioned in Jude 9 and Revelation 12:7.

Daniel 11 Kings of the North and the South

Daniel's visions showed him the way the course of history would go, with one nation defeating another and taking power. A Greek king would rule with great power (Daniel 11:3), but his kingdom would be divided into four parts (Daniel 11:4). That's exactly what happened when Alexander the Great's four generals fought over his kingdom after his death.

Daniel 12 The Time of the End

Daniel's prophecies ended with a view of the end of time, when there will be more trouble than has ever happened before. At that time, however, those people whose names are written in the Book of Life will be saved (Daniel 12:1).

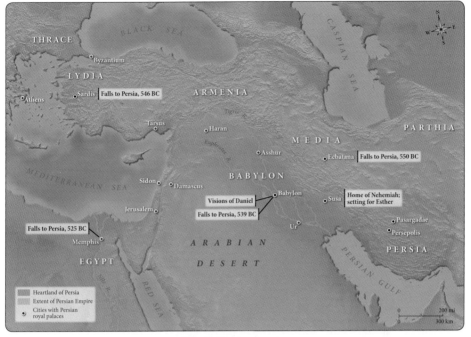

THRACE

BLACK SEA

Byzantium

LYDIA

Sardis | Falls to Persia, 546 BC

Athens

ARMENIA

Tarsus

Haran

Tigris R.

Euphrates R.

Asshur

MEDIA

Ecbatana | Falls to Persia, 550 BC

PARTHIA

CASPIAN SEA

MEDITERRANEAN SEA

Sidon

Damascus

BABYLON

Babylon

Visions of Daniel

Falls to Persia, 539 BC

Jerusalem

Susa | Home of Nehemiah; setting for Esther

Ur

Pasargadae

Persepolis

Falls to Persia, 525 BC

Memphis

ARABIAN

DESERT

EGYPT

Nile R.

RED SEA

PERSIA

PERSIAN GULF

Heartland of Persia
Extent of Persian Empire
Cities with Persian royal palaces

0   200 mi
0   300 km

Map 7. Persian Empire

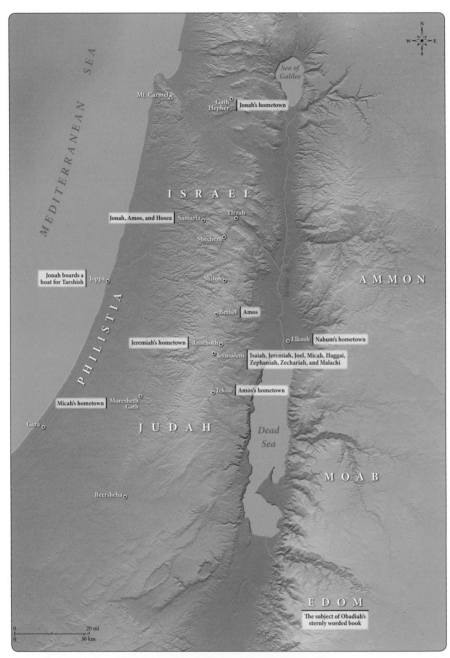

Map 8. Prophets Who Wrote Books of the Bible

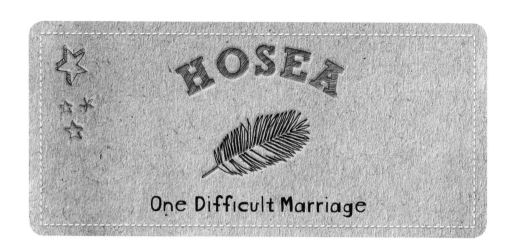

HOSEA

One Difficult Marriage

Hosea's marriage is a picture of a God who loves his people even though they have been unfaithful to him. God longs for his people to turn to him so that he can forgive them and show his love to them again. The faithful prophet, Hosea, devoted his life to trying to make the people see that God still loved them.

Writer:
Hosea

Place:
Israel

People:
Hosea

Why Is It Important?

The book of Hosea reveals that God's love for you is greater than anything you could ever do, any sin you could ever commit, any wrong way you could ever turn. As long as you turn to him for forgiveness, he's waiting and willing to show his love to you.

Some Stories in Hosea:

Hosea Gets Married and Has Kids: Hosea 1

Hosea Buys His Wife Back: Hosea 3

Hosea 1–3 Hosea's Wife and Children

Israel, God's bride, had turned away from him and given herself to the worship of other gods. God commanded Hosea to marry a woman who wouldn't be faithful to him. Hosea's marriage was a picture of God's relationship with Israel. Hosea's children's names pictured the coming punishment for sin. But though the people would be punished, they wouldn't be forgotten. Hosea changed two of his children's names: Lo-Ammi ("Not my people") becomes Ammi, "My people," and Lo-Ruhamah ("Not pitied") becomes Ruhamah, "My loved one."

Hosea Hosea 1:1

Hosea was God's messenger to the northern kingdom of Israel. The name *Hosea* means "salvation." God told him to marry a woman named Gomer. Hosea knew even before he married her that his life with her would be a difficult one. But he did as God asked.

Jezreel Hosea 1:4

Jezreel was Gomer's first child. God told Hosea to name the boy Jezreel. Jezreel was the place where a terrible killing had taken place. God wanted the people to know that judgment for that event was coming.

Be Wise—Memorize!
Hosea 2:23 "I will show my love to the one I called Not My Loved One. I will say, 'You are my people' to those who were called Not My People. And they will say, 'You are my God.'"

Hosea 4 Words against Israel

The list of the people's sins was horrifying. Punishment was on the way. Hosea told Judah to take a lesson from what was about to happen in Israel (Hosea 4:15). But Judah only listened a little and then continued her own slide into sin. It would be another hundred years before her punishment came.

Hosea 5 Judgment against Israel

The priests, kings, and people had all rebelled against God (Hosea 5:1). Punishment was coming for sure (Hosea 5:9).

Hosea 6–7 Israel Doesn't Repent

The words of Hosea 6:1 sound sincere. The people seemed sad for their sins. But they quickly turned away from God again and ignored his call to leave their sin behind.

Hosea 8 A Windstorm Is on the Way

Like an eagle circling overhead, Assyria circled Israel, looking for an opportunity to invade and destroy her. God would allow the armies of Assyria to capture Israel because of the people's sins.

Hosea 9–10 Punishment

The history of the Israelites was one of turning away from God and then toward him. But as time went on, they turned away more and more. When God found them in the desert in their early history, their relationship was sweet, like the first figs on a tree (Hosea 9:10). But now, because of "many evil things" (Hosea 9:15), such as their "god that looks like a calf" (Hosea 10:5), they would be punished.

Hosea 11:1–11 God's Love

Just like parents who don't stop loving their children even when they must punish them, God didn't stop loving Israel. Even though the people had made up their minds to turn away from God (Hosea 11:7), he still pitied them and ached for them to turn back to him (Hosea 11:7–8).

Hosea 11:12–12:14 Israel's Sin

Hosea told the Israelites that their secret agreements with both Assyria and Egypt—to play them against each other—would only bring disaster.

Hosea 13 God's Anger

The people had added the worship of the idol Baal to their calf worship. They had even sacrificed their children to him. Such terrible sins could not be ignored.

Be Wise—Memorize!
Hosea 14:9 The ways of the LORD are right. People who are right with God live the way he wants them to.

Hosea 14 Israel Will Return

Amazingly, all was not lost. Eventually Israel would return. Like a wayward bride who returns to her husband, Israel would return to God and he would bless them.

JOEL

A Plague of Locusts

They came pouring down on the land like a rain shower. Grasshoppers—a shocking plague of them. They ate everything in sight. No food was left for people or animals. The prophet Joel said that this plague of locusts would come if the people of Judah did not turn back to God. But in Joel's book punishment was combined with God's plan to restore his people. Joel said that God would pour out the Holy Spirit on them. How wonderful that God's judgment is always mixed with his mercy!

Writer:

Joel

Place:

Judah

People:

Joel

Why Is It Important?

Joel says that God will come and pour out his Holy Spirit on his people, and this happened when the Holy Spirit came after Jesus went back to heaven (Acts 2:1-4). The power and filling of the Holy Spirit can help you today. With the power of the Spirit in your life, you can live faithfully for God, not continually turning away from him as the Israelites did in the Old Testament.

Some Lessons in Joel:

Repentance Is Most Important: Joel 2:13

The Holy Spirit Will Come: Joel 2:28-29

Joel 1:1–2:27 The Plague of Locusts

Suffering came in the form of a horrible famine caused by a plague of locusts and a long time without rain. The plague brought the people to their knees, and they cried out for help. God heard their cries, removed the locusts, and promised good times.

Joel Joel 1:1

Joel was a messenger of God to Judah. He prophesied not only about what would happen to Judah because of her sins but also about how the Holy Spirit would someday be poured out on all people.

Locusts Joel 1:4

Locusts are huge grasshoppers. They flew over in large, dark clouds, settled down, and then ate every green thing in sight. Locusts are mentioned more often than any other insect in the Bible. They were used at times as a punishment for the people's sins, as they were here in Joel and in Exodus 10. But at times, they were also used as food (Mark 1:6).

Joel 2:28–3:21 The Day of the Lord

These verses pictured a time when God's Word, the message of Jesus, and the work of the Holy Spirit would all come together and bring people to God. That time is today!

Be Wise—Memorize!

Joel 2:28–29 "I will pour out my Spirit on all people. Your sons and daughters will prophesy. Your old men will have dreams. Your young men will have visions. In those days I will pour out my Spirit on those who serve me, men and women alike."

AMOS

A Shepherd's Prophecies

Amos, a shepherd and a prophet from Judah, brought a message for his brothers in Israel. Their hard treatment of the poor and weak was not pleasing to God. God has always been concerned for the poor, and he gave Israel some clear rules for taking care of them. He never wanted rich people to hurt poor people. Which is exactly what was happening. Israel's many sins were bringing them closer and closer to the day of punishment.

Writer:

Amos

Place:

Judah

People:

Amos

Why Is It Important?

God saw rich people in Israel being unkind, unjust, and unfair to poor people, and God wanted them to know that he wasn't going to let their sins go unpunished forever.

Some Lessons in Amos:

Selfish Women and Their Punishment: Amos 4:1-3

Watch for Good Things: Amos 5:14-15

A Basket of Ripe Fruit: Amos 8:1-7

Amos 1–2 Israel and Her Neighbors Are Doomed

Amos started his book with a look, not only at Israel, but also at her neighbors. None of them measured up to what God wanted.

Amos Amos 1:1

Amos was not an educated preacher or priest. He was not a person with royal blood. Amos was just a shepherd in Judah. But God came to him with a message for the people in Israel. Like the other prophets, Amos told the people that God was angry with them for worshiping idols. But his main point was that their mistreatment of the poor was making God furious.

Tekoa Amos 1:1

Tekoa is a city in Judah, south of Jerusalem. The region around Tekoa was good for raising sheep. Amos was a shepherd (Amos 1:1). It must also have been a good place for growing fig trees. Amos took care of fig trees (Amos 7:14).

Amos 3 Judging Israel

The sins of Israel were obvious to God. Though the rich sat on their beds and couches (Amos 3:12) and thought nothing bad would ever happen to them, God promised that their punishment was coming.

Amos 4 Israel Has Not Returned to God

Amos compared the spoiled women of Samaria with cows in the rich grazing land of Bashan (Amos 4:1). They didn't care that their selfish, greedy lives hurt the poor people around them. Just as the wicked people of Sodom and Gomorrah (Amos 4:11) had been punished for their sins, these people would also be punished for their sinful behavior.

Be Wise—Memorize!
Amos 5:15 Hate what is evil. Love what is good.

Amos 5 Look to God and Live

There was a way out! If God's people would turn to him, obey his commands, and turn away from sin, he would forgive them. But Amos wanted to be sure that the changes weren't just on the outside. They truly had to change their hearts and honestly desire to love and obey God.

Amos 6 Harsh Words

Amos had really harsh words for those who lived grandly and thought their lifestyle would go on forever and ever. He urged them to look at other doomed nations and consider their own future. Their pride would keep them from turning to God. They would be the first to be punished.

Amos 7 Visions of Destruction

Amos had three visions of the destruction that was coming to Israel. Locusts would come and eat all the food (Amos 7:1–3), and fire would burn and destroy what the locusts left behind (Amos 7:4–6). Then God held up a plumb line. It showed that the people of Israel were crooked. They were not straight and strong. Like so many times before, destruction would follow because of their sins.

Plumb Line Amos 7:7–9

A plumb line is a long string or cord with a heavy weight tied to one end. Builders held the line up against a wall to make sure it was straight.

Amos 8 A Basket of Ripe Fruit

The kingdom was ripe for ruin—like a basket of ripe fruit. Amos repeated the causes: greed, dishonesty, and mistreatment of the poor. Over and over again, the Bible makes it clear that there is no way to escape the consequences of continual sin.

Amos 9 Future Glory

Amos again predicted that exile was coming (Amos 9:1–8). Within thirty years, it happened. God's final message through Amos was that David's kingdom, which the northern kingdom had rejected, would recover and rule—not over one nation only but over a world of nations in final, eternal glory.

OBADIAH

Edom Is Doomed

O badiah is a little book with a big punch aimed right at Edom—a country near Judah. The people of Edom were distant relatives of the people of Judah. When the Babylonian armies defeated Judah and destroyed Jerusalem, Edom cheered. The people of Edom were even cruel enough to turn over some of the people of Judah to the Babylonians. They looted the cities of Judah after the armies of Babylon left. Obadiah wanted Edom, as well as the people of Judah, to know that God saw the way the people of Edom treated the people of Judah. He would punish them for it.

Writer:
Obadiah

Place:
Probably Judah

People:
Obadiah

Why Is It Important?
Just as surely as Judah was punished for its sins, God would punish Edom for its crimes against God's people.

Some Lessons in Obadiah:
God Is in Control: Obadiah 1–21

Obadiah 1–21 Edom Is Doomed

Obadiah prophesied that Edom would be destroyed forever. It would be as if it had never existed (Obadiah 10, 16, 18). But some people of Israel would be left and would return to live in Judah (Obadiah 17, 19, 20). As the years passed, the people of Edom were slowly defeated. The nation grew smaller and smaller. Eventually they disappeared completely.

Edom Obadiah 1

Edom was a country near Judah. Esau, the brother of Jacob, founded the nation of Edom (Genesis 36:1, 8). The people of Edom and the people of Israel were bitter enemies.

Obadiah Obadiah 1

Obadiah was a prophet of God. Nothing is known about his background. His name means "servant of God."

JONAH

A Fishy Prophet

Toss. Splash. Glub. Gulp. Jonah is the famous prophet who spent three days in the belly of a huge fish. That's what most people remember about this book. But Jonah's message from God was even more amazing than surviving a cruise in a fish. It was a message of love and forgiveness to a people who were more sinful than we can imagine. The people of Nineveh were the enemies of Jonah's people. He would rather see God destroy them than forgive them. No wonder he ran away!

Writer:

Jonah

Place:

Joppa and Nineveh

People:

Jonah and the people of Nineveh

Why Is It Important?

Jonah shows us that nobody is beyond hope and that God willingly forgives anyone who turns to him, no matter what the sin might be.

Some Stories in Jonah:

Running Away: Jonah 1:1–3

Rocking the Boat: Jonah 1:4–16

Swallowed by a Fish: Jonah 1:17

Jonah Prays and a Fish Vomits: Jonah 2

Nineveh Repents: Jonah 3

Jonah 1 Jonah on the Run

Jonah had his vision from God and quickly decided to run in the opposite direction. God told Jonah to go to Nineveh, to the east. Jonah was afraid and instead choose to disobey God. He started out for Tarshish, a city as far west as he could go.

Nineveh Jonah 1:2

Nineveh was the capital of the Assyrian Empire. The people of Assyria were defeating and destroying the northern kingdom of Israel where Jonah lived.

Joppa Jonah 1:3

Joppa was a city on the Mediterranean Sea. It was the main port for getting things to Jerusalem by sea. The cedar wood that was used to build the first and second temple was shipped to Jerusalem by way of Joppa (2 Chronicles 2:16; Ezra 3:7). It was natural that Jonah would think of Joppa when he was planning his getaway.

Modern-day Joppa, now known as the city of Jaffa

Tarshish Jonah 1:3

Tarshish was about as far from Jerusalem as Jonah could go by ship. It was a city in what is now Spain, way on the west side of the Mediterranean Sea.

Fish Jonah 1:17

Most of the time the Bible talks about the fish that people ate (Numbers 11:5; John 21:12–13). This verse in Jonah is the only one about the person a fish ate! Nobody knows for sure what sort of fish swallowed Jonah. It could have been a whale or some unusual fish large enough to swallow a human being.

Jonah 2 Jonah's Prayer

Jonah spent most of his time in the fish praying to God, thanking him that he hadn't died.

Jonah 3:1–9 Nineveh Turns to God

When Jonah preached to the people of Nineveh, he spoke in the name of the God of Israel—the nation that the people of Nineveh intended to destroy. But the people took Jonah seriously. They told God they were sorry for their sins.

Jonah 3:10–4:4 Disappointed Jonah

Jonah had not come to see the people of Nineveh turn to God. He had come to announce that God was going to destroy them. But God was pleased when the people of Nineveh asked for forgiveness, so he didn't destroy them. Jonah was disappointed when God was kind to his enemies.

Jonah 4:5–11 God's Love

God wanted Jonah to understand his love for people other than the Israelites. God set up a situation that would help Jonah see God's love for all of his creation. A vine grew up over the place where Jonah sat, protecting Jonah from the hot sun. The next day, God made the plant die. Now Jonah was angry because his protection from the sun was gone. Just as Jonah mourned the loss of the vine, God mourned when any of the people he created were lost. He still does.

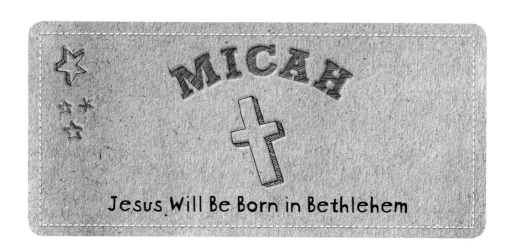

MICAH

Jesus Will Be Born in Bethlehem

Micah spoke in Judah—the southern kingdom. Under King Ahaz, he saw how wicked the government of Judah had become. Under Hezekiah, Micah watched Jerusalem and the people turn back to God. Micah's message was to both Israel and Judah—mainly their two capitals, Samaria and Jerusalem. He tells them that their sins are about to bring punishment. The cities would be destroyed, and the people taken captive. But Micah also told the people that God would not forget them. At some point in the future, he would bring them back to their homeland.

Writer:
Micah

Place:
Judah

People:
Micah

Why Is It Important?
Micah is a reminder of the greatness of God's love—that he loves us enough to forgive our sins and bless us when we turn to him.

Some Lessons in Micah:
A Promised Ruler Is Coming: Micah 5:2–5
What God Wants: Micah 6:6–8
Who Is Like God?: Micah 7:18–20

Micah 1 Judging Samaria and Jerusalem

Samaria was the capital of the northern kingdom of Israel. Samaria's rulers had led God's people deep into idol worship. They had set up calf idols at two towns in Israel, Dan and Bethel, two hundred years before (1 Kings 12:25–33). Now the people also worshiped Baal and the other idols of their neighbors. The southern kingdom of Judah, with its capital in Jerusalem, had not fallen as deeply into idol worship, but the people had not been completely faithful to God. Destruction was coming to both nations.

> ### Micah Micah 1:1
> Micah was a messenger from God who lived in the town of Moresheth, about thirty miles southwest of Jerusalem.

Micah 2–3 Cruel Rulers

In addition to worshiping idols, the leaders of the people were cruel in their treatment of poor people (Micah 2:2). Even while doing these terrible things, they basically said, "Hey! We're okay, aren't we? Doesn't God live here with us?" (Micah 3:11). Like God was a good-luck charm of some sort.

Micah 4 God's Kingdom Is Coming

Micah turned quickly to a future time when wars would cease. Then, just as quickly, Micah turned back to his own time and announced that the people would be taken as captives to Babylon (Micah 4:10). It was an amazing prophecy since Assyria, not Babylon, was the world power at that time.

Micah 5 A Ruler from Bethlehem

With Jerusalem surrounded by the Assyrians, Micah talked about a deliverer from Bethlehem. In a way, the angel of God who delivered Jerusalem from the destruction of the Assyrians (2 Kings 19:35) was a picture of Jesus, who delivers all human beings from the destruction of sin.

Micah 6 Judging Israel

Micah again listed the sins of the people of his time. They weren't thankful to God. They pretended to love God, but they really didn't. They were dishonest and worshiped idols. All would be punished.

Micah 7 A Future Vision

Micah was sad because of the people's sins. He warned them that they would be punished. But he ended his book with a vision of the future when God, with his people, would rule.

NAHUM

The Doom of Nineveh

Like the prophet Jonah, Nahum prophesied about the city of Nineveh. But Nahum did it without the ride in a fish. Nahum spoke about one hundred years after Jonah. Though the people of Nineveh had turned to God when Jonah preached there, they must have slowly swung back to their sinful ways. Nahum wanted his hearers to be sure they understood that God is merciful and kind, but he is also just. He will wait as long as he can to send punishment. But when people don't turn to him, his justice demands that their sins be punished.

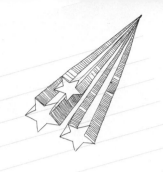

Writer:
Nahum

Place:
Judah

People:
Nahum

Why Is It Important?

God is slow to anger, and his mercy is great for those who turn to him and ask for forgiveness. But those who don't ask God to forgive their sins must eventually be punished.

Some Lessons in Nahum:

God Is Just: Nahum 1:3

God Is Loving: Nahum 1:7

Nahum 1–3 Nineveh Will Be Gone

Throughout these three chapters, Nahum sometimes talked *about* Nineveh and other times *to* Nineveh. Nineveh fell to the Babylonians only a short time after Nahum's prophecy. The city was so completely destroyed that it was never rebuilt.

Nahum Nahum 1:1

Nahum was God's messenger to the people of Nineveh. His name means "comfort." Little else is known about him.

Elkosh Nahum 1:1

Nahum was from the town of Elkosh. The town was probably located somewhere in southern Judah, but no one knows for sure.

Be Wise—Memorize!
Nahum 1:7 The LORD is good. When people are in trouble, they can go to him for safety. He takes good care of those who trust in him.

HABAKKUK

Habakkuk Argues with God

Habakkuk just didn't understand. How could God allow sinful people to go unpunished? And how could he use a nation even more wicked to punish Judah? Where is the justice in that? Habakkuk honestly admitted to God that he couldn't figure him out. But in the end, Habakkuk realized that he simply had to trust God.

Writer:
Habakkuk

Place:
Judah

People:
Habakkuk

Why Is It Important?
God's ways are so much bigger and higher (and smarter!) than our ways that it's impossible for us to understand. But it's not impossible to trust him.

The Lesson in Habakkuk:
Trusting God No Matter What: Habakkuk 3:17–18

Habakkuk 1:1–11 Habakkuk Complains

Habakkuk complained when God allowed his own nation to be destroyed for its wickedness by a nation that was even more wicked. Habakkuk could not see the justice in that. God's answer was that he did have a purpose.

Habakkuk 1:12–2:20 Habakkuk Complains Again

Habakkuk knew that Judah deserved to be punished for her sins. But he asked God for more information. God told Habakkuk that Babylon, which would destroy many nations, would someday be destroyed itself.

Habakkuk 3 Habakkuk Prays

Habakkuk asked God to perform miracles in order to save his people as he had done in the past. But Habakkuk knew that no matter what happened, God was in control and could be trusted.

Be Wise—Memorize!
Habakkuk 2:4 "The one who is right with God will live by faith."

ZEPHANIAH

God's Great Day Is Coming

The messenger Zephaniah speaks to the people of Judah during the reign of King Josiah. Josiah tries to bring about reform in Judah. Zephaniah tells the people that unless they turn back to God soon, judgment will come. Many people listened to Josiah and Zephaniah—but not all of them. A few years after Zephaniah's ministry, the Babylonians came. They destroyed Jerusalem and took many of the people back to Babylon with them.

Writer:
Zephaniah

Place:
Judah

People:
Zephaniah

Why Is It Important?
Zephaniah declared God's judgment, not just on Judah, but also on all the surrounding nations because of their idol worship. They were all punished.

The Lesson in Zephaniah:
Punishment Paves the Way for a New Beginning:
Zephaniah 1-3

Zephaniah 1:1–2:3 The Day of the Lord

The Day of the Lord is mentioned over and over in Zephaniah (Zephaniah 1:7–10, 14–16, 18; 2:2–3; 3:8). It would be a day of terror and would come on Judah and her neighbors very soon. Only twenty years after Zephaniah spoke these words, Babylon invaded Judah and carried away its people as captives to Babylon.

Zephaniah Zephaniah 1:1

Zephaniah was a messenger of God to the people of Judah. Zephaniah spoke during the reign of King Josiah, who tried to bring reform to Judah. Zephaniah's great-great-grandfather was King Hezekiah, so he was part of the royal family of Judah.

Baal, Molech, Stars Zephaniah 1:4–5

Molech was the god of the Ammonites, Judah's neighbors. Solomon had introduced the worship of Molech in Judah in order to please some of his wives (1 Kings 11:7). The worship of Molech involved the horrible practice of child sacrifice. The people of Jerusalem worshiped the stars, something else that was common among their neighbors.

Zephaniah 2:4–3:8 Judah and Its Neighbors

Within twenty years all the countries listed in these verses—including Assyria, the terror of the world, with its proud capital of Nineveh—would be destroyed by Babylon.

Zephaniah 3:9–20 Redemption and Peace Follow God's Judgment

These verses talk about a time of peace after the storm of the invasion. Zephaniah ended by assuring the people that God wouldn't forget them completely. He would bring some of his people back home to Judah to live. Besides the return of the Jews to Judah, this chapter also speaks to the age of peace at the end of time (Revelation 20:4–6).

Be Wise—Memorize!
Zephaniah 3:17 "The LORD your God is with you. He is the Mighty Warrior who saves you."

HAGGAI

Build the Temple First

About twenty years before Haggai came on the scene, fifty thousand Jews returned to Judah from Babylon. They begin to rebuild the temple but quickly stopped when their neighbors opposed them. The temple lay in ruins for years while the people built their own houses and businesses. Haggai wanted them to see the error of their ways. The best way to live life is to put God first. The Jews in Judah needed to put God's house before their own houses.

Writer:
Haggai

Place:
Judah

People:
Haggai

Why Is It Important?
In order for God to bless the people of Judah, they needed to put him and his house first.

The Lesson in Haggai
Rebuilding Their Own Houses Instead of God's:
Haggai 1:9

Haggai 1 Working on the Temple

The foundation of the temple had been put in place fifteen year earlier (Ezra 3:10). But nothing more had been done since that time. The people had lost interest. God, speaking through Haggai, told them that this was the reason their crops were so poor. Haggai's message stirred the people to action. In less than a month, work on the temple had begun again.

> **Haggai** Haggai 1:1
> God's messenger to the people who had returned from Babylon to Judah.

Haggai 2 God's House

Within a month, the old foundations of the temple had been cleared. The outline of the building could be seen. It was the middle of winter, and the people were busy rebuilding God's temple. The crops they had planted had not yet grown or been harvested. Through Haggai, God promised to bless their crops from then on.

Be Wise—Memorize!
Haggai 2:19 "From this day on I will bless you."

ZECHARIAH

God's Big Plans

Flying baskets, flying scrolls, chariots. Zechariah's visions churn with action. The temple in Jerusalem was being rebuilt. But the people were sad. This temple would not be great when compared with Solomon's temple. But Zechariah wanted them to continue to work. Through his visions from God, he showed them the wonderful plans God had for them and for the city.

Writer:
Zechariah

Place:
Judah

People:
Zechariah

Why Is It Important?
God's plans for his people are almost always bigger than anything they can imagine.

Some Stories in Zechariah:
Measuring Up: Zechariah 2
Clean before God: Zechariah 3
God's Big Plans: Zechariah 4
A Scroll That Flies: Zechariah 5:1-4
A Basket That Flies: Zechariah 5:5-11
Racing Chariots: Zechariah 6:1-8
Israel's Enemies Destroyed: Zechariah 9:1-12:9

Zechariah 1:1–6 Return to the Lord

Zechariah didn't want the people to forget that they had been punished for turning away from God. He didn't want them to repeat their parents' mistakes. As they heard Zechariah, the people realized that God had given them what they had deserved, and they promised to follow him faithfully.

Zechariah Zechariah 1:1
Zechariah was God's messenger to Judah while they were rebuilding the temple. He was probably born in Babylon and returned to Judah while still a young man.

Zechariah 1:7–17 Men on Horses

These horsemen went out over the earth. They returned to report that the world was at peace. Under King Darius of Persia, the world was at rest for a time. He allowed the Jews to rebuild their city and their temple. The end of the vision declared a bright future for Jerusalem.

Zechariah 1:18–21 Four Horns, Four Workers

The four horns are a picture of the nations that had destroyed Israel and Judah. The four skilled workers are a picture of those who would destroy the nations represented by the four horns. It was Zechariah's way of saying that the world powers of the day would be broken and that Judah would again become strong. God is on the throne, even when his people are defeated.

Zechariah 2 A Measuring Line

This wonderful chapter pictures a Jerusalem full of people. It will be a rich city and a safe one. No walls will be needed, since God himself will protect it.

Measuring Line Zechariah 2:1
A measuring line is a standard length of rope or cord for measuring distances.

Zechariah 3 Joshua the High Priest

This vision points ahead to the salvation from sin that Jesus would offer. Joshua's clothes were filthy, showing the sin of the people. His dirty clothes were removed, meaning that the people's sins were forgiven and God accepted them. This was a picture of a time when the power of Jesus would make everyone clean before God.

Zechariah 4 Lampstand and Olive Trees

The people working on the temple got pretty discouraged at the small work they were doing (Zechariah 4:10). God wanted them to realize that their work wasn't the point. His work was. He had big plans for them and for the temple.

Zechariah 5:1–4 A Flying Scroll

A large scroll, like a huge unrolled wall map, flew overhead. Written on it were the sins of the people. All those who would not turn back to God and ask forgiveness would be destroyed.

Zechariah 5:5–11 A Flying Basket

Zechariah saw a basket with a woman inside it. Two other women picked it up and took it out of the land. The woman in the basket is a picture of sin being removed from the land.

Zechariah 6:1–8 Four Chariots

The chariots were God's messengers of judgment. They wandered over the earth and carried out God's judgment on his enemies.

Zechariah 6:9–15 A Crown for Joshua

Joshua, a priest, is crowned as a king. This is probably a sign that in Jesus both the royal and priestly family lines would become one. Jesus would be both king and priest.

Zechariah 7–8 Fasting

For seventy years the people had been fasting in the fourth, fifth, seventh, and tenth months (Zechariah 8:19) to mourn the destruction of the temple. Now that it looked as though they were going to have a temple again, they had a question. Should they keep fasting? Zechariah reminded them that their fasts had a good purpose. He wanted to be sure they didn't fast just because it was the thing to do. That wasn't enough. They had to fast because their hearts were sorry for their sins and because they wanted to grow closer to God.

Be Wise—Memorize!
Zechariah 10:12 "I will make my people strong. They will live in safety because of me."

Zechariah 9:1–12:9 Judgment on Enemies

All through the centuries, Israel has had many enemies. Even today, nations oppose the Israelites. These chapters cover a number of enemies, past, present, and future, and explain that anyone who opposed God's people opposed God and would be punished.

Jesus in the Old Testament Zechariah 9:9

Jesus fulfilled this prophecy of Zechariah when he rode into Jerusalem on the colt, or baby, of a donkey (Matthew 21:1–5).

Zechariah 12:10–14:21 Israel's Future

These verses can be understood many ways. But everyone would agree with one thing. In the end, when time is no more, Jesus will reign as King of Kings and Lord of Lords over everyone and everything.

Jesus in the Old Testament

Zechariah 12:10–14

This prophecy of Jesus told how he would suffer and be "pierced." His hands and feet were pierced with nails when he was killed on the cross in Jerusalem. Many in Jerusalem that day were filled with horror and sorrow when they saw what had been done to Jesus.

Man riding a donkey in Israel

MALACHI

Following God with All Their Hearts

When Malachi spoke to the people, they had been back in Judah from Babylon for about one hundred years. The new temple had been built. The wall of Jerusalem had been rebuilt. Time in Babylon had cured the people of their worship of idols. But they still tended to ignore God's house. The priests were lazy. The people brought inferior sacrifices. They weren't giving to God as he had commanded. These Jews, favored by God above all other nations, sat and waited for the Messiah. They thought he would restore Judah to its earlier glory—as it had been under King David. Malachi told them that the Messiah would come, but his coming would mean judgment for them rather than glory.

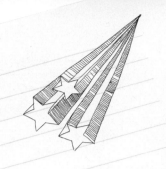

Writer:
Malachi

Place:
Judah

People:
Malachi

Why Is It Important?
Being lazy about worshiping God is not true worship at all. Giving God only half of our hearts and selves isn't enough.

Some Stories in Malachi:
God Deserves Your Best: Malachi 1
Robbing God: Malachi 3:8-12

Malachi 1 Giving God the Best

Instead of giving God the best they had, the people were bringing what was not so good. They brought gifts to God that they wouldn't think of giving even to the country's governor (Malachi 1:8). Instead of perfect animals for the sacrifice, they brought animals that were blind and sick—something God had told them not to do.

Malachi 2:1–9 A Word for Priests

Priests were not teaching the people to do right. Because the priests themselves didn't care about bringing the best to God, the people didn't care either. God would not ignore that sort of laziness in worship for long.

Malachi 2:10–16 Being Unfaithful to God

Men were divorcing their wives in order to marry women who worshiped other gods. The people noticed that the wicked nations around them were doing better than they were. So they were asking, "What's the use in serving God?" They didn't understand. The very fact that they weren't serving God faithfully was the problem.

Malachi 2:17–3:5 Judgment Is Coming

Malachi wanted the people to know that God would not allow this situation to continue forever. The coming day of judgment would show them whether it paid to serve God.

Malachi 3:6–18 Robbing God

Malachi changed the subject and spoke about how the people were stealing from God. When they didn't give God their tithes, they were robbing him. According to Moses, a tenth of all their income was God's property, and the giver had no more right to it than to another person's property (Leviticus 27:30). Note also that God promised good things—big time!—to those who faithfully gave to him.

Tithe Malachi 3:8

A tithe is a tenth of something. God wanted his people to bring to him the first tenth of everything they earned and everything they harvested. If they earned $10, God wanted them to return to him the first $1. Many Christians today still give a tithe to God as a way of putting God first in their lives.

Malachi 4 The Day of the Lord

Malachi ended his book by emphasizing that the Day of the Lord was for sure. God would judge those who had ignored him. And he would reward those who had faithfully followed him.

Malachi

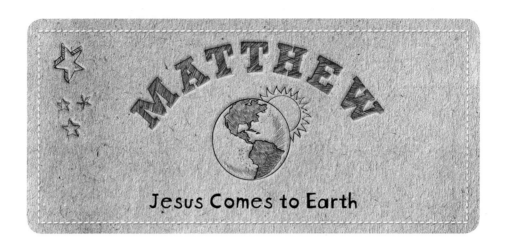

MATTHEW

Jesus Comes to Earth

It's him! It's him! Jesus, God's Son and the Savior of the world, has come. Matthew, one of Jesus' twelve disciples, wrote his account of Jesus to show God's people how Jesus fulfilled all that the Old Testament prophets had said about the Messiah. You see, Jesus wasn't exactly what the Jewish people were expecting their Messiah to be. They were expecting a king who would save them and rule over them on earth. Jesus is a king, but it wasn't time for him to rule here on earth—the issue of sin had to be settled first.

In his book, Matthew refers to Old Testament verses that predicted Jesus' birth, life, and death with amazing detail hundreds of years before they all happened. In fact, Matthew quotes from the Old Testament more than any other New Testament writer. Matthew probably first wrote his book in Hebrew for the Jewish people. It is thought that years later (around AD 60), he translated it into Greek so that non-Jews could also read and understand it.

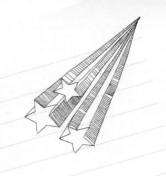

Writer:
Matthew

Place:
Around Galilee

Why Is It Important?
The book of Matthew shows us how Jesus came to earth to fulfill the prophecies of the Old Testament and be our Messiah.

Some Stories in Matthew:
Jesus Is Born: Matthew 1:18–25
Tempted in the Desert: Matthew 4:1–11
Jesus Miraculously Feeds Five Thousand People: Matthew 14:13–21
Jesus Enters Jerusalem: Matthew 21:1–11
Eating Together for the Last Time: Matthew 26:17–30
Arrested!: Matthew 26:47–56
Jesus Dies: Matthew 27:32–56
Alive Again!: Matthew 28:1–10

Matthew 1:1–17 Jesus' Family

Matthew begins his book by tracing Jesus' family all the way back to Abraham. He wants his readers to know that God had planned for Jesus to come to earth from the beginning.

Matthew 1:18–25 Jesus Is Born

When Joseph discovered that Mary was going to have a baby, he knew it wasn't his child. They were only "betrothed" at this time, not yet married. That means they had promised to marry each other. Today we would say they were "engaged to be married" but they were not married yet. An angel visited Joseph and told him that the baby was God's Son. So Joseph married Mary. He was a good husband to Mary and a good father to God's Son, Jesus.

Be Wise—Memorize!
Matthew 1:23 "The virgin is going to have a baby. She will give birth to a son. And he will be called Immanuel."

Joseph Matthew 1:18–25

Joseph, Jesus' father on earth, was a carpenter. Joseph didn't want to hurt Mary when he found out that she was pregnant with Jesus. He was going to quietly divorce her. (At that time, you had to get a divorce even if you were just engaged.) But an angel came and told Joseph that Mary's baby would be Jesus, the Savior. So he married her and cared for her and Jesus.

Mary Matthew 1:18–25

Mary was Jesus' mother. An angel came to tell Mary that she would have a baby and the baby would be Jesus (Luke 1:27–38), the Savior of the world. She was probably a young teenager when this happened, but she was willing to do whatever God wanted.

Jewish Wedding Tradition Matthew 1:18–25

Most Jewish parents arranged with other Jewish parents for their children to be married to each other. The parents would agree on all the conditions of the marriage. Then they would have a big party and announce to everyone that their children were getting married. The soon-to-be bride and bridegroom were usually teenagers and continued to live with their parents until their wedding a year or more later. During this time the bridegroom would prepare a house for his bride. When all was ready, the bridegroom would come to get her, and the wedding would take place. It was during their engagement that the angel came to tell Mary that she would have baby Jesus.

Jesus as Immanuel Matthew 1:23

All through history, God's purpose was to get a closer relationship with his people. Now he actually came and lived with them. Jesus was God's Son and also a human being. He lived and loved and worked on earth just like other people. But Jesus was also God. "Immanuel," the name the angel gave to Jesus, means "God is with us."

Matthew 2:1–8 Wise Men Visit

These wise men lived in a country to the east of Israel. When they saw the special star in the sky, they knew it was the sign that a king had been born. So they left home and followed it. First, they visited Herod, who was king at that time. Herod knew nothing of this new king, and the news scared him. He asked the teachers in Jerusalem where this king was going to be born. They said the Old Testament prophets had promised that the Messiah and King of the Jews would be born in Bethlehem.

Bethlehem Matthew 2:1–8

Bethlehem is the town where Jesus was born. Jacob's favorite wife, Rachel, was buried there (Genesis 35:19), and Ruth, whose story is told in its own book of the Old Testament, lived there (Ruth 1:22), as well as King David. Jesus' parents were from the town of Nazareth. They went to Bethlehem because the Roman governor had ordered all of the people of Judah to be counted. Mary and Joseph had to go to Bethlehem to be counted because Joseph was from the family line of David, and David was from the town of Bethlehem.

Herod Matthew 2:1–12

Herod, part of the line of rulers of Judea, was king when Jesus was born. When the wise men came to him to discover where this "king of the Jews" had been born, Herod reacted with anger and fright. He killed all babies in Bethlehem under the age of two years. But Jesus escaped to Egypt with his parents.

Matthew 2:9–12 Wise Men Worship Jesus

In Bethlehem, the wise men worshiped Jesus and gave him gifts with special meaning. The gold represented royalty and predicted that Jesus would be a king. The incense was used by high priests during prayers in the temple and foretold that Jesus would be a high priest. The myrrh was a spice that was often used as an oil in preparing bodies for burial. It foretold of Jesus' death. Then an angel came and warned the wise men not to go back to Herod as he had asked. So they went back to their homes a different way.

Matthew 2:13–15 Run to Egypt

An angel came to Joseph and told him what evil things Herod was planning. So Joseph took Mary and Jesus away to Egypt.

Matthew 2:16–18 Babies of Bethlehem Killed

It didn't take long for Herod to realize that the wise men weren't coming back to tell him about Jesus. He was so angry that he ordered his soldiers to kill all the baby boys in Bethlehem.

Matthew 2:19–23 Return from Egypt

An angel came to Joseph again and told him it was safe to return to Israel. Joseph and Mary, along with baby Jesus, didn't go to Bethlehem, but to their hometown of Nazareth.

Matthew 3 Jesus Is Baptized

This story is also found in Mark 1:1–11 and Luke 3:1–22. John the Baptist, who wore clothes made of camel's hair, told the people they needed to turn back to God. He told them that Jesus would be coming soon. One day, as John preached, Jesus walked up. John splashed into the river and baptized Jesus. As Jesus stood in the water, the Holy Spirit came on him in the form of a dove. God spoke from heaven so everyone there heard that Jesus was God's Son.

Baptism Matthew 3:13–17

Baptism is a special act that uses water to show that a person has been made pure and clean, and his or her sins have been forgiven because of Jesus' work on the cross.

Camel Matthew 3:4

Camels were the trucks of the desert. They carried people and goods all over the world during Bible times. They could carry heavy loads and travel long distances without water. The hair from camels was also used to make tents and very rough clothing. John the Baptist wore clothes made of camel's hair.

Matthew 4:1–11 Jesus Is Tempted

Right after Jesus' baptism, Satan came to him in the desert. He tried to get Jesus to listen to him. But Jesus knew Satan only wanted to defeat him and God. Jesus used the words of the Bible to defeat Satan instead. Afterward, "angels came and took care of him."

Matthew 4:12–17 Jesus Begins His Work

Matthew told of Jesus' work in Galilee, the area around Jesus' hometown of Nazareth.

Capernaum Matthew 4:13

Capernaum was a town on the Sea of Galilee. Jesus lived there and traveled from there out into Galilee to do his work.

Matthew 4:18–22 Calling Simon, Andrew, James, and John

(See the note on Mark 1:16–20.)

Matthew 4:23–25 Jesus Heals Sick People

Sick people. Deaf people. People with leprosy. Blind people. Wherever Jesus went, these people followed him. Jesus felt sorry for them and healed them. Just like that! Sick people were well. Deaf people could hear. Leprosy was gone. Blind people could see. When no one else could make someone well, Jesus could!

Matthew 5:1–12 Jesus Gives Blessings

Jesus said that people who are humble, patient, pure, peaceful, and hungry for what is right, would be blessed. These blessings, also called Beatitudes, are the beginning of what most people call Jesus' Sermon on the Mount.

Beatitudes Matthew 5:3–11

Words of blessing. Jesus told his followers what kind of people would be blessed. These are called beatitudes. If you read them, you'll find out what kind of person Jesus wants you to be.

Matthew 5:13–16 Salt and Light

Salt gives food flavor and makes it last longer. Light shows the way. Jesus wanted believers to be the salt and light of the world. Believers make the world a better place to live. They shine their light so others can find their way to God.

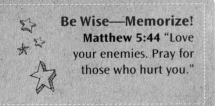

Be Wise—Memorize!
Matthew 5:44 "Love your enemies. Pray for those who hurt you."

Matthew 5:17–48 Jesus and the Law

Jesus came to fulfill and expand on God's laws. His life and teachings gave the laws even deeper meaning than before. In the Ten Commandments, God said not to murder. Jesus went deeper and said not to hate.

Matthew 6–7 More Teachings

Jesus continued his sermon with lots of teachings on how Christians should live and what things should be important to them. Getting rich on earth isn't as important for believers as storing up riches in heaven by serving God here on earth. Jesus told believers that they shouldn't worry. It gets them nowhere, and God will always be there to take care of them. To end his sermon, Jesus told a story about wise and foolish builders. Those who listen and follow Jesus are wise and build their lives on the rock of his teaching. Those who don't follow him are foolish.

Fasting Matthew 6:16–18

Fasting means to purposely go without eating for a specific amount of time. People fast when they pray for forgiveness or for some special, specific thing. Fasting helps people clear their minds of everyday things and think more about their praying.

> **Be Wise—Memorize!**
> **Matthew 7:7** "Ask, and it will be given to you. Search, and you will find. Knock, and the door will be opened to you."

Matthew 8:1–4 Healing a Man with a Skin Disease

(See the note on Mark 1:40–45.)

Matthew 8:5–13 The Commander's Servant

(See the note on Luke 7:1–10.)

Matthew 8:14–15 Peter's Mother-in-Law

(See the note on Mark 1:29–31.)

Matthew 8:16–17 Jesus Heals Many

(See the note on Mark 1:32–34.)

Matthew 8:18–22 Foxes Have Holes

(See the note on Luke 9:57–62.)

Matthew 8:23–27 Jesus Stops a Storm

Crash! Splash! Rock! Boom! The disciples were terrified. The storm was so bad they thought they were going to drown. But Jesus stood up and told the storm to stop. The disciples were shocked when the storm obeyed!

Matthew 8:28–34 Jesus Heals Two Men Controlled by Demons

(See the note on Mark 5:1–20.)

Matthew 9:1–8 Jesus Heals a Man Who Can't Walk

(See the note on Mark 2:1–12.)

Matthew 9:9–13 Jesus Calls Matthew

(See the note on Mark 2:13–17.)

Matthew 9:14–17 About Fasting

(See the note on Mark 2:18–22.)

Matthew 9:18–26 Jesus Raises Jairus's Daughter

(See the note on Luke 8:40–56.)

A Dead Girl Lives Matthew 9:18–19, 23–26

Not only could Jesus heal people who were sick, but he could bring dead people back to life. That's the most amazing thing of all. Can you picture how happy this little girl's mom and dad must have felt? Jesus saw that the girl's parents had great faith, and he loved them enough to do something that would make them happy.

Matthew 9:27–31 Jesus Heals Two Blind Men

Back in the Old Testament, the prophet Isaiah predicted that the Messiah (Jesus) would heal the blind (Isaiah 35:5). In this story, blind men call out to Jesus using the title "Son of David." This was a popular Jewish title for the coming Messiah. By calling Jesus "Son of David," the blind men were declaring that they believed that Jesus was the Messiah. Jesus healed them because of their faith in him. Jesus heals us too when we believe in him.

Matthew 9:32–34 Jesus Heals a Man Who Can't Speak

(See the note on Mark 7:31–37.)

Matthew 9:35–38 Traveling in Galilee

(See the note on Mark 1:38–39.)

Matthew 10 The Disciples Are Sent Out

This event is also told in Mark 6:7–13 and Luke 9:1–6. Jesus' teachings contained some wonderful advice for Christians. When they tell others about Jesus, they shouldn't expect it to be easy. However, they can depend on God to take care of them.

Disciples Matthew 10:1–4

Disciples are special students of a teacher. Jesus invited twelve men to follow him and become his disciples. Many people followed Jesus. But he spent more time with these twelve men and taught them things he didn't teach the others.

Tax Collectors Matthew 10:3

Jewish people who collected taxes from other Jews and sent the money to Rome. The Jews hated tax collectors for a couple of reasons. First, because tax collectors often cheated the Jews and kept part of the money for themselves. And second, the Jews looked on tax collectors as traitors because they were willing to work for the Romans.

Matthew 11:1–19 Jesus and John the Baptist

John the Baptist was in prison. Jesus was very popular, but John was wondering if Jesus was really and truly the Messiah, the one for whom the Jews had all been waiting. Jesus didn't think less of John because he was uncertain. Jesus' answer was so clear and so loving. He basically said, "Take a look at what's happening! Blind people see. Deaf people hear! The good news is being preached."

Matthew 11:20–24 Watch Out!

Jesus spoke against three cities: Korazin, Bethsaida, and Capernaum. He had done many of his miracles in and around these cities. But the people refused to turn away from their sin and believe in him.

Matthew 11:25–30 Take a Rest

What kind words Jesus spoke here. Jesus loves people enough to give them not only salvation (which would truly be enough) but also love and rest and kindness.

Matthew 12:1–8 Picking Grain on the Sabbath

(See the note on Mark 2:23–27.)

Matthew 12:9–14 Healing on the Sabbath

(See the note on Mark 3:1–6.)

Matthew 12:15–21 Many Miracles

No cars, buses, trains, or planes. These people walked many miles to find Jesus and be healed.

Matthew 12:22–37 Jesus and Beelzebub

This event is also told in Mark 3:22–30 and Luke 11:14–26. Jesus healed a man who was controlled by a demon and couldn't see or speak. This healing was so amazing that the Pharisees said Jesus must have been working with Beelzebub (Satan) to do such miracles.

The Pharisees hated Jesus. But they couldn't deny his miracles. There were just too many, and they were too well known for the Pharisees to say they didn't happen. So they had a choice. Either they accepted the miracles as coming from God's power or claimed they were from Satan's power. If they were from God, then the Pharisees had to believe in Jesus. If Jesus were for real, it would mean they were no longer in control. Their pride would not allow them to see Jesus as the true Messiah. So they said his power came from Satan.

> **Beelzebub** Matthew 12:22–28
> The prince of all demons. The devil. He is also known as Satan.

Matthew 12:38–45 The Sign of Jonah

This event is also told in Luke 11:29–32. What were the Pharisees thinking? After they accused Jesus of working miracles through Satan's power, they asked him for a sign—another miracle. Jesus promised that they would see an even more amazing sign: Jesus would rise from the dead. Jesus called this "the sign of the prophet Jonah." Jonah was in the stomach of a fish for three days. Jesus would spend three days in a grave and then rise again.

Matthew 12:46–50 Jesus' Mother and Brothers

This event is also told in Mark 3:31–35 and Luke 8:19–21. When Jesus pointed to his disciples and said that they were his mother and brothers, he wasn't trying to hurt his mother. He was simply saying that following God's will is more important that being with relatives.

Matthew 13:1–23 The Story of the Farmer

This story is also told in Mark 4:1–20 and Luke 8:4–15. The seed the farmer spread on the ground was a symbol of God's Word. This story teaches that some people would accept the good news of Jesus and others wouldn't. Some people would not even listen. Others would accept it but soon fall away. Some would hold on longer but gradually lose interest. And some would hold on until their lives showed what the good news of Jesus was all about.

Parable Matthew 13:1–23

Parables are stories that have a special meaning. Jesus told many common stories. The people remembered the stories easily. Sometimes the meaning behind the story was clear. Sometimes the meaning was difficult to understand.

Matthew 13:24–30 The Story of the Weeds

Jesus told his followers that his "good news" would be told throughout the world, but not everyone would accept it. The bad (weeds) would remain along with the good (wheat) until the end of the world.

Matthew 13:31–35 The Stories of the Mustard Seed and Yeast

These stories are also told in Mark 4:30–32 and Luke 13:18–21. These two stories were much alike. They showed that Jesus' kingdom would start out small, but it would grow until it became the biggest and most important thing in the world.

Matthew 13:36–43 Explaining the Story of the Weeds

When Jesus was alone with his disciples, he answered their questions. He explained to them what the story of the weeds meant (see the note on Matthew 13:24–30).

Matthew 13:44–46 Hidden Treasure and a Pearl

Jesus told two stories that showed that knowing him was worth more than anything else in the world.

Matthew 13:47–52 The Story of the Net

Jesus told a story about fishermen who caught good fish and bad fish in their nets. They kept the good fish and threw away the bad fish. At the final judgment, the same thing will happen. Those who love and follow Jesus will be saved, and those who don't love Jesus will be tossed aside and punished.

Matthew 13:53–58 Jesus Visits Nazareth

(See the note on Mark 6:1–6.)

Matthew 14:1–12 John the Baptist Is Killed

(See the note on Luke 3:1–20.)

Matthew 14:13–21 Feeding Five Thousand Men

Jesus fed five thousand men plus all the women and children who were with them. He didn't even have to go to the store! He just took a little boy's lunch of five loaves of bread and two fishes. He blessed it and had his disciples pass it out to the people. There was enough to feed all those people—with a basketful of leftovers for each of the twelve disciples!

Matthew 14:22–36 Jesus Walks on Water

(See the note on John 6:16–21.)

Walking on Water Matthew 14:22–36

Have you ever tried to walk across the water of a swimming pool? Or a puddle in your driveway? Can't do it, can you? You sink right in. But Jesus was so powerful that even a lake couldn't stop him from walking where he wanted to go. He just walked across the top of the water!

Matthew 15:1–20 Clean and Unclean

(See the note on Mark 7:1–23.)

Matthew 15:21–28 The Woman from Canaan

(See the note on Mark 7:24–30.)

Matthew 15:29–39 Feeding Four Thousand People

(See the note on Mark 8:1–9.)

Matthew 16:1–12 The Yeast of the Pharisees

(See the note on Mark 8:10–21.)

Pharisees/Sadducees Matthew 16:1–4

The Pharisees and Sadducees were well-educated leaders of the Jewish religion. They read the Bible and carefully followed the laws. They seemed to think God would be pleased if they were better than other people. When Jesus taught that it was more important to be loving and kind than to follow each tiny little law, the Pharisees and Sadducees became his enemies.

Matthew 16:13–20 Peter Says Jesus Is the Christ

This event is also told in Mark 8:27–29 and Luke 9:18–20. Peter had accepted Jesus as the Messiah about three years earlier (John 1:41–42). A year later, he called Jesus "Lord" (Luke 5:8). Six months after that, he called Jesus "the Holy One of God" (John 6:69). Now he announced that Jesus was the Christ, God's Son.

Peter Matthew 16:16

Peter was one of Jesus' disciples. He was a rash and outgoing man. He would often just blurt out what was on his mind. That sometimes got him into trouble. But he also realized Jesus was the Christ—and wasn't afraid to say so.

Matthew 16:21–28 Jesus Tells about His Coming Death

(See the note on Mark 9:30–32.)

Matthew 17:1–13 On a Mountain

(See the note on Mark 9:2–13.)

Matthew 17:14–20 Jesus Heals a Boy

(See the note on Mark 9:14–29.)

Matthew 17:22–23 Jesus Again Tells about His Death

(See the note on Mark 9:30–32.)

Matthew 17:24–27 Jesus Pays His Taxes

This tax was paid by every male in Israel for the upkeep of the temple. Jesus asked Peter if the son of a king usually paid taxes, and Peter said no. Jesus was saying that because he was God's Son, he really didn't need to pay the tax. But Jesus chose to pay the tax so he wouldn't make anyone angry. Here's the funny part of the story: Jesus, being God's Son, was able to make the tax money miraculously appear in a fish's mouth! Perhaps Jesus was laughing a bit when he told Peter to go fishing. Peter pulled up one special fish and found the exact amount of money to pay the tax.

Matthew 18:1–6 Who Is Greatest?

(See the note on Luke 9:46–48.)

Matthew 18:7–14 Things That Lead People to Sin

(See the note on Mark 9:42–50.)

Matthew 18:15–35 About Forgiveness

Jesus compared our sins against God with the sins others commit against us. God has forgiven us of so much—"millions of dollars" (Matthew 18:24). We, then, can and should forgive others the little bit they have sinned against us—"a few dollars" (Matthew 18:28).

Matthew 19:1–12 Question about Divorce

This teaching about divorce is also found in Matthew 5:31, Mark 10:2–12, and Luke 16:18. Jesus taught that one man and one woman, married for life, is God's will.

Matthew 19:13–15 Little Children

(See the note on Luke 18:15–17.)

Matthew 19:16–30 The Rich Young Man

(See the note on Luke 18:18–30.)

Be Wise—Memorize!
Matthew 19:14 Jesus said, "Let the little children come to me. Don't keep them away. The kingdom of heaven belongs to people like them."

Matthew 20:1–16 The Story of the Workers

In this story, Jesus taught this principle: Those who think they are first in this world are going to find themselves last in heaven. Heaven and earth are so different that many of the humblest Christians— those who spend their lives serving others like Jesus did—will have the high places in heaven.

Matthew 20:17–19 Jesus Again Tells about His Death

(See the note on Mark 9:30–32.)

Matthew 20:20–28 A Mother Asks Jesus a Favor

Jesus reminded his disciples as well as this mother that his work was not about who would be the most important. He reminded them that the key to a reward in heaven would be how believers loved and served others here on earth.

Matthew 20:29–34 Blind Men at Jericho

(See the note on Luke 18:35–43.)

Matthew 21:1–11 Jesus Enters Jerusalem

This event is also told in Mark 11:1–11, Luke 19:29–38, and John 12:12–19. As the people shouted and sang in praise, Jesus entered Jerusalem on the Sunday before his death. He knew the religious rulers had decided to put him to death. He also knew that this was part of God's plan—and he was ready for it. Jesus rode on the colt of a donkey because it was foretold that the Messiah would come that way (Zechariah 9:9). The people joyfully danced and sang along the way into Jerusalem.

Matthew 21:12–17 Jesus Clears the Temple

This story is also told in Mark 11:12–19 and Luke 19:45–48. Jesus went to the temple on the Monday before he died. He was angry when he saw the buying and selling that was going on there. Can you picture it? Tables overturned and money rolling along the floor. Animals running underfoot. Jesus told the people that they were misusing God's house.

Matthew 21:18–22 A Fig Tree Dies

This story is also told in Mark 11:12–14, 20–26. This fig tree died as a lesson to the disciples. Truth is more important than appearances. The fig tree appeared to have fruit—but it didn't. People who appear to believe—but really don't—will end up just like the fig tree.

Matthew 21:23–27 By What Authority?

This is also told in Mark 11:27–33 and Luke 20:1–8. The religious rulers were bitter because so many people were following Jesus instead of listening to them. They did everything they could to embarrass Jesus with trick questions. But he easily answered each one, often turning the question back on the religious leaders.

Matthew 21:28–32 The Story of the Two Sons

This story was for the religious leaders in Israel. The leaders rejected Jesus. But ordinary people—people who the religious leaders thought didn't deserve God's grace—accepted God's forgiveness.

Matthew 21:33–46 The Story of the Renters

This story is also found in Mark 12:1–12 and Luke 20:9–19. This story probably gave the Jews quite a shock. The story said they would reject their Messiah, who was actually Jesus himself.

Vineyard Matthew 21:33

A vineyard is a place where farmers grow grapes. In Israel during Bible times, a wall of stones or bushes with thorns often surrounded a vineyard to protect the fruit from wild animals.

Matthew 22:1–14 The Story of the Wedding Dinner

This story has the same point as the story of the renters. (See the note on Matthew 21:33–46.) God's people, the Jews, had rejected God and his messengers. Now, for a time, they themselves would be rejected, and other people would be invited to become God's people through believing in Jesus.

Matthew 22:15–22 Taxes to Caesar

(See the note on Mark 12:13–17.)

Matthew 22:23–33 When the Dead Rise

(See the note on Mark 12:18–27.)

Matthew 22:34–40 The Most Important Commandment

(See the note on Mark 12:28–34.)

Matthew 22:41–46 Son of David

(See the note on Mark 12:35–37.)

Matthew 23 Judging the Pharisees and Teachers of the Law

Jesus didn't have much good to say about the Pharisees and the teachers of the law. He called them things like "pretenders" (Matthew 23:15), "blind guides" (Matthew 23:16), and "poisonous snakes" (Matthew 23:33)! Jesus saw their hearts, and he didn't like what he saw.

Matthew 24 Signs of the End

These teachings can also be found in Mark 13 and Luke 21. Jesus taught about the destruction of Jerusalem, his own return, and the end of the world. Jesus' words about Jerusalem were fulfilled in less than forty years. The grand buildings of marble and gold were so completely destroyed by the Roman army in AD 70 that one writer said it looked as if no one had ever lived there.

Matthew 25:1–13 The Story of Ten Bridesmaids

This story means just one thing. We need to keep our minds on Jesus and be ready when he comes.

Lamp Matthew 25:1

There were no lightbulbs or electricity in Bible times. Lamps were little clay containers that held a bit of oil and a wick that would burn and produce light. It was important to keep enough oil in the lamp so the wick wouldn't go out.

Oil lamp perched on a stone

Matthew 25:14–30 The Story of Three Servants

The man in this story gave his servants a gift of money. He wanted them to use it to make more money. Jesus has given you gifts too. You may not have thousands of dollars like the servants in this story, but you do have something you can use for Jesus. Maybe you have the gift of kindness. Well, then, be kind! Or maybe you have a musical gift. Be sure to use it! Do you have the gift of sharing Jesus' love with others? Be sure to do that whenever you can. Whatever your gift may be, use it for Jesus!

Matthew 25:31–46 Sheep and Goats

Jesus uses sheep and goats to show that what you do here on earth matters. If you live for him, you are a sheep and will live forever with him. The goats are those people who don't love Jesus and will live forever separated from him.

Matthew 26:1–5 The Plot to Kill Jesus

(See the note on Mark 14:1–2.)

Matthew 26:6–13 A Woman Pours Perfume on Jesus

(See the note on Mark 14:3–9.)

Matthew 26:14–16 Judas's Terrible Deed

(See the note on Mark 14:10–11.)

Matthew 26:17–35 The Last Supper

This story is also told in Mark 14:12–25, Luke 22:7–38, and John 13–14. This supper was held the night before Jesus died. Jesus and his disciples shared the Passover supper, as the Jews had been doing for hundreds of years. The Passover pointed toward Jesus, who would soon himself become the lamb whose shed blood would save us. (Read Exodus 12 for more information on the first Passover.)

Matthew 26:36–46 Jesus in Gethsemane

Gethsemane was the garden area where Jesus often went to pray with his disciples. They went there after eating their last supper together. While they were praying, Jesus was arrested and taken away.

Matthew 26:47–56 Jesus Is Arrested

(See the note on John 18:1–14.)

Matthew 26:57–68 Before the High Priest

(See the note on Mark 14:57–68.)

Matthew 26:69–75 Peter Says He Doesn't Know Jesus

(See the note on John 18:15–27.)

Matthew 27:1–2 Jesus Is Led Away

(See the note on Mark 15:1–20.)

Matthew 27:3–10 Judas Hangs Himself

(See the note on Mark 14:10–11.)

Matthew 27:11–25 Before Pilate

Pilate asked Jesus if he was the king of the Jews. He wanted to know if Jesus was a rebel against Rome. Pilate found no reason to punish Jesus. Even Pilate's wife urged him to leave Jesus alone. But Pilate was too afraid of the Jewish leaders to do nothing. So he handed Jesus over to them.

Pilate Matthew 27:11–26

Pilate was the governor of Israel, who had been appointed by the government in Rome. Pilate could see that Jesus didn't deserve to die. But he was too weak-willed and afraid of the people of Jerusalem to set him free. He sent Jesus to be killed.

Matthew 27:26 Jesus Is Whipped

Prisoners were often whipped before they were put to death.

Matthew 27:27–31 Making Fun of Jesus

When the Jews tried Jesus, they made fun of him (Luke 22:63–65). Herod and his soldiers laughed and made fun of Jesus (Luke 23:11). While Jesus was on the cross, the robbers and the leaders of the Jews made fun of him (Matthew 27:41–44). Pilate's soldiers did the same.

Matthew 27:32 Simon of Cyrene

Jesus was weak and tired from a night of horror. He had not gone far when he became too weak to carry his cross any farther. Simon was forced to carry the cross from there. Simon was probably a Jew who had come to Jerusalem for the Passover.

> **Cyrene** Matthew 27:32
>
> Cyrene was an important city in North Africa. Many Jews lived there. Today Cyrene is just a small town.

Matthew 27:33–56 Jesus Is Crucified

You can also find this story in Mark 15:21–41, Luke 23:32–43, and John 19:17–30. Amazing events took place as Jesus spent his last hours on the cross. The land was dark for three hours. The earth shook, and the curtain in the temple was torn right down the middle. The bodies of many holy people were raised from the dead, showing that the power of death had been broken. Even the commander of the Romans who crucified Jesus could see that Jesus was someone special, the Son of God (Matthew 27:54).

> **Temple Curtain** Matthew 27:51
>
> A heavy curtain hung in the temple that enclosed God's presence in the Most Holy Room (see Exodus 26:33–34). It separated people from God's presence. Because of their sin, people would have been burned up in the presence of God. With Jesus' death, the total price had been paid for all sins. God's people were made righteous by Jesus' sacrifice and can now go right into God's presence.

Matthew 27:56–61 Jesus Is Buried

(See the note on John 19:38–42.)

Matthew 27:62–66 Guarding the Grave

(See the note on Matthew 28:11–15.)

Matthew 28:1–8 Women Visit the Tomb

This story is also told in Mark 16:1–8, Luke 24:1–12, and John 20:1–3. These women had spices to put on Jesus' body so it wouldn't smell so bad as time passed. They obviously didn't think he would rise again. They started out when it was still dark and reached the tomb when the sun was just coming up. When they arrived, they saw an angel sitting on the stone in front of the open tomb.

Matthew 28:9–10 Jesus Appears to the Women

In a time when women were not highly thought of, Jesus appeared first to them, even before he visited his disciples! Jesus appeared to Mary Magdalene when she was alone at the tomb. A little later, he appeared to several other women. Jesus loved these women who had helped him throughout his time on earth.

Matthew 28:11–15 The Guards

The guards were terrified of what they experienced when Jesus rose from the dead—angels, earthquakes, and an empty tomb. They went to the priests and told them what had happened. The priests didn't want this story to go any further. So they gave the guards lots of money to say they had fallen asleep and didn't see what happened. Many people believed the guards' story. But many also believed the truth—Jesus was alive!

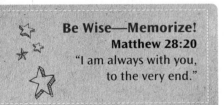

Be Wise—Memorize!
Matthew 28:20
"I am always with you, to the very end."

Matthew 28:16–20 Jesus Appears to His Disciples

It's hard to understand how one person can be with millions and billions of people at the same time. Yet Jesus said it, and it's true. No matter how weak or small or unimportant you may think you are, you are important enough that Jesus promised to be with you. Now. Next week. Next year. Forever.

MARK

Jesus Shows His Power

Mark showed us Jesus as a human being, one who loved and helped those around him. Mark tells us what Jesus *did* rather than what Jesus *said*. He doesn't record many of the teachings of Jesus. But he records hundreds of Jesus' actions. In the first chapter, Mark tells how Jesus healed the sick. Mark may have been brought to Jesus through Peter. He probably wrote this book from stories Peter told him about Jesus. Mark traveled with Paul and Barnabas as a missionary. He was the son of a woman named Mary, whose home in Jerusalem was a meeting place for Jesus' disciples (Acts 12:12). It is thought that Mark wrote his book sometime between AD 60 and 70, before the Romans destroyed Jerusalem.

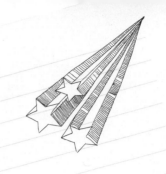

Writer:
John Mark, most often called Mark

Place:
Around Galilee

Why Is It Important?
Mark draws a picture of Jesus and his awesome supernatural power, recording one miracle after another.

Some Stories in Mark:
The Healer Begins His Work: Mark 1:29–34
Stopping a Storm: Mark 4:35–41
Jesus Heals a Sick Woman: Mark 5:24–34
A Widow Gives a Little: Mark 12:41–44
Pouring Perfume on Jesus: Mark 14:1–11
Jesus Dies and Rises Again: Mark 15:33–16:8

Mark 1:1–8 John the Baptist Prepares the Way

Mark starts his book with quotes from the Old Testament. He skips the story of Jesus' birth and jumps right into John the Baptist getting the people ready for Jesus to come.

Mark 1:9–11 John Baptizes Jesus

(See the note on Matthew 3.)

Mark 1:12–13 Jesus Is Tempted

(See the note on Matthew 4:1–11.)

Mark 1:14–15 Jesus Works in Galilee

Jesus had been preaching in the area around Jerusalem. But the Pharisees were becoming angrier and angrier with him, and Herod had put John in prison. Since he had work to do before his death, he thought it best to travel away from dangerous Jerusalem.

Mark 1:16–20
Calling Simon, Andrew, James, and John

This event is also told in Matthew 4:18–22 and Luke 5:1–11. Jesus called these four fishermen—two sets of brothers—to come and follow him.

> **Be Wise—Memorize!**
> **Mark 1:17** "Come. Follow me," Jesus said. "I will make you fishers of people."

Mark 1:21–28 Driving Out an Evil Spirit

This event is also told in Luke 4:31–37. This evil spirit controlled the body of the man in order to torture and destroy him. The demon knew that Jesus was God's Son, even when the people around didn't know it. Jesus commanded the demon to be quiet and come out. The demon obeyed. Jesus would not let the demon tell others who he was. He wanted to show the people that he was the Messiah by his miracles and teachings before he told the people that he was God's Son.

Mark 1:29–31 Healing Peter's Mother-in-Law

This story is also told in Matthew 8:14–15 and Luke 4:38–39. This account of healing is interesting because it tells us that Peter was married.

Mark 1:32–34 Jesus Heals Many

These events are also told in Matthew 8:16–17 and Luke 4:40–41. The news about healing the man with an evil spirit and Peter's mother-in-law spread all over the city. Great crowds came with their sick, and Jesus healed them. They were attracted by his miracles. Jesus' love for the people and his willingness to take care of them drew huge numbers.

Jesus Our Healer Mark 1:32–34
While Jesus was on earth, he spent a lot of his time healing people who were sick. He still does. He still notices when people are struggling with problems, sickness, discouragement, weakness, and fatigue. And he still heals them. He cares just as much about you today as he cared about the people he met when he was on earth.

Mark 1:35–37 Praying Alone
This story is also told in Luke 4:42–43. It had been a busy day. Jesus had probably healed several hundred people. Now it was time to get away from the people and get in touch with God.

Mark 1:38–39 Traveling in Galilee
Jesus made many trips around Galilee preaching and healing the sick. After these trips, he often returned to Capernaum, a town on the northwestern shore of the Sea of Galilee.

Mark 1:40–45 Healing a Man with a Skin Disease
This story is also told in Matthew 8:1–4 and Luke 5:12–16. After healing a man, Jesus told him to show himself to the priest. This was required by law for people with skin diseases (Leviticus 13–14). Jesus also told the man not to talk about his healing. He wanted to keep the crowds from getting out of control. The point of the miracles was to show God's love, not to gain power or fame.

Mark 2:1–12 Jesus Heals a Man Who Can't Walk
Talk about determined! These four friends didn't let a crowd stop them. When they couldn't get to Jesus through the door, they went through the roof! Their faith in Jesus' power to heal their friend and their will to get to Jesus pleased him. Jesus first met the man's spiritual needs—"Son, your sins are forgiven"— and then his physical needs. Pharisees and teachers of the law came from Jerusalem to check out Jesus. Before their angry eyes, he boldly offered to forgive the man's sins and heal him. This proved that he was God's Son. Jesus' actions amazed the people but only made the Pharisees angrier. If all that Jesus was saying was true, they'd be out of a job. They were very proud of their religious power and authority—they didn't want to lose it.

Mark 2:13–17 Calling Matthew

Jesus had chosen four fishermen to join him. Now he called a tax collector to be his disciple. Levi was also known as Matthew.

Matthew Mark 2:14

Matthew was one of Jesus' twelve disciples. Matthew was a tax collector, a job that most people hated. When Jesus said, "Follow me," Matthew had an amazing response. Without hesitating for even one minute, Matthew dropped what he was doing and followed Jesus.

Mark 2:18–22 Fasting

This teaching is also found in Matthew 9:14–17 and Luke 5:33–38. The three pictures Jesus uses—the groom, the torn clothing, the old wineskins—seem to mean that there are times when fasting is proper. But fasting is not always necessary, nor is it always the best way to express love for God.

Mark 2:23–27 The Sabbath Day

This event is also told in Matthew 12:1–8 and Luke 6:1–11. God had commanded that his people rest on the Sabbath. But through the years, the priests and rulers added more and more rules to God's laws. The Sabbath was more a day of trouble than a day of rest. The people had to work at not working! Jesus showed he was God's Son when he said he was Lord of the Sabbath.

Mark 3:1–6 Healing on the Sabbath

This event is also told in Matthew 12:9–14 and Luke 6:6–11. The Pharisees were pretty picky about the Sabbath. When on the Sabbath Jesus healed a man who had a weak and twisted hand, they made plans to kill Jesus. It's hard to believe that the Pharisees thought Jesus' act of kindness was a crime.

Mark 3:7–12 Crowds Follow Jesus

The crowds followed Jesus for two reasons. They wanted their sick to be healed. And they had begun to understand that Jesus was God's Son.

Sea of Galilee Mark 3:7

The Sea of Galilee was a large lake in the area of Galilee. The Jordan River flows into its northern end and out its southern end. Cold air blows down from the hills around it and causes sudden, powerful storms. Many of the events recorded by Mark took place around the Sea of Galilee.

Mark 3:13–19 The Twelve Chosen

(See the note on Luke 6:12–16.)

Mark 3:20–30 Jesus and Beelzebub

(See the note on Matthew 12:22–37.)

Mark 3:31–35 Jesus' Mother and Brothers

(See the note on Matthew 12:46–50.)

Mark 4:1–20 The Story of the Farmer

(See the note on Matthew 13:1–23.)

Mark 4:21–25 A Lamp on a Stand

(See the note on Matthew 5:13–16.)

Mark 4:26–29 The Story of the Growing Seed

Jesus told this story so that his people would know that his kingdom would grow slowly and quietly until time for the harvest. Only Mark recorded this story.

A boat on the Sea of Galilee

Mark 4:30–34 The Mustard Seed

(See the note on Matthew 13:31–35.)

Mark 4:35–41 Jesus Stops a Storm

This story is also told in Matthew 8:23–27 and Luke 8:22–25. With just a few simple words, Jesus showed his disciples that he had power over all creation. The disciples were afraid. But Jesus was in control, even when he was sleeping.

Mark 5:1–20 Healing a Man Controlled by Demons

You'll also find this miracle in Matthew 8:28–34 and Luke 8:26–39. When Jesus asked the demon his name, it answered "Legion." A legion was a Roman army unit of six thousand men. No wonder the man was so violent! The demons in the man knew right away who Jesus was. Notice that the people wanted Jesus to get out of their country. He had healed this insane man but destroyed their pigs.

Demons Mark 5:9
Demons are evil spirits—workers and messengers of Satan. They oppose God's work in any way they can. They sometimes entered human beings, like they did with the two men in this passage. But Jesus has more power than any demon.

Galilee Mark 5:1
An area in northern Israel. Jesus spent most of his time working there. Also, most of Jesus' disciples were from towns in Galilee.

Mark 5:21–43 Raising Jairus's Daughter
(See the note on Luke 8:40–56.)

Mark 6:1–6 A Visit to Nazareth
This story is also told in Matthew 13:53–58. Jesus had brothers and sisters, but at that time, the brothers did not believe in him (John 7:5). Later they did come to believe in him. Two of Jesus' brothers, James and Jude, wrote New Testament letters. The other two brothers were Joseph and Simon.

Nazareth Mark 6:1
Nazareth, the town where Jesus was reared, was located in the area of Galilee. Jesus preached his first message in the synagogue at Nazareth.

Mark 6:7–13 The Disciples Are Sent Out
(See the note on Matthew 10.)

Mark 6:14–29 John the Baptist Is Killed
(See the note on Luke 3:1–20.)

Mark 6:30–44 Jesus Feeds Five Thousand Men
(See the note on John 6:1–15.)

Mark 6:45–56 Jesus Walks on the Water
(See the note on John 6:16–21.)

Mark

Mark 7:1–23 Clean and Unclean

This story is also told in Matthew 15:1–20. This hand-washing rule was not intended to make dirty hands clean. It was a religious practice that the teachers of the law had invented. It was not part of God's law. Jesus taught that real cleanness is *inside* the heart—not on the *outside* of the body.

Mark 7:24–30 The Woman from Canaan

This story is also told in Matthew 15:21–28. A woman from Canaan asked Jesus to heal her daughter. Jesus answered by talking about dogs and children and bread. He was teaching that the good news (the bread) should first go to the Jews (the children). The woman understood what Jesus was saying. But she still asked for a "crumb" of the bread. Her faith amazed Jesus, and he gave her what she wanted. When she got home, her daughter was free from the demon.

Mark 7:31–37 Jesus Heals a Man Who Can't Speak

Jesus was now back in the area where the people had tried to make him king just a few weeks earlier. It was here that he touched a man's eyes and ears. Then he spoke, and the man could speak and hear. He told the man to keep quiet. Jesus didn't want to draw attention to himself at that time.

> **Healing a Man Who Can't Speak or Hear** Mark 7:31–37
> Most often Jesus' miracles were done with just a word. But Mark here included some interesting information. Jesus touched the man's eyes and ears. Then Jesus spoke and the man could speak and hear. Jesus did many miracles all through his work on earth.

Mark 8:1–9 Jesus Feeds Four Thousand

This story is also told in Matthew 15:29–39. This probably was near where Jesus had fed five thousand men and their families a few weeks before. Matthew added that it was at a time when Jesus was healing many people.

Mark 8:10–21 Yeast of the Pharisees

This story also appears in Matthew 16:1–12. Jesus returned to Galilee, and his enemies met him there. They wanted to make him look foolish in the eyes of the people. They asked for a miracle. For two years, Jesus had been healing huge numbers of people. He had fed thousands of people on two different occasions. And still they wanted a sign. Jesus was also bothered when his own disciples didn't seem to understand. So he scolded them for worrying about food while they were with him.

Yeast Mark 8:15

Yeast is put into bread to make it rise. It goes all through the dough. Jesus used yeast to describe how wrong teaching touches and affects everyone around it.

Mark 8:22–26 Healing a Blind Man

Jesus healed this man at Bethsaida, where he had done many miracles (Matthew 11:21) and near where he had fed thousands of people. He still wasn't ready to draw too much attention to himself. So he told the man to keep quiet.

Mark 8:27–30 Peter Says Jesus Is the Christ

(See the note on Matthew 16:13–20.)

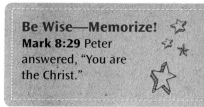

Be Wise—Memorize!
Mark 8:29 Peter answered, "You are the Christ."

Mark 8:31–33 Jesus' Coming Death

(See the note on Mark 9:30–32.)

Mark 8:34–9:1 The Cost of Following Jesus

(See the note on Luke 14:25–35.)

Mark 9:2–13 Jesus' Appearance Is Changed

This story is also told in Matthew 17:1–13 and Luke 9:28–36. This event helped the disciples understand more clearly that Jesus was God's Son. When Moses and Elijah appeared, it was as if God was saying, "See? Everything that's happened before and everything I've said was part of the plan to bring Jesus to earth to die for people's sins."

Transfiguration Mark 9:2–13

Transfiguration is a word used in some Bibles for how Jesus' appearance changed on the mountain. Jesus' clothes were so white they shone brightly.

Mark 9:14–29 Healing a Boy with an Evil Spirit

This story is also found in Matthew 17:14–19 and Luke 9:37–42. The disciples couldn't control this demon. But Jesus came along, and the demon obeyed him and left the boy. (See the note on Mark 5:1–20.)

Mark 9:30–32 Jesus' Coming Death

Up to this time, Jesus had not talked much about his coming death. But from here on, he wanted his disciples to understand what was going to happen to him.

Mark 9:33–37 Who Is the Greatest?

(See the note on Luke 9:46–48.)

Mark 9:38–41 Whoever Is Not Against Us Is for Us

(See the note on Luke 9:49–50.)

Mark 9:42–50 Leading People to Sin

Jesus wants you to be careful how you live so that nothing you do will lead someone else to sin.

Mark 10:1–12 Teaching about Divorce

(See the note on Matthew 19:1–12.)

Mark 10:13–16 Little Children

(See the note on Luke 18:15–17.)

Mark 10:17–31 The Rich Young Man

(See the note on Luke 18:18–30.)

Mark 10:32–34 Jesus' Coming Death

(See the note on Mark 9:30–32.)

Mark 10:35–45 James and John Ask Jesus a Favor

(See the note on Matthew 20:20–28.)

Mark 10:46–52 A Blind Man Sees

(See the note on Luke 18:35–43.)

Mark 11:1–11 Jesus Enters Jerusalem

(See the note on Matthew 21:1–11.)

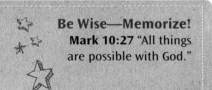

Be Wise—Memorize!
Mark 10:27 "All things are possible with God."

Mark 11:12–19 Clearing the Temple

(See the note on Matthew 21:12–17.)

Mark 11:20–26 The Fig Tree

(See the note on Matthew 21:18–22.)

Mark 11:27–33 Questioning Jesus' Authority

(See the note on Matthew 21:23–27.)

Mark 12:1–12 The Story of the Renters

(See the note on Matthew 21:33–46.)

Mark 12:13–17 Paying Taxes to Caesar

This event is also told in Matthew 22:15–22 and Luke 20:20–26. The Pharisees were trying to trap Jesus into saying something against the Roman government. That would give them an excuse to hand Jesus over to Pilate. But Jesus couldn't be trapped. His answer showed that Christians should obey their government. But the government should keep its nose out of religious things.

> **Caesar** Mark 12:17
>
> Caesar was the name of a famous royal family in Rome. It also became the title of the emperors of Rome. For example, the emperor of Rome when Jesus was born was not called King Augustus but Caesar Augustus (Luke 2:1).

Mark 12:18–27 Marriage When the Dead Rise

This event is also found in Matthew 22:23–33 and Luke 20:27–40. The Sadducees were educated and wealthy. They did not believe the dead would ever rise again. They were trying to trick Jesus into saying a man could have many wives in heaven—when God's law allowed only one on earth. Jesus settled the matter instantly and simply by saying that there will be no marrying in heaven.

Mark 12:28–34
The Great Commandment

This teaching is also found in Matthew 22:34–40. Jesus' first great commandment is found in Deuteronomy 6:4–5. The second is found in Leviticus 19:18. Note that Jesus put God first and neighbors second. The most important thing in life is how much we love God. Is he first in your life? Above everything and everyone else?

> **Be Wise—Memorize!**
> **Mark 12:30** "Love the Lord your God with all your heart and with all your soul. Love him with all your mind and with all your strength."

Mark 12:35–37 The Son of David

This story is also told in Matthew 22:41–46 and Luke 20:41–44. The point of the question is: How could a man call his own son "Lord"? Jesus' simple answer delighted the crowds and stumped the Pharisees (Matthew 22:46).

Mark 12:38–40 Watch Out for the Teachers of the Law

(See the note on Matthew 23.)

Mark 12:41–44 The Widow's Gift

This story is also told in Luke 21:1–4. Jesus took the time to point out the widow who gave a couple of pennies in the temple offering. Her gift may have been small, but it was all she had. That made it a gift of great value to God.

> **The Poor Widow** Mark 12:41–44
>
> Just a few pennies. That's all this widow had to her name. Nothing else. And instead of using those to buy food, she offered them to God. She was a dramatic example to Jesus' disciples of what real, honest, and true giving looks like.

Be Wise—Memorize!
Mark 13:31 "Heaven and earth will pass away. But my words will never pass away."

Mark 13
Teachings on the Second Coming

(See the note on Matthew 24.)

Mark 14:1–2 The Plot to Kill Jesus

This event is also told in Matthew 26:1–5 and Luke 22:1–2. The Sanhedrin—the ruling group of Jewish leaders—had decided that Jesus must be put to death (John 11:53). Under Roman rule, the Sanhedrin was given a great deal of authority, but it could not legally kill someone. And Jesus was popular with the people, which also made it difficult to harm him (Luke 22:2). The leaders' opportunity came two nights later. Judas, one of Jesus' disciples, delivered Jesus to them in the night. Then they accused Jesus of opposing the Roman leaders, hoping Rome would put him to death.

Mark 14:3–9 A Woman Pours Perfume on Jesus

This story is also told in Matthew 26:6–13 and John 12:1–11. This seems to have happened on the Saturday evening before Jesus entered Jerusalem for the last time (John 12:2, 12). (See more at the note on John 12:1–11.)

Mark 14:10–11 The Bargain of Judas

This event is also told in Matthew 26:14–16 and Luke 22:3–6. Judas's part was to deliver Jesus to the leaders when there were no crowds around. They didn't dare to arrest him in front of the people. They were afraid the crowds would riot and protect Jesus. Judas led them to Jesus in the evening after the city had gone to sleep.

Jesus knew from the beginning that Judas would betray him. Why Jesus chose Judas to be one of his disciples is a mystery known only to God. In God's eyes, Judas's act was wicked. Jesus said it would have been better for Judas if he had never been born (Matthew 26:24).

Mark 14:12–35 The Last Supper

(See the note on Matthew 26:17–35.)

Mark 14:36–42 Suffering in Gethsemane

(See the note on Luke 22:39–46.)

Mark 14:43–56 Jesus Is Arrested

(See the note on John 18:1–14.)

Mark 14:57–68 Jesus Is Tried

Jesus' trial is also covered in Matthew 26:57–27:31, Luke 22:54–23:25, and John 18:12–19:16. There were two trials. The first was before the Sanhedrin and the high priest—at night. The second was before Pilate, the Roman governor. The Sanhedrin could not carry out a death sentence without the Roman governor's consent.

Mark 14:69–72 Peter Says He Doesn't Know Jesus

(See the note on John 18:15–27.)

Mark 15:1–20 Jesus' Trial Continues

(See the note on Mark 14:57–68.)

Mark 15:21–41 Jesus Is Crucified

(See the notes on Matthew 27:33–56 and John 19:17–37.)

Mark 15:42–47 Jesus Is Buried

(See the note on John 19:38–42.)

Mark 16:1–8 The Women Visit the Tomb

(See the note on Matthew 28:1–8.) This event is also told in Luke 24:1–12 and John 20:1–10. Jesus mentioned Peter apart from the other disciples. After denying Jesus, Peter probably felt like he no longer belonged to Jesus, so he needed this special message. How wonderful of Jesus to give it to him! Jesus later officially took Peter back. (See the note on John 21:15–23.) Jesus' loving

A tomb from the time of Jesus

actions made Peter forever a faithful follower. He never again denied knowing Jesus. Peter's life ended when he died rather than deny Jesus.

Mark 16:9–13 Jesus Appears to Others

This event is also told in John 20:11–18. Jesus also appeared to the other women (Matthew 28:9–10) and to the two disciples traveling on the road to Emmaus. (See the note on Luke 24:13–35.)

Mark 16:14–18 Jesus Appears to the Eleven Disciples

(See also the notes on Luke 24:36–43 and John 20:19–23.) Jesus' command that the disciples go into all the world and preach the good news was given at this time.

Mark 16:19–20 Jesus Goes Up to Heaven

(See the note on Luke 24:44–53.)

LUKE

Jesus Loves and Teaches

The book of Luke tells more stories and teachings of Jesus than any other book. Luke records more about Jesus' birth. He also covers his boyhood, something no other book does. Sometimes Luke tells completely new stories. Sometimes he just adds interesting details to the stories found in Matthew, Mark, and John. You'll see Jesus at work, teaching and healing and loving those who followed him. Luke wants his readers to know that Jesus came to save not just the Jews but all people of the world. Luke was Paul's friend and a doctor. Perhaps Luke's training as a doctor taught him to write down important details. His book includes more details than the others about Jesus' life and ministry. Luke probably wrote his gospel about the year AD 60.

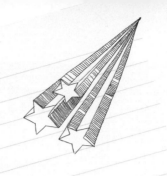

Writer:

Luke

Place:

Around Galilee

Why Is It Important?

Reading Luke will give you a clear picture of Jesus as a man, as well as the Son of God

Some Stories in Luke:

Jesus Is Born: Luke 2:1-7

Baby Jesus Visits the Temple: Luke 2:21-40

Boy Jesus Visits the Temple: Luke 2:41-52

John Prepares Jesus' Way: Luke 3:1-18

The Story of the Good Samaritan: Luke 10:25-37

The Story of the Lost Son: Luke 15:11-31

Jesus Goes to Heaven: Luke 24:50-53

Luke 1:1–4 Introduction

Others had already written down the story of Jesus. Luke looked carefully through those records. He also talked to people who had been with Jesus during his time on earth. Then he carefully wrote down the story of Jesus based on the facts. Luke's book was sent to a man named Theophilus (Luke 1:3). His name means "lover of God." It is not known just who he was. He was probably an important Roman official. He may have been one of Luke's converts in Philippi or Antioch. Perhaps he paid to publish the books of Luke and Acts for all to read.

Luke 1:5–25 John the Baptist

Luke is the only gospel that tells the story of the birth of John the Baptist. In the world at that time, someone would be sent ahead to prepare the way for the visit of a king. While old Zechariah was taking his turn serving as a priest in the temple, an angel notified him that he and his

> **Be Wise—Memorize!**
> **Luke 1:37** "Nothing is impossible with God."

wife, Elizabeth, would have a boy. This boy would prepare the way for Jesus. Elizabeth was quite old and had never had children. So when the angel told Zechariah that he would have a son, Zechariah at first didn't believe him. Because of this unbelief, the angel took away Zechariah's voice until John was born.

Luke 1:26–38 The Announcement to Mary

God ignored the powerful and famous families around Jerusalem. He went instead to an unknown woman from a poor home in a little village in Galilee. Mary was probably just a young teenager at that time and engaged to marry a man named Joseph. It was Jewish custom for girls to marry when they were quite young. At first, she was scared of the angel. But the message he brought was amazing. By the power of the Holy Spirit, Mary would become pregnant and give birth to the Messiah!

Luke 1:39–56 Mary Visits Elizabeth

Mary and Elizabeth were relatives (Luke 1:36). Elizabeth was pregnant with John—later to be called John the Baptist. As soon as she saw Mary, before Mary had even told her what had happened, Elizabeth's baby jumped inside her. Elizabeth knew right away that Mary was going to have Jesus. Mary stayed with Elizabeth for three months (Luke 1:56), probably until John was born. Then she returned to Nazareth.

Luke 1:57–80 John the Baptist Is Born

As soon as Zechariah named his son John, Zechariah could speak again. The people knew this was a special baby. They wondered what would happen as John grew older.

Luke 2:1–5 The People Are Counted

The Roman government wanted a list of all the people in Israel so that they could make sure they got the right taxes from them. Each family had to go to his or her family's town. For Joseph, who was from the family of David, that meant going to Bethlehem.

Luke 2:6–7 Born in a Barn

Nazareth was a hundred miles from Bethlehem. What a long and hard trip for Mary! All the rooms in Bethlehem were filled with other travelers. So Joseph and Mary camped in a barn. That night, the Savior of the world was born. Mary lovingly wrapped him up and put him in a manger, a place for animal feed.

Christmas—December 25 Luke 2:8

Today we celebrate Jesus' birthday on December 25—Christmas. But nothing in the Bible supports that date. It first appeared in the fourth century as the date of Jesus' birthday.

Luke 2:8–20 The Shepherds

Suddenly, an angel appeared to the shepherds who were keeping watch of their flocks in the hills around Bethlehem. The angel explained, "A Savior has been born to you; he is Christ the Lord." The angel was declaring that the baby was the long-awaited "Christ" (or "Messiah"), a deliverer sent by God. No wonder the shepherds jumped up and ran into Bethlehem to see Jesus!

Luke 2:21–38 Baby Jesus at the Temple

After the birth of a son, a Jewish woman had to wait forty days and then offer a sacrifice in the temple. The priests would then declare her to be clean again. This was according to the Jewish laws of Leviticus. She was to offer a lamb and a dove. But if she could not afford these, she could offer two pigeons or doves (Leviticus 12:2–8). Jesus' parents brought two pigeons as a sacrifice.

Simeon Luke 2:25

Simeon was a "good and godly" old man in Israel. God had told him he would see the Messiah before he died. When he saw baby Jesus in the temple, he praised God. Simeon prophesied that Jesus was a king over all. He would be a light to those who were not Jews (known as Gentiles), as well as to the people of Israel. Jesus fulfilled this prophecy in his ministry to both the Jews and those who weren't Jews.

Anna Luke 2:36–38

Anna was an old woman in the temple, who had been a widow for most of her life. She was a prophetess, and she spent her time in the temple praying. When Jesus' parents brought him there, she knew right away who he was. She told those around her, "This is the one we've been waiting for!"

Luke 2:39 Returning to Nazareth

Luke left out the events recorded in Matthew 2:1–21—the visit of the wise men, the escape to Egypt, the killing of the infants in Bethlehem, and the return from Egypt. He picked up the story when Mary and Joseph returned to Nazareth.

Luke 2:40 Jesus' Childhood

The Bible says little about Jesus' childhood. We do know that Jesus was the oldest of about seven children. His father was a carpenter. He probably had his share of family chores to do. But other than the visit to the temple when he was twelve, we only know that he grew and became strong and was very wise.

Luke 2:41–52 Jesus Visits Jerusalem at Age Twelve

Jesus was twelve years old. This was probably his first trip to Jerusalem, other than when he was first born (see Luke 2:22). Jesus was so interested in what the teachers had to say that he didn't even notice when his parents left for home. And they didn't notice that he was missing until they stopped for the night. It must have been a large group of friends and family traveling together. Jesus' parents seemed sure their boy was somewhere among them. They knew he was able to take care of himself until evening. Besides, in those days friends were like family—they would keep an eye on Jesus.

Jesus' knowledge of the Old Testament (Luke 2:47) at the age of twelve astounded the great teachers of the temple. Jesus lived

> **Be Wise—Memorize!**
> **Luke 2:52** Jesus became wiser and stronger. He also became more and more pleasing to God and to people.

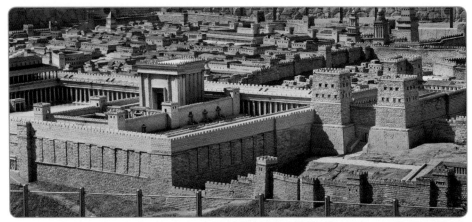

A model of the temple that Jesus would have visited

by God's Word and quoted from it throughout his life on earth. Isn't it interesting that Jesus was gone for three days? Perhaps that pictured the three days he would be in the grave before he came back to life.

Luke 3:1–20 John the Baptist

The preaching of John is also told in Matthew 3:1–12, Mark 1:1–8, and John 1:6–8, 19–28. John lived alone in the wild area west of the Dead Sea. This strange, rugged, holy man of the desert stood on the banks of the Jordan and shouted that the Deliverer whom the Jews had been waiting for was coming. John's preaching was hugely popular and successful. The whole land was stirred up by his words alone, since he did not perform any miracles (John 10:41). Great crowds came to be baptized by him (Matthew 3:5). Even the wicked King Herod liked to listen to him (Mark 6:20). John roused the nation and presented to them the Son of God. His work was done. About a year after he baptized Jesus, John was put in prison by Herod.

John the Baptist Luke 3:2–3

The man God sent to prepare the way for Jesus. John preached to the people and told them they needed to be forgiven for their sins. He told them that Jesus was coming and would bring them the forgiveness they needed.

Luke 3:19–20 Herod Antipas Throws John the Baptist in Jail

Herod the Great had three sons: Herod Antipas, Herod Philip, and Archelaus. Herod Antipas divorced his wife and married his niece, Herodias. This was a problem because Herodias was already married to her uncle Herod Philip. John the Baptist scolded Herod Antipas for marrying his brother's wife. Herod Antipas didn't like to be criticized by John the Baptist, so he had him locked up in jail. Herodias held a grudge against John the Baptist and later asked Herod Antipas to have John killed.

Luke 3:21–22 Jesus Is Baptized
(See the note on Matthew 3.)

Luke 3:23–38 Jesus' Family
(See the note on Matthew 1:1–17.)

Luke 4:1–13 Satan Tempts Jesus
(See the note on Matthew 4:1–11.)

Luke 4:14–30 Jesus Is Rejected at Nazareth

Jesus' powerful speaking amazed the people of Nazareth. They could hardly believe that this was the boy they had watched grow up. Even in that small town, Jesus had lived so quietly and was from such a lowly family that the people barely knew him (Luke 4:22). However, some of the things Jesus said offended them so badly that they flew into a rage and tried to kill him.

> **Synagogue** Luke 4:16
>
> A synagogue is the place where the Jews went to worship on the Sabbath. Before going away as captives to foreign lands, the Jews worshiped only in the temple in Jerusalem. When they returned to Israel, they rebuilt the temple, but they also built synagogues in their small towns where they worshiped each week. But they still went to the temple in Jerusalem for important feasts and worship days.

Luke 4:31–37 Healing a Man with an Evil Spirit
(See the note on Mark 1:21–28.)

Luke 4:38–39 Healing Peter's Mother-in-Law
(See the note on Mark 1:29–31.)

Luke 4:40–41 Jesus Heals Many
(See the note on Mark 1:32–34.)

> **Be Wise—Memorize!**
> **Luke 4:8** "Worship the Lord your God. He is the only one you should serve."

Luke 4:42 Praying Alone

(See the note on Mark 1:35–37.)

Luke 4:43–44 Good News of God's Kingdom

(See the note on Mark 1:38–39.)

Luke 5:1–11 Calling Peter, James, and John

(See the note on Mark 1:16–20.)

Luke 5:4–11 Lots of Fish

The disciples hadn't caught any fish during the night (the usual time for fishing). But when Jesus said to put their nets back into the water, they did it. They caught so many fish that their nets started to break! They hauled the fish into the boats, but they had so many that they were in danger of sinking. Jesus didn't just give them a little or even a normal amount of fish. He gave them more than they had ever caught before—maybe so they would know *for sure* that this was a miracle.

Luke 5:12–16 Healing a Man with a Skin Disease

(See the note on Mark 1:40–45.)

Luke 5:17–26 Healing a Man Who Can't Walk

(See the note on Mark 2:1–12.)

Luke 5:27–32 Calling Levi (Matthew)

(See the note on Mark 2:13–17.)

Luke 5:33–39 A Question about Fasting

(See the note on Mark 2:18–22.)

Luke 6:1–11 Jesus Is Lord of the Sabbath

(See the notes on Mark 2:23–27 and Mark 3:1–6.)

Luke 6:12–16 Jesus Chooses Twelve Disciples

Before making his final choice on the twelve disciples, Jesus spent all night praying to God. These twelve men would be the ones to spread the good news all over the world after Jesus went back to heaven. The New Testament tells only a little about their work in Israel, Asia Minor, Greece, and Rome. In about

AD 62, Paul said that the good news of Jesus had reached the known world (Colossians 1:23). It took these men only thirty years to spread the gospel. Most of the disciples ended up being killed for their faith in Jesus.

Luke 6:17–49 The Sermon on the Plain

This sermon is sometimes called the "Sermon on the Plain" because Luke begins with a description of Jesus "standing on a level place." Jesus was constantly teaching. He probably covered these same teachings several times in different places.

Luke 6:20–26 Blessings

(See the note on Matthew 5:1–12.)

Luke 6:27–30 Love Your Enemies

"Love your enemies"? Does that seem impossible? Many think so. But that's no excuse not to do as Jesus said. God will help you love those who offend and hurt you. It would be impossible if you had to do it on your own. But with his help, anything is possible.

> **Be Wise—Memorize!**
> **Luke 6:27** "Love your enemies. Do good to those who hate you."

Luke 6:37–42 Judging Others

This teaching can also be found in Matthew 7:1–5. Too bad it's so easy to judge others, isn't it? It really is easier to see the bit of wrong in someone else's life and ignore the huge wrongs in our own lives. Instead of finding fault with others, Jesus wants us to forgive and become givers.

Luke 6:43–49 Building on the Rock

This story is also told in Matthew 7:24–29. Jesus wanted his listeners to take his teachings seriously. Like they're building on sand, those who listen but don't follow will be disappointed in the end. But like they're building on a rock, those who listen and follow will be saved.

Luke 7:1–10 The Roman Commander's Servant

This story is told also in Matthew 8:5–13. This Roman officer was called a centurion. He was in charge of one hundred soldiers. At that time, Israel had been under Roman control for about one hundred years. Most Roman officers were cruel. A few, however, were good men. The first Gentile to be received into the church was a Roman officer named Cornelius (Acts 10). This story is amazing because of the Roman commander's great faith. He knew that Jesus needed only to speak words of healing and his servant would be healed.

Luke 7:11–17 Jesus Raises a Widow's Son

This is one of three times Jesus raised someone from the dead. The others are the daughter of Jairus (Mark 5:21–43) and Lazarus (John 11:1–44). Jesus may have raised others as well (Luke 7:22). No one asked Jesus to do this miracle. He did it because he felt sorry for the boy's mother. She had lost her husband, and now she had lost her only son. Jesus knew her life would be very hard without a son. So he raised her son back to life.

Luke 7:18–35 Messengers from John

(See the note on Matthew 11:1–19.)

Luke 7:36–50 A Sinful Woman

Banquets at this time were public affairs. Jesus would have been resting on a couch, his face toward the table, his legs stretched out behind him. So the woman could reach his feet easily. Try to picture the woman kneeling at Jesus' feet, crying so hard that her tears wet his feet along with the perfume. She dried his feet with her long hair. It was all to show Jesus how much she loved him. The others at the banquet were probably annoyed and embarrassed—but not Jesus. He treated the woman with kindness. He forgave her sins and sent her on her way.

Luke 8:1–3 Women Who Helped Jesus

These women traveled from town to town with Jesus and his disciples. They graciously provided service to the group, probably by doing things like gathering food, cooking and serving meals, and doing laundry. Three women are named here, but there were probably many others. Jesus had called seven demons out of Mary (called Magdalene). She was one of the women present at Jesus' crucifixion (Matthew 27:56). Nothing further is known of Susanna. Joanna was married to King Herod's steward. Her husband's job was to manage all the staff at King Herod's royal palace. Joanna belonged to the group of Jesus' closest friends. She was among those at the tomb (Luke 24:10).

Luke 8:4–18 The Parable of the Farmer

(See the note on Matthew 13:1–23.)

Luke 8:19–21 Jesus' Mother and Brothers
(See the note on Matthew 12:46–50.)

Luke 8:22–25 Jesus Stops a Storm
(See the note on Mark 4:35–41.)

Luke 8:26–39 Healing a Man Controlled by Demons
(See the note on Mark 5:1–20.)

Luke 8:40–56 Raising Jairus's Daughter
This story is also told in Matthew 9:18–26 and Mark 5:21–43. (See the note on Luke 7:11–17.)

Luke 9:1–9 The Twelve Disciples Sent Out
(See the note on Matthew 10.)

Luke 9:10–17 Feeding Five Thousand Men
(See the note on John 6:1–15.)

Luke 9:18–20 Peter Says Jesus Is the Christ
(See the note on Matthew 16:13–20.)

Luke 9:21–27 Jesus' Coming Death
(See the note on Mark 9:30–32.)

Luke 9:28–36 Jesus' Appearance Is Changed
(See the note on Mark 9:2–13.)

Luke 9:37–43 Healing a Boy with an Evil Spirit
(See the note on Mark 9:14–29.)

Luke 9:43–45 Jesus Again Tells of His Coming Death
(See the note on Mark 9:30–32.)

Luke 9:46–48 Who Is the Greatest?
Jesus told his disciples about his coming death, and what did they do? They argued about who would be greatest in his kingdom. How sad! They just didn't seem to understand. But Jesus had patience with them.

Luke 9:49–50 He's Not One of Us!

This story is also told in Mark 9:38–40. Jesus scolded John for trying to stop a man who was doing miracles in the name of Jesus. It was just because John didn't know the man.

Luke 9:51–56 Samaritans Do Not Welcome Jesus

The Samaritans' rude treatment of Jesus made James and John furious. Their reaction clearly showed why Jesus had nicknamed them the "Sons of Thunder" (Mark 3:17).

Luke 9:57–62 Foxes Have Holes

Jesus said the same thing to another man who offered to follow him (Matthew 8:19–22). Probably he had given this answer many times. He wanted people to know that following him would not be easy. Are you surprised at Jesus' answer to the second and third men? You have to look a bit deeper to see what he really meant. Jesus knew that the second man wanted to go home and take care of his father until he died, which could have been years. The man wanted to put off serving Jesus until later. The same is true of the third man. Jesus wanted them—and you—to know that following him should always be the first and most important part of your life.

Luke 10:1–16 Jesus Sends Out Seventy-Two

Jesus sent these disciples out to be sure everyone in the nation knew that the Messiah had come. They went ahead of him, toward Jerusalem, four or five months before his death.

Luke 10:17–24 The Return of the Seventy-Two

The success of the seventy-two disciples seemed to be a message to Jesus that Satan would certainly be defeated. But notice that Jesus warned them not to celebrate because evil spirits obeyed them. Instead, he wanted them to be glad because they were saved by Jesus and were promised an eternal home in heaven (Luke 10:20).

Luke 10:25–37 The Story of the Good Samaritan

This is one of the most beautiful stories of kindness in all history. Luke had just told how the Samaritans didn't welcome Jesus (Luke 9:52–53). This story was Jesus' response. He makes a Samaritan the greatest example of love and kindness.

Luke 10:38–42 Mary and Martha

Jesus was now getting close to Jerusalem. Mary and Martha lived in Bethany, about two miles from Jerusalem. So Jesus stopped for a visit. Martha welcomed him and then kept on working. What she did wasn't wrong. She just had her priorities out of order. Following and listening to Jesus are far more important than any busywork.

Luke 11:1–4 The Lord's Prayer

There is a longer form of this prayer in Matthew 6:9–13. Jesus wanted to give a good pattern for prayer for his people to follow.

Luke 11:5–13 More on Prayer

(See the note on Luke 18:1–8.)

Luke 11:14–26 Jesus and Beelzebub

(See the note on Matthew 12:22–37.)

Luke 11:27–28 The Word of God

Everywhere we look, we see and hear *words*. All those words can easily drown out the only true word—God's Word.

> **Be Wise—Memorize!**
> **Luke 11:9–10** "Ask, and it will be given to you. Search, and you will find. Knock, and the door will be opened to you. Everyone who asks will receive. He who searches will find. And the door will be opened to the one who knocks."

Luke 11:29–32 Signs

(See the note on Matthew 12:38–45.)

Luke 11:33–36 The Lamp

(See the note on Matthew 5:13–16.)

Luke 11:37–54 Warnings

(See the note on Matthew 23.)

Luke 12:1–12 Words of Warning and Hope

The religious people of Jesus' day were more concerned about what those around them thought than what God thought. They did things just to look good (Matthew 6:1–18).

Luke 12:13–21 The Story of the Rich Man

Notice that Jesus didn't get involved in this man's selfish family argument. Instead, he told a story about the results of being greedy. The rich man was foolish in God's eyes (Luke 12:20).

Luke 12:22–34 Riches in Heaven

If you're a Christian, your real home is in heaven. Jesus taught that believers shouldn't think mostly about their lives here on earth. He wanted them to think more about their future lives in heaven. He said that if we think mostly about our future with him, everything we need will be provided for us.

> **Lily** Luke 12:27
> A plant with large flowers shaped like trumpets. Jesus said the lily is more beautiful than even Solomon in all his beautiful clothes and golden jewels.

Luke 12:35–48 Be Ready

Jesus was talking to believers. He wants them to be faithful and ready for him to come back anytime.

Luke 12:49–59 Peace on Earth?

Jesus came to bring peace. But he knew that those who chose to follow him would have problems with those who didn't. He wanted the people to understand how important it is to decide to follow God before it's too late.

Luke 13 Some Lessons

Jesus told about a fig tree that didn't grow fruit (Luke 13:6–9) to show that God would be patient with his people—but only for so long. He healed a woman on the Sabbath (Luke 13:10–17) and shamed the Pharisees, who were saying that healing is work and shouldn't be done on the Sabbath.

When asked if only a few would be saved (Luke 13:22–30), Jesus answered that many who expected to be saved would be sadly disappointed. He said the door to salvation was narrow, and not many would go through it. Jesus ended these lessons by crying, "Jerusalem, Jerusalem" (Luke 13:34–35). He was sad. The very nation he had come to save would reject him.

Luke 14 More Teachings

Jesus went to the house of a Pharisee to eat on the Sabbath (Luke 14:1–6). While there, he healed a man who was sick. Funny, isn't it, that the Pharisees had no problem feasting on the Sabbath, but to heal a sick person was considered wrong. (See the note on Mark 3:1–6.)

Jesus had a lot to say to people who think they are more important than others (Luke 14:7–14). He said they should think about others first, rather than themselves. Jesus then told a story about a big banquet (Luke 14:15–24). The people who were invited gave lots of silly excuses for not coming. People did the same thing when Jesus invited them to follow him. They gave one excuse or another for not following. They would rather have what they could see right now than pay attention to what would last forever.

Jesus ended these teachings with hard words (Luke 14:25–35). Following Jesus would be tough. The people didn't seem to understand that. When Jesus said that those who followed him would have to hate their families, he meant that *he* would have to be first in their lives—not that they should actually hate their mother or brother or sister. The Bible clearly teaches us to love our families. But Jesus does mean that if a choice must be made between him and family, he must come first. When we love Jesus first, loving our family and friends will always be easier.

Luke 15 Lost Sheep, Coin, Son

This chapter, following the tough words of Luke 14, is like peace after a storm. The point of both is that Jesus wants to be first in the lives of his people. But, once he *is* first, he's full of love and kindness for them. They may stumble and stumble and stumble, but as long as they keep their faces turned toward him, he will forgive and forgive and forgive. Jesus told three stories to picture this teaching. A lost sheep, a lost coin, and a lost son— they were all found. Jesus will never give up on those who love him.

Be Wise—Memorize!
Luke 15:10 "There is joy in heaven over one sinner who turns away from sin."

Luke 16:1–18 The Story of the Clever Manager

Jesus said hard things about the love of money. Greed is a dangerous sin. It makes people think more about what they want than about what they need or what they have. It becomes something that people put first in their lives instead of Jesus. God knows that we need money to survive in this world. Having money is not bad unless we put more trust in it than in Jesus. If we put him first in our lives, he will provide for all that we need and want.

Luke

Luke 16:19–31 The Rich Man and Lazarus

Jesus told of a talk between Abraham and Lazarus after their deaths. The story clarified certain issues about what happens to us after we die. First, when those who believe in Jesus die, angels come and take them to heaven. Second, those who don't love and follow Jesus end up suffering (Luke 16:23). Third, after a person dies, he or she can't decide to follow Jesus in order to get to heaven. It's simply too late.

Luke 17:1–10 Forgiveness and Faith

Jesus taught that believers should forgive each other, even if it's seven times a day (see also Matthew 18:21–22). When the disciples heard this, they cried to Jesus, "Give us more faith!" They knew they didn't have enough faith to be that forgiving. Jesus told them even a little faith would get great things done for God.

Mustard Seeds Luke 17:6

Mustard seeds are itsy, bitsy, teeny, tiny seeds. Jesus said that's all the faith it takes to do great things!

Luke 17:11–19 Jesus Heals Ten Men

When ten men with leprosy (or some other skin disease) came to Jesus, he healed them all. He told them to go show themselves to the priests to prove they were no longer unclean (Leviticus 13–14). As they were on their way, their skin was healed. They were all amazed. But only one was amazed enough to come back to thank Jesus for healing him.

This great story shows how gladly Jesus used his power to do good, even for those who didn't bother to thank him. By his actions, he pictured for his disciples the sort of kind and loving heart he had just been talking about. (See the note on Luke 17:1–10.)

Skin Diseases/Leprosy Luke 17:12

When the Bible talks about leprosy, it can mean several different skin diseases. Leprosy caused a person's skin to get hard and then drop off, often causing victims to be deformed. According to the law, people with skin diseases had to live away from other people to keep the disease from spreading. They lived lonely lives. They missed their families, and their families missed them.

Luke 17:20–37 The Coming Kingdom

Jesus wanted the Pharisees to know that God's kingdom wasn't something on the outside of a person—kings or palaces or power—it was something on the inside, in a person's heart. Then Jesus' thoughts moved to the future. He told the disciples about the wonderful day when he would come back to earth in power and glory.

Luke 18:1–8 The Widow Who Wouldn't Give Up

Jesus told this story to show that God loves it when his people don't give up on praying for something. The widow in this story went over and over again to see a judge. She asked him for the same thing every time. Finally, she wore him down, and he gave her what she wanted. God does better. He hears, and sometimes his answers come quickly. When they don't, this story shows that we should not give up but keep on praying.

Luke 18:9–14 The Pharisee and the Tax Collector

The Pharisees thought they were so good already that they didn't need God. But the tax collectors knew differently. They knew they were sinners and needed God's forgiveness. That made it much easier for them to take that first step toward him. God wants us to understand how much we need him—like the tax collectors did.

Luke 18:15–17 Little Children

This story is also told in Matthew 19:13 and Mark 10:13–16. The disciples did not think children were important enough to bother with. That made Jesus angry. He loved children (Mark 10:13–14). Here Jesus taught that only people who humble themselves like little children will be found in heaven.

Luke 18:18–30 The Rich Young Ruler

This story is also told in Matthew 19:16–30 and Mark 10:17–31. Jesus told this young man to give up everything he had. Jesus wanted the young ruler to put Jesus first in his life instead of his money and power. But this young ruler was too much in love with his riches to be of any use in the kingdom of Christ. Jesus just wants us to put him first in our lives.

The eye of a needle (Luke 18:25) is thought by some to be the small town gate for people who are walking. The only way a camel could go through would be by kneeling and crawling through, almost impossible for a camel to do. Others think Jesus meant a real needle. Either way, Jesus meant it would be very difficult for a person who trusts in riches to get to heaven. But then he went on to remind his listeners that what is impossible for people is always possible for God!

Luke 18:31–34 Jesus' Death

(See the note on Mark 9:30–32.)

Luke 18:35–43 Jesus Heals a Blind Man

This story is also told in Matthew 20:29–34 and Mark 10:46–52. Just before he healed the blind man, Jesus told his disciples—for the fifth time—that he was on his way to be crucified (Luke 18:31–34). But they still did not understand what he was talking about (Luke 18:34). Perhaps they were still expecting him to become a king and rule on earth.

Luke 19:1–10 Zacchaeus

Zacchaeus was more than just a "wee little man." He was the main tax collector in the Jericho area. He was willing to look foolish in order to see Jesus, and he climbed a tree to see the Lord. Zacchaeus had stolen money from almost everyone. But when he met Jesus, he decided to pay everyone back and live a righteous life.

Sycamore Tree Luke 19:4

A sycamore is a large tree with sweet fruit. Its branches spread wide and close to the ground. That made it an easy tree for Zacchaeus to climb.

Luke 19:11–28 The Story of the Three Servants

This story is similar to the story in Matthew 25:14–30. It teaches the same general truth. God cares how we use our time, our gifts, and our money.

Luke 19:29–44 Jesus Enters Jerusalem

(See the note on Matthew 21:1–11.)

Luke 19:45–48 Clearing the Temple Area

(See the note on Matthew 21:12–17.)

Luke 20:1–8 By What Authority?

(See the note on Matthew 21:23–27.)

Sycamore tree

Luke 20:9–19 The Story of the Renters

(See the note on Matthew 21:33–46.)

Luke 20:20–26 Paying Taxes to Caesar
(See the note on Mark 12:13–17.)

Luke 20:27–40 The Dead Will Rise
(See the note on Mark 12:18–27.)

Luke 20:41–44 David's Son
(See the note on Mark 12:35–37.)

Luke 20:45–47 Beware of the Teachers of the Law
(See the note on Matthew 23.)

Luke 21:1–4 The Widow's Offering
(See the note on Mark 12:41–44.)

Luke 21:5–38 Teachings on the End
(See the note on Matthew 24.)

Luke 22:1–2 The Plot to Kill Jesus
(See the note on Mark 14:1–2.)

Luke 22:3–6 Judas Agrees to Betray Jesus
(See the note on Mark 14:10–11.)

Luke 22:7–38 The Last Supper
(See the note on Matthew 26:17–35.)

Luke 22:39–46 Suffering on the Mount of Olives
This event is also told in Matthew 26:36–46, Mark 14:32–42, and John 18:1. Jesus had come to earth from heaven knowing that his death on the cross was at the end of the road. He went to Jerusalem knowing what was ahead. But now that shocking thing was right before him. Not only would he die a horrible death, but he would also be separated from God. Jesus knew that he would be taking on the sin of the whole human race. It required separation from his Father. It made even Jesus, the Son of God, ask the question, "Lord, is there any other way?" But there was no other way. Jesus came to defeat death and pay the price for sin so that people could be close to God.

Jesus spent a long time in prayer—so long that his disciples fell asleep. His suffering was so great that he sweat drops of blood. He was so weak that God sent an angel to strengthen him (Luke 22:43–44).

Mount of Olives Luke 22:39

The Mount of Olives is the highest of the hills east of Jerusalem. It got its name from the olive groves that covered it. Jesus went to pray in a garden at the foot of the Mount of Olives.

Garden of Gethsemane on the Mount of Olives

Luke 22:47–53 Jesus Is Arrested

(See the note on John 18:1–14.)

Luke 22:54–62 Peter Says He Doesn't Know Jesus

(See the note on John 18:15–27.)

Luke 22:63–23:25 The Trial of Jesus

(See the note on Mark 14:57–68.)

Luke 23:26 Simon of Cyrene

(See the note on Matthew 27:32.)

Luke 23:27–31 Crying at the Cross

On the way to Calvary, some women followed Jesus and cried about what was happening to him. He told them not to cry for him but for their people. He knew the pain that the people who rejected him would face.

Luke 23:32–49 Jesus Is Nailed to a Cross

(See the notes on Matthew 27:33–56 and John 19:17–37.)

Luke 23:32–43 The Two Criminals

At first both criminals mocked Jesus (Matthew 27:44). But one changed his mind and seemed to understand that Jesus' kingdom was not of this world. Even Jesus' disciples didn't fully understand that! Jesus was dying, and they thought his kingdom was dying with him. A criminal understood Jesus better than his own friends did! Jesus' great love for sinners was shown to this criminal when Jesus promised he would see the man in paradise.

Luke 23:50–56 Jesus Is Buried
(See the note on John 19:38–42.)

Luke 24:1–10 The Women at the Tomb
(See the note on Matthew 28:1–8.)

Luke 24:11–12 Peter Runs to the Tomb
(See the note on John 20:3–10.)

Luke 24:13–35 Jesus Appears to Two Men
Jesus met these men in the afternoon on the road from Jerusalem to Emmaus. In the early morning hours, he had already appeared to several women (Matthew 28:9–10; Mark 16:9–11; John 20:11–18). These two men had heard that the tomb was empty but didn't realize that Jesus had risen.

Luke 24:36–43 Jesus Appears to the Disciples
(See also the notes on Mark 16:14–18 and John 20:19–23.) Thomas, one of Jesus' disciples, was absent (John 20:24). Note the disciples' joyous belief (Luke 24:34), and yet some were also disbelieving (Luke 24:41), even after Jesus had shown them his hands and feet. They wanted to believe, but what had happened was just so far beyond what they expected and what they could imagine.

Luke 24:44–53 Returning to Heaven
This event is also told in Mark 16:19 and Acts 1:3–11. Jesus' forty days of work after he rose from the dead were finished. His mission on earth was finished. Angels were waiting to take him back to God's throne. The disciples now fully believed all that had happened and what it meant. They went back to Jerusalem, as Jesus had commanded them to do. And they went shouting and singing and worshiping God.

JOHN

Jesus Is God's Son

John, one of Jesus' disciples, wrote this book to make sure people understood that Jesus wasn't just a man. He was God. John told of Jesus' miracles, which proved that Jesus was God's Son. But John told more of what Jesus said than of what Jesus did. John talked about how Jesus is the light of the world. He told how Jesus is the only way to eternal life. In a world where people worshiped many gods, John introduced the one God worthy of worship—his Son, Jesus.

John's father's name was Zebedee (Matthew 4:21). His mother seems to have been Salome (Matthew 27:56; Mark 15:40), who may have been a sister of Mary, Jesus' mother. If that was true, then John was Jesus' cousin. They probably knew each other as boys growing up in Galilee. John wrote his book around AD 60.

Writer:

John

Place:

Judea

Why Is It Important?

It shows that Jesus is God. And because that is true, we know his work here on earth and his death for our sins have great meaning.

Some Stories in John:

Jesus Goes to a Wedding: John 2:1-11

Jesus and Nicodemus: John 3:1-21

Walking on Water: John 6:16-21

Raising Lazarus: John 11:1-44

Peter Says He Doesn't Know Jesus:
  John 18:15-18, 25-27

Jesus Dies: John 19:28-30

Jesus Appears to His Friends: John 20

John 1:1–5 Jesus Is God

Word. Life. Light. All these words refer to Jesus. Jesus was there in the beginning. He was with God when the world was made. And he is now "God with us" in the world.

John 1:6–13 The Light of the World

John 1:6 introduces John the Baptist, who was sent from God to prepare the way for Jesus. Whenever this book uses the name "John," it means John the Baptist, not John the writer of the book. John the Baptist came "as a witness to the light." Jesus called himself the light of the world (John 8:12; 9:5; 12:46). As the light of the world, he lights up the way to God.

John 1:14–18 Jesus as a Human Being

God became a man in order to win people to himself. Jesus came and lived as you live. He came as a man in order to give you a better picture of the kind of God he is. God is like Jesus. Jesus is like God.

John 1:19–34 John Prepares the Way for Jesus

John skipped right over Jesus' birth. He began his story with John the Baptist. John told the people that Jesus was coming. John said he wasn't even good enough to tie Jesus' shoe—something that was a servant's job (John 1:27). Then he called Jesus "the Lamb of God" (John 1:29). John was telling the people that Jesus would be the sacrifice for their sins.

Be Wise—Memorize!
John 1:29 John said, "Look! The Lamb of God! He takes away the sin of the world!"

John 1:35–51 The First Disciples

Jesus called John, Andrew, Simon, Philip, and Nathanael (also called Bartholomew) to be his disciples. These five had been prepared for Jesus' coming by the preaching of John the Baptist.

> **Messiah** John 1:41
> Messiah is one of the names of Jesus. It means "anointed one" or "Christ."

John 2:1–11 Water Changed into Wine

Jesus' first public miracle was to turn water into wine. His mother Mary asked him to do it. They were at a wedding in Cana, which was near Galilee. The host had run out of wine for the guests to drink. Jesus lovingly told his mother that his time hadn't yet come. He meant that he didn't want people to know who he was just yet. Mary seemed to understand. She simply told the servants to obey him. To help out, Jesus turned the water in six large jars into wine.

Cana John 2:1

Jesus performed his first miracle in the small town of Cana. It was located in the area of Galilee.

Jars John 2:6

People in Bible times used large jars made of clay or stone to store lots of things. Jesus had some men put water into large stone jars. Each huge jar probably held about as much as two tanks of gas in a car. Jesus turned all that water into wine.

John 2:12–25 Jesus Clears the Temple Area

Jesus cleared the temple twice, three years apart. This one happened at the beginning of his ministry. The other happened at the end (Matthew 21:12–16; Mark 11:15–18; Luke 19:45–46). The first time, Jesus drove out sheep and cattle; the second time he drove out traders. Jesus' first act as he began his work was to challenge the religious leaders of the day. Jesus did so many miracles at this time that lots of people were ready to accept him as the Messiah. But he wasn't ready to show them who he was or how he would work as the Messiah.

John 3:1–21 Nicodemus

Jesus had made a huge impact on Jerusalem. Nicodemus, an important man and a Pharisee, came to talk to Jesus at night. He was interested, but he didn't want anyone else to know. Jesus told Nicodemus he had to be born again in order to be saved. Two years later, Nicodemus defended Jesus (John 7:50–52). Later still, he and Joseph of Arimathea buried Jesus (John 19:39). Nicodemus was a secret disciple in the early days of his faith. But later, when even Jesus' disciples had run away, he risked his life to care for Jesus' body.

John 3:22–36
Jesus and John the Baptist

Soon Jesus had a larger following than John. Some of John's disciples were jealous of Jesus' success. John reminded them that Jesus would become more important and he would become less important (John 3:30).

Be Wise—Memorize!
John 3:16 "God loved the world so much that he gave his one and only Son. Anyone who believes in him will not die but will have eternal life."

John 4:1–42 The Samaritan Woman

The Samaritan woman did not expect to see a man at the well at that time of the day. She also didn't expect a Jew to talk to her. This is the only time before his trial that Jesus clearly said he was the Messiah. How interesting that the religious leaders in his own country didn't accept Jesus. But these Samaritans—people despised by the Jews—did accept him.

Samaritans John 4:22

Seven hundred years before Jesus, when Assyria defeated the northern kingdom of Israel, they took the people of Israel captive and moved people from other defeated countries into Israel. The few Israelites who were left behind married the foreign people who moved into their land. This new group of people became known as Samaritans. The Jews hated the Samaritans because they were no longer a pure Jewish people.

John 4:43–54 The Official's Son Healed

Cana and Capernaum were almost twenty miles apart. Jesus performed this miracle from a distance. He did not need to see or touch the child to heal him. The official's faith was so great that he left for home as soon as Jesus said his son was healed.

John 5 Healing a Disabled Man

A pool in Jerusalem called Bethesda had special healing powers. Sick people would sit and lie all around it waiting for an angel to come and stir the water of the pool. When that happened, the first sick person in the pool was healed. One man was too sick to make it into the waters. This man did not see Jesus as his healer. The man could only think about the healing power of the pool. Jesus healed the man, who did not even know who Jesus was. Jesus didn't need the man's permission or even his faith in order to heal him. Later Jesus told the man to "stop sinning" (John 5:14). The results of sin are much worse than sickness of the body.

John 6:1–15 Feeding Five Thousand Men

This is the only one of Jesus' miracles that is described in all four gospels (Matthew 14:13–33; Mark 6:32–52; Luke 9:10–17). Jesus told the disciples to pick up the leftovers (John 6:12–13). The Jews thought of bread as a gift from God, so they were careful not to waste any. What's amazing is that there were leftovers after feeding five thousand men and their families from a little boy's lunch—Jesus went above and beyond to prove his power. This miracle made a great impression. The people were ready to make Jesus king (John 6:14–15).

Baskets John 6:13

There were twelve big baskets of leftover fish and bread after the feast Jesus created from a little boy's lunch. Baskets were used for just about everything in Bible times. People carried food, meat, and clay in them. They stored things in baskets in their houses. Small, medium, big, huge—baskets came in all sizes. Some were large enough for a man to fit inside (see the story of Paul's escape in Acts 9:25).

John 6:16–21 Jesus Walks on the Water

The disciples got into their boat and headed for the other side of the lake. A strong wind was blowing, and the water was rough. When Peter saw Jesus walking on the water, he wanted to try it too (Matthew 14:28). But after only a few seconds on the water, he began to sink. Jesus said he had too little faith.

John 6:22–71 Jesus the Bread of Life

Jesus spent a lot of time healing the sick and doing other miracles. But his real purpose in coming into the world was to save people from their sin. When he told them that, they began to lose interest. As long as he fed and healed their bodies, they thought he was great. They were looking for a king, not a Savior.

Bread John 6:35

Bread in Bible times was different than the bread we eat today. The loaves were flat, and the bread was coarse. Jesus said he was the bread of life. He meant that he would fill up anyone who was hungry to know about him.

Judas John 6:71

Judas, one of the disciples, followed Jesus all during his work on earth. But in the end, he turned Jesus over to his enemies.

John 7 In Jerusalem Again

Jesus went to Jerusalem again. Knowing the plan to kill him (most people seemed to know about it, John 7:25), Jesus stayed hidden right up until he appeared in the middle of the crowds in the temple. Then he began his speech by referring to their plot to kill him (John 7:19–23). When the rulers heard this, they sent officers to arrest Jesus. But the officers were amazed by what Jesus said (John 7:46), and they never got around to arresting him!

John 8:1–11 The Woman Caught in Sin

The Pharisees tried to trap Jesus by asking what they should do with this sinful woman. If Jesus said that she should be stoned, he would be going against Roman law, which did not allow the Jews to carry out death sentences. On the other hand, if he said that she should go free, he would be ignoring Moses' laws. Instead of answering, Jesus wrote in the sand. No one knows what he wrote—perhaps the names of the men in the crowd who were guilty themselves of sin! In the end, everyone left because of guilt or fear. Jesus told the woman to go and be sure not to continue sinning (John 8:11).

Be Wise—Memorize!
John 8:12 "I am the light of the world. Those who follow me will never walk in darkness. They will have the light that leads to life."

John 8:12–59 Jesus Continues Teaching

Jesus' statements about the rulers made them so angry they tried to stone him (John 8:59). Some of Jesus' harshest words were spoken to the religious leaders who refused to believe in him.

John 9 Jesus Heals a Man Born Blind

On this visit to Jerusalem, Jesus did another amazing miracle on the Sabbath (John 9:14). He healed a man who had been blind from birth.

John 10:1–21 Jesus the Good Shepherd

Jesus called himself the good shepherd of all those who would accept and follow him. He said he would carefully and lovingly take care of his people, just as a shepherd takes care of his sheep.

John 10:22–39 The Jews Don't Believe

The people asked Jesus to tell them if he was the Christ. He said he had already told them, but they wouldn't believe. They picked up stones to throw at him, but Jesus escaped.

John 10:40–42 Beyond the Jordan River

Jesus crossed the Jordan to get away from those who were trying to kill him. He stayed there for about two months. The area had many people. It was under Herod's rule and out of reach of the Jerusalem officials.

John 11 Jesus Raises Lazarus

Jesus' friend Lazarus died and was put into a tomb. No one thought they'd ever see him alive again. But Jesus knew better. He called Lazarus and told him to walk out of the tomb. Everyone was amazed at what Jesus did that day.

Lazarus was the third person Jesus raised from the dead (Jairus's daughter, Mark 5:21–43; the widow's son, Luke 7:11–17; and then Lazarus). This miracle brought the Sanhedrin to a final decision to kill Jesus (John 11:53).

View from inside what is said to be the tomb of Lazarus

Jesus, the Son of God John 11:27

Martha knew that Jesus was someone special. More than that, she knew he was God's Son.

Sanhedrin John 11:47

The Sanhedrin was the ruling group of Jews during Roman times. They were elders, or teachers of the law, or priests.

John 12:1–11 Supper at Bethany

Lazarus, Martha, and Mary must have been a wealthy family. The perfume Mary poured on Jesus was, for most people, equal to about a year's pay. Jesus probably had spoken of his coming death. Mary seemed to understand what he was saying. So she poured the rich perfume over his feet and wiped them with her hair. Jesus knew she was trying to tell him how her heart ached. He said her deed would never be forgotten. While Mary showed Jesus her love for him, the Jewish leaders continued to plot to kill him. More and more people were following Jesus, especially since he had raised Lazarus. The leaders planned to kill Lazarus also (John 12:10).

> **Be Wise—Memorize!**
> **John 11:25–26** "I am the resurrection and the life. Anyone who believes in me will live, even if he dies. And those who live and believe in me will never die."

Martha John 12:2

Martha was a friend of Jesus. She was a sister to Mary and Lazarus. Jesus must have been a guest in her home several times. Jesus corrected her when she complained that Mary wasn't helping her with all the work in the kitchen (Luke 10:38–42).

John 12:12–19 Jesus Enters Jerusalem

(See the note on Matthew 21:1–11.)

John 12:20–36 Some Greeks Come to See Jesus

When Jesus was told that some Greeks wished to meet him, he answered with some thoughts on his death. He didn't look forward to what was ahead. But he knew this was why he had come to earth. His only goal was to bring glory to God's name.

John 12:37–43
The Unbelief of the Jews

Even though he did wonderful miracles in front of them, the Jewish rulers refused to believe in Jesus. According to John, their hardhearted reaction fulfilled the words of Isaiah (see Isaiah 53:1; 56:10).

John 12:44–50 Jesus' Final Temple Message

Jesus probably gave these teachings on Tuesday. It was his last day in the temple.

John 13:1–30 The Last Supper

All through their time with Jesus, the disciples had argued about who would have the most important place when Jesus became king. Jesus had said over and over that he was going to die, but the disciples just didn't get it. Jesus finally got down on his knees and washed their feet, the act of a slave. He wanted them to understand that he had called them to serve, not to rule.

Then Jesus pointed out the disciple who would turn him over to his enemies (John 13:21–30). Judas kept his secret so carefully that none of the disciples suspected him. Judas now knew that Jesus knew his secret. But with a heart of steel, he left to carry out his terrible act.

John 13:31–14:31 Jesus Comforts His Disciples

The end had come. Jesus was ready for it. He dreaded the pain, but probably more he dreaded the moment when he would be separated from God—the moment when he would take on himself all of our sins. But through all the sorrow, he kept his eye on the joy beyond the pain. The disciples were puzzled when Jesus said he was leaving them. Peter thought maybe Jesus meant he was going on a dangerous mission. Peter offered to follow, even to die if it came to that. But Jesus kindly told Peter that he didn't know what he was saying.

> **Be Wise—Memorize!**
> John 14:6 "I am the way and the truth and the life. No one comes to the Father except through me."

Jesus then went on to give the disciples some comfort for the terrible times that were coming. He was going to prepare a place for them—a heavenly place. The people as well as the place had to be prepared. Jesus said he would send the Holy Spirit to comfort, train, and lead his people homeward.

John 15–16 Teachings on the Way to Gethsemane

The disciples were confused and upset by what was happening. Jesus did his best to comfort and prepare them for what was ahead. He wanted them to remember what he had taught them. He told them he loved them (John 15:9) and that they needed to love each other (John 15:12). He said they would be sad for a while, but their sorrow would turn to joy (John 16:20). He would send the Holy Spirit to comfort them and take them through the times and work ahead (John 16:13). Then Jesus lovingly called his disciples his "friends" (John 15:15). Jesus directed his words to his disciples, but they were meant for all those who would believe on him through the years— including you!

> **Be Wise—Memorize!**
> **John 16:33** "In this world you will have trouble. But cheer up! I have won the battle over the world."

John 17 Jesus Prays

Jesus ended these last teachings by praying for himself, for his disciples, and for all believers. Jesus came to save the world, but his special interest was in those who believed in him.

John 18:1–14 Jesus Is Arrested

This story is also told in Matthew 26:47–56, Mark 14:43–56, and Luke 22:47–53. Judas guided Roman soldiers, along with officials from the high priest, into the darkness of the garden where Jesus was praying. Judas kissed Jesus so the soldiers would know who to arrest. As the soldiers and officials came close, Jesus made them all fall to the ground. He wanted to make sure they understood that they could not take him against his will. He would go only when he was ready. Peter jumped right into the fight, drew his sword, and cut off the ear of one of the officials. But Peter's bravery would soon turn to fear.

John 18:15–27 Peter Says He Doesn't Know Jesus

Only a short time before, Peter had been willing to fight all the Roman soldiers alone. He certainly wasn't a coward. A whirl of emotions tore at Peter's soul that night. As Peter was denying that he knew Jesus, a rooster began to crow— just as Jesus had predicted (see John 13:38). That sound broke Peter's heart.

John 18:28–19:16 Jesus before Pilate

(See the notes on Matthew 27:11–25 and Mark 14:57–68.)

John 19:17–37 Jesus Is Crucified

(See the note on Matthew 27:33–56.) The soldiers broke the legs of the two men who were crucified with Jesus (John 19:32). They would die more quickly if they couldn't push themselves up on their legs.

Golgotha John 19:17

Golgotha was the place outside of Jerusalem where Jesus was killed on a cross. It was also called Calvary. Golgotha means "skull." The hill either looked like a skull or was called that because of the killings that took place there.

John 19:38–42 Jesus Is Buried

Joseph of Arimathea and Nicodemus were both members of the Sanhedrin and secret disciples of Jesus. Now, when Jesus had died, they both came out boldly to care for his body. Joseph of Arimathea went to Pilate to ask for Jesus' body, and then he took the body and buried it in his own tomb.

John 20:1–2 Mary Magdalene Goes to the Tomb

Other women were with her. (See the note on Matthew 28:1–8.)

Mary Magdalene John 20:1

Mary Magdalene was one of the women who followed Jesus throughout his time on earth. She was the first person who saw Jesus alive after he rose from the dead.

John 20:3–10 Peter and John Run to the Tomb

This story is also told in Luke 24:11–12. First to the tomb after the women, Peter and John may have been staying at a place closer to the tomb than the other disciples. Perhaps they were at John's home, where Jesus' mother also was staying (John 19:27).

John 20:11–18 Jesus Appears to Mary Magdalene

Mary Magdalene was alone at the tomb. The other women and Peter and John had left. She cried. She sobbed. She had no thought that Jesus was alive. Although Jesus had said that he would rise on the third day, she hadn't understood. When Jesus appeared it only took one word for her to know he was her Lord. Jesus called her name, "Mary." In that instant Mary's sadness turned to the greatest joy she had ever known.

A little later, Jesus appeared to the other women (Matthew 28:9–10). That afternoon he appeared to two men on the road to Emmaus (Luke 24:13–32), then later still to Peter (Luke 24:34).

John 20:19–23 Jesus Appears to His Disciples

That night, Jesus appeared to ten of his disciples in Jerusalem. Thomas wasn't with them (John 20:24). Jesus' appearances are recorded three times: John 20:19–23, Mark 16:14–18, and in Luke 24:36–43. Jesus' body looked the same, with the marks on his hands, feet, and side. He ate food. But his body had changed. He now had the power to pass through walls, to appear and disappear whenever he wanted.

John 20:24–31 Jesus Appears Again to the Eleven Disciples

Without seeing Jesus with his own eyes and touching him with his own hands, Thomas was having trouble believing that Jesus had risen from the grave. When Jesus appeared again when Thomas was with the disciples, he invited Thomas to touch the scars on his hands and feet so that Thomas would believe. Jesus said, "Blessed are those who have not seen me but still have believed" (John 20:29).

John 20:30–31 Purpose of the Book

John clearly stated here why he wrote this book. He wanted to show his readers that Jesus is God's Son and that Jesus is God.

John 21:1–14 A Last Miracle

The disciples had gone back to Galilee, as Jesus had told them to do (Matthew 28:7, 10; Mark 16:7). While waiting to see what would happen next, they went back to fishing. One morning, when they had caught no fish, Jesus came and told them to put their nets on the other side of the boat. Just one little change, and they caught more fish than their nets could hold.

John 21:15–23 Jesus Takes Peter Back

Three times Jesus asked if Peter loved him. Three times Peter answered that he did. Jesus asked this question three times, once for each of the three times Peter had denied knowing him. Jesus told Peter to feed God's sheep. Peter's business was no longer fishing. It was being Jesus' disciple and spreading the good news. Jesus then talked about how Peter would die. Some say that when Peter was going to be put to death on a cross, he asked to be hung upside down. He didn't think he was worthy to die as Jesus had died.

John 21:24–25 The End

John ended his book with a beautiful statement about Jesus' work on earth. If all Jesus had done—all the teachings and miracles and loving acts—had been written down, the whole world wouldn't have room for all the books.

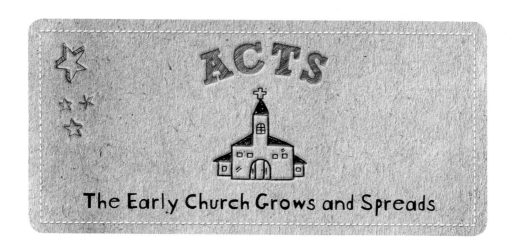

The Early Church Grows and Spreads

With a wind that rushed through the room and tongues of flame that sat on heads, Jesus' promise of the Holy Spirit came true. Jesus had gone back to heaven, and his followers had waited in Jerusalem for the Holy Spirit, just as Jesus had told them to do. When the Holy Spirit arrived, he gave the disciples power and courage. Jesus' followers spread the good news all through Jerusalem, through Judea, then through the entire world. Their amazing deeds, brave actions, and clear teaching made many decide to believe in Jesus. The book of Acts tells the story of the spread of the good news of Jesus and the beginning of the church.

Writer:
Luke

Place:
Around the Mediterranean Sea

Why Is It Important?
The book of Acts reminds us over and over again
that we are Jesus' witnesses in the world today.

Some Stories in Acts:
The Holy Spirit Arrives: Acts 2:1-13
Stephen Is Stoned: Acts 7:54-60
Philip Tells a Man about Jesus: Acts 8:26-40
Saul Is Saved: Acts 9:1-19
Peter Visits Cornelius: Acts 10
Freed from Prison by an Angel: Acts 12:1-10
Shipwrecked!: Acts 27:27-44

Acts 1:1–11 The Forty Days

Can you picture what it must have been like? You saw Jesus die. Then you saw him alive again. You talked to him and ate with him. How amazing and wonderful those days must have been! For forty days, Jesus appeared to his disciples. He wanted to make sure that they knew he was truly *alive*. After the forty days were over, Jesus told his disciples to wait for the Holy Spirit in Jerusalem. Then they watched as he was taken up into the clouds.

Acts 1:12–26 The Upper Room

Jesus' followers waited for the Holy Spirit together in an upstairs room in Jerusalem. Jesus' mother, Mary, was with them (Acts 1:14). This is the last time she is mentioned in the Bible.

Be Wise—Memorize!
Acts 1:8 "You will be my witnesses from one end of the earth to the other."

While they waited, the disciples chose someone to replace Judas. Judas died after he turned Jesus over to his enemies (Acts 1:18). The disciples prayed and then threw lots, kind of like rolling dice, knowing that God would use the result to give them clear direction. Matthias was chosen to take Judas's place among the twelve disciples.

Acts 2:1–13 The Holy Spirit Arrives

The sound of wind roared through the room. A mass of flames appeared and then separated. A small flame settled on the head of each person. Everyone began to speak in languages they had never learned. The Holy Spirit had arrived, just as Jesus said he would.

Thousands of people from many different countries (fifteen different nations are named in Acts 2:9–11) were in Jerusalem at that time. They heard Jesus' followers speak to them in their own languages. The disciples were completely surrendered to the control of the Holy Spirit.

Acts 2:14–36 Peter's Sermon

Bold, impulsive Peter jumped up and spoke for all of them. He explained that the Old Testament was being fulfilled before their eyes. God had said he would pour out his Spirit on all people (Joel 2:28–32). He called everyone to turn to Jesus for forgiveness. Then they, too, would receive the Holy Spirit (Acts 2:38).

Acts 2:37–47 The Newborn Church

Of those who heard the disciples preaching in different languages that day, about three thousand believed in Jesus. Those people were the beginning of the church. They shared everything—money, food, love, and praise for the God who had saved them. Because of their good example, new people were saved every day.

Acts 3 Peter's Second Sermon

When the Holy Spirit came, the tongues of fire and the sound of the wind quickly drew a crowd together. That crowd heard Peter preach his first sermon. Several days passed. The crowds returned home. The city quieted down. Then one afternoon Peter entered the temple. He healed a beggar who was known by almost everyone. This guy had been at the temple gate begging every day. His healing filled the city with fresh excitement. Crowds gathered, and Peter spoke to them again. Peter said the man was healed through the power of Jesus, who died and rose again. The number of believers grew to five thousand (Acts 4:4).

Be Wise—Memorize!
Acts 2:44 All the believers were together. They shared everything they had.

Acts 4:1–31 Peter and John in Prison

The rulers were worried about all that was happening. They arrested Peter and John and ordered them to stop speaking about Jesus. Peter answered them with grand boldness (Acts 4:9–12, 19–20). This was the Peter who in the same place and before the same people had said he didn't know Jesus. Now he stood tall and strong before them and said he had to obey God, not the rulers (Acts 4:19–20).

Acts 4:32–35 The Church Continues to Grow

The warning of the rulers made no dent on the church's enthusiasm. The believers continued to love each other and tell others about Jesus. The church kept on growing.

Acts 4:36–37 Barnabas

Barnabas's real name was Joseph. The disciples gave him the name *Barnabas*, which means "son of help." He must have been a great help and encouragement to earn a new name. He sold a field and gave the church all the money he received.

Acts 5:1–11 Ananias and Sapphira

Ananias and Sapphira lied. They didn't have to give anything to the church, but they sold some property, brought part of the money, and then lied by saying it was all they had gotten in the sale. Their sin was not that they didn't give all the money, but that they lied—they said they gave everything when they didn't.

They died for their sin, as an example for all time of how much God hates lying. God doesn't strike people dead every time they lie. If he did, people would be falling down dead all the time. But this event was a warning. God doesn't want people to try to look better on the outside than they are on the inside.

Acts 5:12–42 The Disciples Are Put in Prison Again

The rulers were amazed at the growing power of the Jesus they had put to death. They arrested the disciples again. They wanted to stone them, but Gamaliel convinced the Sanhedrin to let them go. Note how Peter continued to act bravely before the rulers (Acts 5:29–32). The rulers had the disciples whipped before letting them go. The disciples went on their way, happy because they had been chosen to suffer for Jesus (Acts 5:41–42).

> **Be Wise—Memorize!**
> **Acts 5:29** "We must obey God instead of people!"

Gamaliel Acts 5:34

A Pharisee and a member of the Sanhedrin. The Sanhedrin wanted to put Peter and the other disciples to death for preaching about Jesus. Gamaliel said they should be careful and let the men go. If what the disciples said was true, the Sanhedrin would be fighting against God. How right he was!

Acts 6:1–7 Seven Leaders Are Chosen

The church grew so fast and the disciples got so busy that they just couldn't keep up. The disciples were the ones who had been with Jesus during his time on earth. The only way to make that story known was by talking about it from morning until night. Seven other men were chosen to care for the physical needs of the church people—like serving food to the widows.

Acts 6:8–15 Stephen

Men from one of the Jerusalem synagogues began to argue with Stephen. But since he was filled with the Holy Spirit, his wisdom was just too great for them. Since they couldn't win an argument with Stephen, they hired some men to lie about him. He was arrested and brought before the Sanhedrin.

Acts 7 Stephen Dies

Wise and brave Stephen spoke to the Sanhedrin. He began with an Old Testament history lesson and ended with sharp words for their stubborn refusal to believe (Acts 7:51–53). They rushed at him like wild beasts. Stones began to fly. Stephen died as Jesus had died, saying, "Lord! Don't hold this sin against them!" (Acts 7:60).

Almost as a side note, Acts 7 ends with the information that Saul was there, agreeing that Stephen should be killed. Here is one of the turning points of history. Young Saul, who would later become known as Paul, saw all that was happening in the new church. And he saw Stephen die. Saul's rage against believers made him seek them out and put them in prison. But deep down inside, God was working, making Saul ready for his great vision on the road to Damascus (Acts 26:14). Saul was the one man who, more than any other, spread the good news across the world. His work altered the course of history.

Stephen Acts 7:59–60

Stephen was a wise man. He defended faith in Jesus before the Jewish leaders of his day. He was the first believer to die for his faith.

Acts 8:1–4 The Church Scatters

The attack on the young church, triggered by the stoning of Stephen, was wild and cruel. The believers scattered, taking with them all that the disciples had taught them.

Acts 8:4–40 Philip's Work

God sent Philip to preach the good news in Samaria. The people of Samaria believed. Even Simon, who was famous for his magic, believed and was baptized. God then sent Philip south, where he met and baptized a man from Ethiopia. Through that man, the news of Jesus made its way into Africa.

Philip Acts 8:12–13

Philip was one of the men chosen to make sure the widows in the early church got the help they needed (Acts 6:1–5). He told people about Jesus wherever he went.

Simon the Evil Magician Acts 8:9

A man with great magical power. Simon lived in Samaria. He was amazed at the powers and preaching of Philip.

Acts 9:1–30 Saul Believes

Saul was from the tribe of Benjamin (Philippians 3:5), which means that he was born into a Jewish family. He was born in Tarsus (Acts 21:39), an important city of the old Greek Empire. He was also born a Roman citizen (Acts 22:28) of a powerful and influential family. So Saul was Jewish, Greek, and Roman. He was trained as a Jewish Pharisee, which meant he was devoted to serving God by strict obedience to the Jewish law. Because of this, Saul did not believe that Jesus was the Son of God. He hated the people who followed Jesus and wanted to destroy the church. But one day, when he was on the way to Damascus, Saul saw a vision of Jesus. From that moment on, Saul served Jesus with a devotion few in history can match.

Damascus Acts 9:3

Damascus was a city north of Israel. It was the capital of one nation after another for thousands of years.

Saul/Paul Acts 9:17–18

Saul became the greatest preacher, teacher, and missionary of all time. Saul started out hating Christians and trying to get them killed (Acts 8:1). Then Jesus appeared to Saul on his way to Damascus, and Saul believed that Jesus was the Son of God (Acts 9:1–20). Saul, later known as Paul, spent the rest of his life teaching others about Jesus. He was hurt and put in prison many times for his work (2 Corinthians 11:23–27). Paul wrote a number of the books of the New Testament. In thirty years of ministry, he won huge numbers of people to Christ. While not recorded in scripture, tradition says that in Rome around AD 68, Paul was killed for his faith in Jesus.

Barnabas Acts 9:27

An early believer from Cyprus. When the church in Jerusalem was afraid of Paul and not sure he had truly become a believer, Barnabas took Paul's side. He told the church all that had happened to Paul. Barnabas went with Paul on his first missionary trip.

Acts 9:31–43 Peter in Joppa

Peter stayed in Joppa for some time. While there he raised Dorcas, also called Tabitha, from the dead—a miracle that led many to believe.

Joppa Acts 9:36

Joppa was a walled city on the Mediterranean Sea, located about thirty-five miles west of Jerusalem. Anything that came to Jerusalem by sea came through Joppa.

Acts 10 Peter and Cornelius

Until now the good news had been preached only to Jews, Samaritans, and others who followed the Law of Moses. Cornelius was an officer of the Roman army in Caesarea. God told Cornelius to send for Peter (Acts 10:5). God also sent a vision to urge Peter to go (Acts 10:9–23). And God poured his Holy Spirit on these men who weren't Jews but now were believers (Acts 10:44–48). After this,

Peter understood God's plan that the news of Jesus wasn't just for Jews. Peter then baptized Cornelius and the others.

Caesarea Acts 10:1

Caesarea, the Roman capital of Palestine, was built by Herod the Great. Peter (Acts 10), Philip (Acts 21:8), and Paul (Acts 24–25) all spoke of Jesus there. Paul was in prison there for two years.

Ruins at Caesarea by the Sea

Acts 11:1–18
Peter Explains What Happened

The rest of the apostles approved Peter's acceptance of Cornelius into the church, but only after Peter explained that it was God's doing.

Acts 11:19–30
The Church at Antioch

After the stoning of Stephen, believers who ran from Jerusalem went to Antioch and started a new church there. At first this church had only Jewish Christians (Acts 11:19). Before too long, some Greeks believed in Jesus and were baptized. The church in Jerusalem heard about it. They sent Barnabas to Antioch to let them know they approved. Many people who weren't Jews joined the church (Acts 11:24).

Barnabas then went to Tarsus, found Saul, and brought him to Antioch. God had called Saul to tell those who weren't Jews about Jesus (Acts 22:21). Saul became an active leader in the church at Antioch. When the church at Antioch sent a gift to the church in Jerusalem, Barnabas and Saul were chosen to take it to them.

Christians Acts 11:26

Followers of Jesus were first called *Christians* in the city of Antioch. Before that, Christians were often called followers of the Way (Acts 9:2).

Antioch Acts 11:26

Antioch was the capital of the Roman province of Syria. It was a busy city, and many came there to trade. One of the first major churches outside of Jerusalem was in Antioch.

Acts 12 James Is Killed; Peter Is Put in Prison

James, the brother of John, was the first of Jesus' twelve disciples to die. Later, when Herod put Peter in prison, the church prayed hard for him. His feet and hands had been chained to the prison wall. During the night, an angel appeared. The chains fell off Peter's hands and feet, the prison doors swung open, and Peter walked out—free! God then struck down Herod (Acts 12:23).

Rhoda Acts 12:13

Oops! Rhoda was a servant who was so surprised to see Peter at the door that she forgot to let him in the house. Many believers were in the house praying for Peter to be freed from prison. Now here he was, and they couldn't believe it!

Acts 13–14 Paul's First Missionary Trip

Paul had been a Christian now for twelve or fourteen years. He had become a leader in the church in Antioch. The time had come for him to move out to do his work. He would take the truth of Jesus to people all over the world (Acts 22:21). Paul and Barnabas set out from Antioch.

Paul and Barnabas went first to Cyprus, then on to Pisidian Antioch, different from the Antioch in Syria. Paul, as usual, started his work in the synagogue. Some Jews believed, as did many who weren't Jews (Acts 13:43, 48–49). But the unbelieving Jews stirred up trouble and drove Paul and Barnabas out of the city.

Paul and Barnabas stayed in Iconium for quite a long time (Acts 14:3). They performed miracles, and lots of people believed (Acts 14:1). But again, those who didn't believe drove them out of the city.

In Lystra, Paul healed a cripple, and the crowd thought he was a god. Later the people stoned him and left him for dead.

In Derbe, Paul and Barnabas made many disciples before returning to Antioch.

Be Wise—Memorize!
Acts 13:39 "Through him everyone who believes is made right with God."

Cyprus Acts 13:4

Cyprus is an island in the Mediterranean Sea. A large group of Jews lived there.

Iconium Acts 14:1

A city in Asia Minor that Paul visited on several of his missionary trips. Iconium was on the road to Ephesus and Rome.

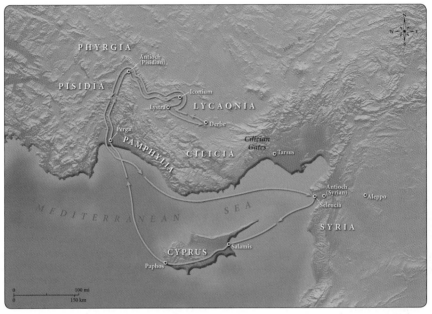

Map 9. Paul's First Missionary Journey

Acts 15:1–35 Church Leaders Meet in Jerusalem

It was time to settle a big question once and for all. God had clearly revealed to Peter that non-Jews could be part of the church without having to obey all the laws of Moses. Some Jewish believers didn't agree, however, and the church was being torn apart by arguing over the issue. At a meeting in Jerusalem, the church leaders decided that those who were not Jews did not have to follow all of the laws of Moses.

Acts 15:36–18:22 Paul's Second Missionary Trip

Paul and Barnabas went their separate ways after disagreeing over whether John Mark should join them on their second trip. Later they worked together again (1 Corinthians 9:6; Colossians 4:10). Silas was Paul's partner on this trip. John Mark went with Barnabas (Acts 15:39–40).

At Lystra, Paul found Timothy and took him along also (Acts 16:1). Paul made his way to Troas and from there to Philippi (Acts 16:11–12). In prison in Philippi, Paul and Silas sang hymns, and God sent an earthquake to open the prison doors (Acts 16:25–26). Paul and Silas were in Philippi only a short time, but many believed (Acts 17:1–9).

In Athens (Acts 17:15–34), Paul met the world's smartest, most well-educated people. It was his biggest challenge yet—to convince these people who worshiped many gods that there was only one God. Paul's message shows his brilliant mind and learning.

Corinth was one of the great cities of the Roman Empire. Paul stayed there a year and a half and founded a great church (Acts 18:11).

Paul then returned to Jerusalem and Antioch. On the way, he stopped in Ephesus, a visit he had wanted to make for some time. He would return to Ephesus on his third missionary trip.

Map 10. Paul's Second Missionary Journey

John Mark Acts 15:36–39

A young man who went on an early missionary trip with Paul and Barnabas. He didn't stay with them through the whole trip, however. When Paul and Barnabas were leaving on another trip, Barnabas wanted John Mark to go and Paul didn't. The disagreement ended up with Barnabas going one way with John Mark and Paul going another way with a new helper, Silas.

Silas Acts 15:40

Paul's partner on his second missionary trip. They traveled part of the time with Timothy.

Macedonia Acts 16:9–10

Macedonia was a Roman province in the area where Greece is today. Paul had a vision of a man from Macedonia begging him to come there and tell his people about Jesus. Paul went right away.

Lydia Acts 16:14

Lydia was a successful businesswoman who sold purple cloth. She heard Paul and Silas speak in Philippi and became a believer. Paul and Silas stayed with her while they were in Philippi.

Berea Acts 17:10

A city in the Roman area of Macedonia. When Paul told the people there about Jesus, they went right to their copies of Scripture to see if what Paul said was true.

Athens Acts 17:21

A famous city in Greece and one of the greatest in the Roman Empire. The people of Athens were well educated. They loved to talk and debate. Paul spoke in their famous place of debate, the Areopagus. Most of the learned men there just thought Paul was "chattering." They chose not to believe in Jesus.

Priscilla and Aquila Acts 18:1–2

Priscilla and Aquila were a husband and wife who were tentmakers living in Corinth. Since Paul was also a tentmaker, he stayed with them when he was in town. When Paul left for Ephesus, they went with him.

Acts 18:23–20:38 Paul's Third Missionary Trip

In Ephesus with a lecture hall as his headquarters (Acts 19:9), Paul spoke in public and from house to house (Acts 20:20), day and night, for three years (Acts 20:31). He supported himself by working as a tentmaker (Acts 20:34). With preaching and miracles (Acts 19:11–12), Paul shook the mighty city of Ephesus to its foundations. Magicians were so awed that they made a great bonfire of their evil books (Acts 19:19). Many who worshiped the false goddess Diana became Christians (Acts 19:23–26). Churches were founded for many miles around the city (Acts 19:10, 26). This was the end of Paul's three missionary trips, which together covered about twelve years.

> **Be Wise—Memorize!**
> **Acts 20:35** "It is more blessed to give than to receive."

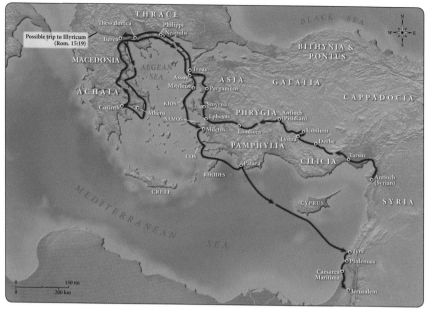

Map 11. Paul's Third Missionary Journey

Apollos Acts 18:24–26

Apollos was a well-educated man from Alexandria. Apollos knew about Jesus and spoke boldly about him. But he didn't know the whole story of Jesus' life and death. Priscilla and Aquila taught him what he needed to know.

Acts 20:7–12 Raised from the Dead

Yawn. Eutychus just couldn't stay awake. Paul talked on and on. Finally, Eutychus fell sound asleep. Problem was, he was sitting in a window—on the third floor. He fell to the ground outside and was killed. Paul hurried down the stairs and threw himself on the young man. Eutychus came back to life. The people were amazed and thankful.

Acts 21:1–16 Paul's Trip to Jerusalem

Paul went to Jerusalem to deliver a gift. Churches in Greece and Asia had gathered money to help the poor believers in Jerusalem (Acts 24:17). The gift showed the love of believers who weren't Jews for believers who were Jews. Some who knew and loved Paul warned him not to go to Jerusalem (Acts 21:4, 12). The Spirit had shown them that Paul would be captured there (Acts 21:10–11). They were afraid Paul would also be killed. But Paul trusted in God's plan for his life—and he went anyway.

Acts 21:17–23:30 Paul in Jerusalem

In Jerusalem, some Jews saw Paul in the temple. They began to yell. In no time, a mob fell on Paul like a pack of wild dogs. Roman soldiers appeared just in time to save him from being beaten to death.

On the stairway to the Roman fort, Paul asked the soldiers to let him speak. He told the angry crowd the story of Christ's appearance to him on the road to Damascus. They listened until he mentioned that God had sent him to tell people who weren't Jews about Jesus. Then the mob began to shout again that Paul should be killed.

The Roman commander brought Paul before the Sanhedrin. Paul's speech there caused another great uproar (Acts 23:9–10). The Roman commander ordered the soldiers to take Paul back to jail.

That night the Lord came to Paul and told him that he would get the chance to tell others about Jesus in Rome (Acts 23:11). Paul had *hoped* he would get to go to Rome (Romans 1:13). But now he *knew* he would get there.

The next day the Jews decided to kill Paul. They said they wouldn't eat or drink until Paul was dead. But Paul's nephew heard about the plot and warned him. It took seventy horsemen, two hundred soldiers, and two hundred men with spears to get Paul safely out of the city.

Acts 23:31–26:32 Paul in Caesarea

Paul spent two years in Caesarea as a prisoner in the palace of the Roman governor (Acts 23:35). Paul used his time there to tell everyone who came to see him about Jesus.

Paul made a deep impression on Felix, the Roman governor. Felix and his wife, Drusilla, spent many hours talking with Paul. But Felix's greed kept him from releasing Paul from prison without a bribe (Acts 24:26).

When Festus replaced Felix as governor, the Jews were still plotting to murder Paul. Festus was sure Paul had done nothing wrong. But he seemed to be planning to turn him over to the Jews. Paul knew that would mean death. So Paul appealed to Caesar (Acts 25:11). As a Roman citizen, Paul had a right to do that.

Festus called on Herod Agrippa to help him with Paul's case (Acts 25:13–26:32). Agrippa, from the hated and cruel family of the Herods, was surprisingly moved by what Paul had to say. But Festus thought Paul was crazy (Acts 26:24). They all agreed, however, that Paul had done nothing wrong (Acts 26:31).

Felix Acts 24:27

A governor of Judea in Roman times. Paul was tried before him. Felix married Drusilla, a woman who was married already and who was a Jew.

Festus Acts 24:27

Governor of Judea after Felix. He also put Paul on trial. He didn't think Paul had done anything wrong. But when Paul said he should be tried in front of Caesar, Festus was very willing to send him to Rome.

Herod Agrippa Acts 25:23

Agrippa was a ruler over much of the area around Jerusalem. Agrippa was a Jew but worked with the Romans. He sided with the Romans even when they destroyed Jerusalem in AD 70.

Bernice Acts 25:23

Bernice was a wicked woman who lived with her brother, Agrippa, as his wife. She heard Paul when he spoke to Agrippa, but she refused to believe in Jesus.

Acts 27:1–28:15 Paul's Trip to Rome

Under guard, Paul began the long and dangerous trip to Rome. The trip was made in three different ships. On one part of the journey, they ran into a terrible storm. After many days, everyone on board thought they were going to die. But God sent an angel to Paul to assure him that he would make it to Rome (Acts 27:24).

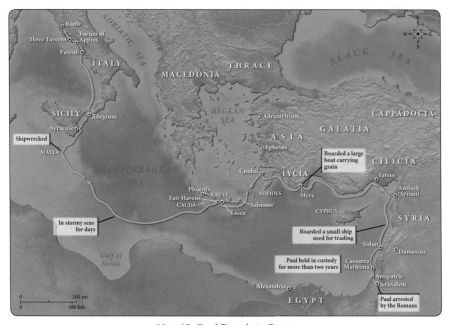

Map 12. Paul Travels to Rome

Malta Acts 28:1

Malta is an island in the Mediterranean Sea. Paul was shipwrecked there when he was on his way to Rome as a prisoner. While on Malta, a poisonous snake bit Paul on the hand. Everyone expected him to get sick and die. But God protected Paul. He wasn't hurt (Acts 28:3–6).

Acts 28:16–31 Paul in Rome

Paul was in Rome at least two years (Acts 28:30). Though a prisoner, he was allowed to live in his own rented house with his guard (Acts 28:16). He could have visitors and could teach those who came about Christ.

Though the Bible doesn't say it, many people believe Paul was found innocent of any crime and perhaps made a fourth missionary trip. He was later arrested again, taken back to Rome, and finally beheaded. Paul's ministry lasted about thirty years. In those years, he won huge numbers of people to Christ.

ROMANS

Saved by Faith

Paul wrote this letter to the Roman Christians to let them know he would be coming to visit them. To get them ready for his visit, he explained the plan of salvation clearly and carefully. First, he looked at all people—those who were Jews and those who weren't Jews—and discovered that all were sinners. Both Jews and non-Jews alike needed to be saved from their sins. Paul then laid out the way that they could be saved. Only through Jesus' work of living and dying and rising again could anyone hope to be saved. The book was probably written in the spring of AD 57 on Paul's third missionary trip.

Writer:
Paul

Place:
Corinth

Why Is It Important?
The book of Romans is the clearest picture in the Bible of God's plan to save people from their sins. Paul carefully used the Old Testament and the events of Jesus' life to show how God worked out the plan of salvation.

Some Teachings in Romans:
Everyone Has Sinned: Romans 3:9–20
Right with God: Romans 3:21–26
New Life in Jesus: Romans 6:1–14
All for Our Good: Romans 8:28–39
Living for God: Romans 12:1–8
Loving Others: Romans 12:9–12

Romans 1–2 Everyone Needs Jesus

Paul began this letter to the Romans by giving a four-sentence outline of his life. Paul served Christ and had been called to preach the good news to all nations. One of the places where Paul wanted to preach was Rome. But he had not yet been able to get there. Paul described for the Romans how sin had reached into every person's life. His picture of sin was as true of the Jews as it was of those who weren't Jews. All people are guilty before God.

The Church in Rome Romans 1:7

Rome was the capital of the Roman Empire. It was a city of great beauty and riches but also great wickedness. The group of Jesus followers in Rome were mostly from Gentile (non-Jewish) backgrounds but there were also some believers who were Jewish. Paul opened his letter to them by reminding them that they are all loved by God and called to be saints. That means that they were "set apart" to God and made "holy" by the Holy Spirit.

Romans 3 Jesus Saves

If Jews were as sinful as all other people, why had there been the need for the Jewish people at all? The answer is that the Jewish nation had come into being to prepare the way for the coming of Christ. Paul made it very clear: Sin must be punished. So God, in the person of Christ, took the punishment for everyone's sin. Over and over again, the book of Romans says that only through Jesus can people be made right with God. Through faith in Jesus' life and death, people who were sinners before God become clean and acceptable to him.

Romans 4 The Faith of Abraham

The promises given to Abraham were given because of his faith in God, not because he followed some strict set of laws. Therefore, those who are truly Abraham's family are those who share his faith.

Righteous Romans 4:3

To be right with God. People can become righteous, or right with God, only through faith in Jesus.

Romans 5 Christ and Adam

Paul asked how one person, Jesus, could die for the sins of millions of people. Paul answered his own question by explaining that the founder of the human race, Adam, was perfect when God made him. But when he sinned, he brought sin to everyone who would be born after him—everyone except Jesus. As one man (Adam) brought sin to the whole human race, so one man (Jesus) brought healing and life. What Adam did, Jesus undid.

Romans 6 Living a New Life

Now Paul asked a tough question. If Christ would forgive sins, why shouldn't we keep sinning and let him keep forgiving? *Unthinkable!* says Paul. People cannot be servants of sin and servants of Christ at the same time. They must choose one or the other. It is not possible to please Christ and continue to live in sin at the same time.

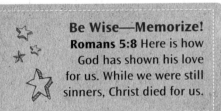

Be Wise—Memorize!
Romans 5:8 Here is how God has shown his love for us. While we were still sinners, Christ died for us.

Romans 7 Struggling with Sin

Paul presented the great human problem—the struggle between a sinful nature, which wants to go its own way, and a spiritual nature, which wants to obey God. People know what is right, yet they sin. They want to obey God, but they don't always do it. In two simple verses Paul expressed how terribly he had failed at obeying God (Romans 7:24) and the happiness he had discovered in the salvation Jesus offered (Romans 7: 25).

Romans 8 The Spirit Gives Life

While believers can depend completely on Christ for their salvation, they should still work every day to obey him more and more. Paul is very clear. In thankfulness for God's grace—the gift of salvation—believers should do everything in their power to live right.

This chapter ends with some of the most comforting words in the Bible. Nothing—and that means just that, *nothing*—can separate us from the love of Christ (Romans 8:31–39). He died for us. He has forgiven us. If we are his, no power on earth or in heaven or in hell can separate us from him.

Glory Romans 8:18
Honor, praise, victory. Believers will experience glory if they believe in Jesus.

Romans 9–11 Israel's Unbelief

Paul was sad because so many Jews refused to believe in Jesus. They hurt the church every chance they got. They made trouble for Paul everywhere he went. Why did God's own people refuse to believe in the Messiah? The Old Testament, Paul told them, said this would happen (Romans 9:25–33). The Jews made their own choice to disobey (Romans 10:1–21). God did not force acceptance of Jesus as the Messiah on them. But Paul made sure to point out that Israel's rejection of Jesus wouldn't last forever. A time will come—no one knows for certain when or where—when all Israel will be saved (Romans 11:26).

Romans 12 Living for God

God's grace gives believers the power to live a life that pleases God. The beauty of God's grace touches believers and transforms their whole outlook on life. Paul went on to list many ways that believers can live for God and then summed it all up with the words, "Don't let evil overcome you. Overcome evil by doing good" (Romans 12:21).

Be Wise—Memorize!
Romans 12:2 What he wants is right. His plan is good and pleasing and perfect.

Romans 13 Obey the Law

Paul urged believers to obey the laws of the country where they live. Believers should be honest and honorable.

Romans 14 Weak and Strong

Paul did not want believers to judge each other in such things as observing special days and eating or not eating certain foods. The food may have been meat that was offered to idols. (See the note on 1 Corinthians 8.)

Romans 15:1–14 Helping Each Other

Paul asked older, more mature Christians to lovingly help newer, weaker Christians. Only when believers worked together would the church grow and become the glorious body God called it to be.

Romans 15:15–33 Paul's Plan to Visit Rome

Paul's plan as a missionary was to preach wherever he went, bit by bit working his way west. Now, after twenty-five years, Paul was ready to go on to Spain with a stopover in Rome on the way (Romans 15:24). Paul arrived in Rome about three years after he wrote this letter.

Romans 16 Personal Matters

In this chapter, Paul sent greetings to some of his close friends.

Phoebe Romans 16:1–2
Phoebe carried the letter to Rome. She probably went on a business trip there.

Priscilla and Aquila Romans 16:3–5
They had formerly lived in Rome (Acts 18:2) and had been with Paul in Corinth and Ephesus. They had returned to Rome, and a church met in their house.

Epenetus Romans 16:5
Epenetus was the first believer in Asia Minor. He now lived in Rome.

Mary Romans 16:6
Mary was one of many women that Paul had as friends. "Mary" was a common name in Bible times. This is not Mary, the mother of Jesus.

Andronicus and Junias Romans 16:7
They were Paul's relatives. They were now old men. They had been Christians longer than Paul and had been in prison with him.

Ampliatus, Urbanus, Stachys, and Apelles Romans 16:8–10
They were Paul's friends.

Aristobulus and Narcissus Romans 16:10–11
They probably had churches that met in their homes.

Herodion Romans 16:11
Herodion was another of Paul's relatives.

Tryphena, Tryphosa, and Persis Romans 16:12
They were three women who had worked hard for the Lord.

Rufus Romans 16:13
Rufus may have been the son of Simon, who bore Jesus' cross (Mark 15:21). His mother treated Paul like a son.

The Last Nine Individuals Romans 16:14–15

The last nine individuals Paul mentioned cannot be identified beyond the fact that they belonged to the church in Rome.

Timothy Romans 16:21

Timothy was one of Paul's most loved partners in his work.

Lucius, Jason, and Sosipater Romans 16:21

They were Paul's relatives.

Tertius Romans 16:22

Tertius was Paul's secretary.

Gaius Romans 16:23

Gaius was the Christian brother in whose home Paul was living at the time and whose home was a general meeting place for Christians in Corinth.

Erastus Romans 16:23

Erastus, the director of public works for the city of Corinth, must have been an important man.

Quartus Romans 16:23

Quartus was another Christian brother.

1 CORINTHIANS

Believers in an Unbelieving World

Paul wrote his letter to the church in Corinth to show them where they had gone wrong in several areas. He was honest but loving in how he wrote to them. He told the people how important it was for them to be pure and loving toward each other. He wanted them to know that the fights they were having were not the way believers should live. He talked about the gifts of the Holy Spirit: what they were and how they should be used in the church. Paul had begun the church in Corinth about three years before he wrote this letter. He loved the people there and wanted them to do what was right. This book was probably written around AD 55 during Paul's third missionary journey.

Writer:

Paul

Place:

Ephesus

Why Is It Important?

The book of 1 Corinthians teaches how Christians should live their lives.

Some Lessons in 1 Corinthians:

Wisdom Comes from God: 1 Corinthians 1:18–2:16

Christians, Stop Sinning!: 1 Corinthians 3

We Are All Important: 1 Corinthians 12:12–31

Love Is Most Important: 1 Corinthians 13

Believers Will Rise from the Dead: 1 Corinthians 15:12–58

1 Corinthians 1 Taking Sides in the Church

These believers weren't especially nice to each other. They took sides over everything: who was the best leader, or who had the best teaching. Paul wanted them to forget their differences and think more about what things they shared.

Corinth 1 Corinthians 1:2

Corinth was a major city in the Roman Empire. It was a rich and beautiful but wicked city. In the time of Paul, about 300,000 free people and about 460,000 slaves lived in Corinth.

1 Corinthians 2 God's Wisdom

The people in Corinth were paying more attention to what some teachers were saying than what God was saying. Paul told them that even their best learning was foolishness compared to God's wisdom.

> **Be Wise—Memorize!**
> **1 Corinthians 2:9** "No eye has seen, no ear has heard, no mind has known what God has prepared for those who love him."

1 Corinthians 3 The Church Is God's

The church is God's. He created it through his Son, Jesus. It doesn't belong to one group or another. Paul reminded the people in Corinth that they were all part of God's church.

1 Corinthians 4 Apostles of Christ

Some of the leaders in the church at Corinth had become proud and stuck up in their attitudes toward Paul. Paul explained his position as an apostle, one who had seen Christ. Then he warned these leaders to be careful.

1 Corinthians 5 Evil People

Paul was amazed at the sin that had crept into the church in Corinth. People were living in sin, and he wanted it to stop. He told them that the offenders should be kicked out of the church if they would not leave their sinful ways behind.

1 Corinthians 6:1–8 Taking Believers to Court

Again, Paul couldn't believe what the Christians in Corinth were doing. They were actually taking each other to court over disagreements. As brothers and sisters in Christ, he told them they should lovingly settle their problems without bringing them before unbelievers in court.

1 Corinthians 6:9–20 More on Sin

Some of the Christians in Corinth were having a hard time adjusting to living a pure life. They were even trying to make it sound like their sins weren't so bad. Paul reminded them that their bodies were temples of the Holy Spirit (1 Corinthians 6:19). They should stay as far away from sin as possible.

1 Corinthians 7 On Marriage

Paul was not married, but he said that those who wanted to get married should do so. He told those church members who were married to unbelievers to stay with their husbands or wives. Maybe by living a good life before their partners, they could lead them to Jesus.

Be Wise—Memorize!
1 Corinthians 6:19
Don't you know that your bodies are temples of the Holy Spirit? The Spirit is in you.

1 Corinthians 8 Food Offered to Idols

There were many gods in Corinth. Much of the meat that was sold in the markets had first been offered to some idol. Some believers didn't think they should eat that meat. Others thought it was all right to eat the meat because believers in Jesus are free from laws about clean and unclean food. Paul warned the Christians to stay out of idol worship. He said that people whose consciences were bothered by eating the meat used in idol worship should not eat it. He may have been referring to believers with Jewish backgrounds, because of their traditions of not eating meat used in sacrifices. But Paul said that those who weren't bothered by this meat (likely the Gentile Christians) could eat it. Paul instructed the Roman church to think of the impact their actions would have on others. He told them not to do something that might lead nonbelievers or people weak in the faith to sin.

1 Corinthians 9 The Rights of an Apostle

This chapter showed how unselfish Paul was. He *could* have let the church in Corinth support him. But he supported himself instead by working as a tentmaker. He said it was a good thing for a church to support its leaders. But he wanted to support himself. He didn't want anyone to think that he might be controlled by those who gave him money to help his ministry.

1 Corinthians 10:1–13 The Danger of Falling

Paul reminded the believers that they should be serious about their faith. Look at the Israelites, he said. The Israelites who were freed from slavery in Egypt were tempted to disobey God. So they never made it to the Promised Land. Those same sins were still a problem. Paul wanted the Corinthians to be careful to obey God. He promised God would be with them to help them stay away from sin.

1 Corinthians 10:14–33 Food Offered to Idols (Again!)

Paul went back to the problem of food that had been offered to idols. He didn't want the believers in Corinth to take part in any of the wicked parties and services for idols, but, he told them, eating the food that had been offered to an idol was not a sin.

1 Corinthians 11:1–16 Women in the Church

In Paul's day, only sinful women would go around without a covering on their heads. Some Christian women, feeling free in Christ, came to church with their heads uncovered. Others were horrified by their actions. Paul told these women not to oppose what was the usual way for women to appear. Believers in Christ that live in a wicked society should be careful to do nothing that keeps the good news from reaching unbelievers.

1 Corinthians 11:17–34 The Lord's Supper

It's a party! Instead of making the Lord's Supper a time of worship, the church in Corinth held a party. People didn't share. Some ate too much, and others got nothing. Paul wanted them to understand how special and sacred these meals were supposed to be.

1 Corinthians 12 Gifts of the Holy Spirit

Paul listed, in 1 Corinthians 12:8–10, the gifts of the Holy Spirit: wisdom, knowledge, faith, healing, miracles, prophecy, speaking in tongues (both earthly and heavenly languages), and explaining tongues. It seemed that the church in Corinth had recently experienced many of these gifts. But instead of being excited and built up, the church argued over what gift was better than another.

Paul explained that each gift is important. He compared the church and the gifts with a body—a body that needs all its parts. If the hand was the only and most important part, what good would that do the rest of the body? In the same way, if only one gift is the best and most important, what good does that do all the others? Paul ended by reminding them that the most important thing was not the gifts, but the love they shared for each other.

1 Corinthians 13 Love

Paul now told the believers in Corinth—and believers today—that the one highest, biggest, most important thing is love. Love is the best way for the church to reach others with the good news of Jesus. Love is the most powerful thing in the world. Everything else in the world will someday be gone—and that includes many of the gifts listed in 1 Corinthians 12. Only a few things will last, and of those things, the best is love.

1 Corinthians 14 Tongues and Prophesying

The church in Corinth had found another thing to argue about! They debated about what was more important: speaking in tongues or prophesying (speaking God's message to other people). Paul said that both were important. But since speaking in other languages couldn't be understood by everyone, perhaps prophesying was more important.

1 Corinthians 15 Believers Will Rise from the Dead

Some leaders in the Corinthian church were also arguing about whether Christians would rise from the dead. Paul very clearly stated that there was no point to being a Christian without the hope of a new life after death. This life is not all there is. No matter what happens to our bodies, as believers we will live on and on and on. We won't need our weak earthly bodies in heaven. We will be given heavenly bodies that will last forever. Those who believe in Jesus have a wonderful future even after they die.

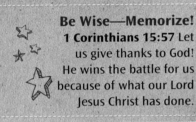

Be Wise—Memorize!
1 Corinthians 15:57 Let us give thanks to God! He wins the battle for us because of what our Lord Jesus Christ has done.

1 Corinthians 16 Personal Matters

Paul urged the believers to give some of their money to the poor believers in Jerusalem. He then said he planned to come and visit them, and he would send Timothy to them also.

Paul had a secretary who wrote down most of his letters for him. But he signed this letter himself (1 Corinthians 16:21). He then added the word *Maranatha* (1 Corinthians 16:22), which means "Come, O Lord."

House Church 1 Corinthians 16:19

Most of the time, believers didn't have churches in which to meet. In Jerusalem, they met in the temple. But in other cities, they usually met in public places or in the homes of believers. This house church met in the home of Aquila and Priscilla.

2 CORINTHIANS

Paul Writes to the Church in Corinth Again

Paul wrote another letter to the church in Corinth, shortly after he wrote
the first one. He poured out his feelings in this letter. He loved the
people at the church in Corinth. He wanted them to understand that he still
wanted what was best for them. He saw them argue and listen to teachers who
told lies. And it hurt him. Paul knew what was best for the church in Corinth,
and he told them all of that in his letter, which was written in the summer of
AD 57.

Writer:

Paul

Place:

Macedonia

Why Is It Important?

False teachers were leading the church in Corinth away from Paul's teachings. Paul jumped in with quick words to guide them away from what wasn't true toward what was true.

Some Lessons in 2 Corinthians:

God Gives Comfort: 2 Corinthians 1:3–11

The Winners' Parade: 2 Corinthians 2:14–3:6

A New Covenant: 2 Corinthians 3:7–18

Paul Has Suffered: 2 Corinthians 6:3–13

Giving Freely: 2 Corinthians 8:1–15

2 Corinthians 1 Comfort in Suffering

Paul began this letter by talking about the comfort God gave him. He had been given comfort from God (2 Corinthians 1:4). Paul was glad that he had escaped safely through difficult times. Then he said he would be coming soon to visit the church in Corinth.

2 Corinthians 2 The Perfume of the Good News

Think for a minute about how perfume works. It's on one person, but all those around can smell it and enjoy it. That's what Paul said believers are—the perfume of Christ, spreading and reaching all those around with the good news (2 Corinthians 2:14–16).

2 Corinthians 3 The Glory of the New Covenant

Paul compared the new covenant of the New Testament, with the old covenant of the Old Testament. The new covenant is written on people's hearts, while the old covenant was written on stones (see Exodus 24:12).

> **Veil** 2 Corinthians 3:13–18
> A thin cloth covering for the face. In the Old Testament, looking at God was like looking through the thin cloth of a veil. But in the New Testament, with Jesus by your side, looking at God is like looking without wearing a veil.

2 Corinthians 4 Paul's Sufferings

In this chapter, Paul talked about how much he suffered in order to bring the world the good news of Jesus. When Paul was saved, Jesus said, "I will show him how much he must suffer for me" (Acts 9:16). And Paul had suffered for Jesus.

2 Corinthians 5 What Comes after Death?

After death comes—Jesus! Paul had just said that the greater the suffering for Jesus' sake on earth, the greater the glory in eternity. Paul had wonderful things waiting for him in heaven. So will all those who believe on Jesus.

> **Be Wise—Memorize!**
> **2 Corinthians 5:17** Anyone who believes in Christ is a new creation. The old is gone! The new has come!

2 Corinthians 6 More on Suffering

Paul continued to list how he had suffered for Jesus. He wanted the people in Corinth to know he had always been Christ's servant.

2 Corinthians 7 The Report of Titus

Earlier, Paul had sent Timothy to Corinth (1 Corinthians 4:17; 16:10). But Timothy wasn't tough enough to handle the problems there. So now Paul sent Titus. Titus went to Corinth and settled many of the problems. Then he reported to Paul that the church was back in line (2 Corinthians 7:7–16).

2 Corinthians 8–9 A Gift for the Church in Jerusalem

Paul now gave some instructions about the collection that he was taking for the persecuted believers in Jerusalem. He took gifts from each of the churches he visited that year. Even the very poor were giving cheerfully. Paul's teachings tell us that we should be giving willingly, regularly, and carefully.

2 Corinthians 10 Paul Speaks Up for Himself

Paul's enemies in Corinth said he was weak. Weak? This was Paul they were talking about! The man who went around turning cities upside down for Jesus was anything but weak. Paul told these enemies that at least he started his own churches instead of causing trouble in churches started by others!

2 Corinthians 11 A Little Foolish Bragging

Paul knew he sounded like he was bragging about all he had done and all he had suffered for Jesus. But his enemies had forced him to do it. He had to defend himself. As a loyal Jew, as a hardworking Christian, and as one who had suffered for Jesus, he had done more than the rest of them put together.

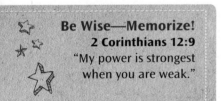

Be Wise—Memorize!
2 Corinthians 12:9
"My power is strongest when you are weak."

2 Corinthians 12 Paul's Painful Problem

No one knows for sure what Paul's painful problem was. Some think there was something wrong with his eyes.

2 Corinthians 13 Coming to Corinth

Paul wrote this letter in the summer and went to Corinth in the fall and winter of AD 57.

GALATIANS

Saved by God's Grace

Problems, problems. Paul started a church in the province of Galatia. The people there followed Jesus with eagerness and excitement. After Paul left, however, some leaders twisted the good news into bad news for the believers. They taught that in order to be a Christian, the people had to follow all the laws of Moses. Paul wrote this letter to explain that Moses' laws were important to Hebrew life and religion. But they were not part of salvation through Jesus. He stressed in this letter, written around AD 57, that people were saved only by faith in Jesus, not by obeying a certain set of rules and laws.

Writer:

Paul

Place:

Probably in Macedonia

Why Is It Important?

The book of Galatians gives a clear explanation of what it means to be saved by faith in Jesus. Following a bunch of rules can't earn salvation for anyone.

Some Lessons in Galatians

Saved by Faith: Galatians 3:1–14

Living by the Spirit: Galatians 5:16–21

The Fruit of the Spirit: Galatians 5:22–26

Doing Good to Others: Galatians 6:1–19

Galatians 1:1–17 No Other Good News

The only good news is the news that we can be saved by faith in Jesus. Any other "good news" is really bad news. Paul was surprised that the people in Galatia so easily turned away from the good news of being saved by faith in Jesus to the bad news of being saved by obeying the laws of Moses.

Galatia Galatians 1:2

Galatia is an area in Asia Minor where the country of Turkey is today. Several cities that Paul visited on his first missionary trip were in the area of Galatia. (See the note on Acts 13–14.)

Galatians 1:18–2:21 Paul and the Other Apostles

Only after he had been a Christian for three years did Paul go back to Jerusalem, where he had once tried to destroy the church (Galatians 1:18). He went back again some years later (Galatians 2:1). During those visits, he met with the apostles there. He gained their approval for his work among people who weren't Jews.

Faith Galatians 2:16

Faith is a hard word to define. You can't see faith or taste it or feel it with your hands. It is a choice to believe that all God says and all Jesus did is right and true and enough to save you from your sins.

Galatians 3–4 Faith or Obeying the Law

Paul started this part of his letter by calling the Galatians "foolish." These were strong words, but Paul clearly thought the Galatians were foolish for setting aside what he had taught them about Jesus' death on a cross and being saved by believ-

> **Be Wise—Memorize!**
> **Galatians 3:26** You are all children of God by believing in Christ Jesus.
>

ing in him. Now they were following other teachers who wanted them to also obey all of the laws of Moses—as if Jesus' death hadn't been enough! Paul set them straight. Only by believing Jesus could they be saved.

Galatians 5–6 Free in Christ

Paul just couldn't understand why anyone would choose to risk his or her salvation by basing it on the work of obeying the law. How much better, he said, to remember that salvation comes only through faith in Jesus. It is the difference between freedom (being saved by faith in Jesus) and slavery (trying and trying to be saved by obeying the law).

But being free in Christ doesn't mean being free to sin. The Holy Spirit gives believers the power to live free in Christ rather than as slaves to sin. The Holy Spirit works in believers' lives and hearts. His work is clear for others to see. Paul calls it the "fruit" of the Spirit: love, joy, peace, patience, kindness, goodness, faithfulness, gentleness, and self-control. Do you know someone who's growing that kind of fruit? Do others know you are a Christian by your fruit?

Be Wise—Memorize!
Galatians 5:22–23 The fruit the Holy Spirit produces is love, joy and peace. It is being patient, kind and good. It is being faithful and gentle and having control of oneself.

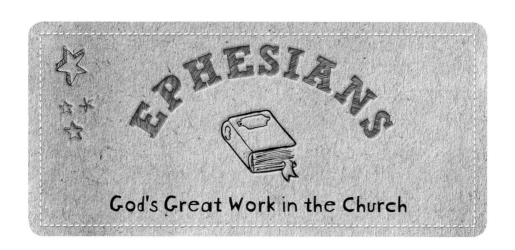

EPHESIANS

God's Great Work in the Church

Idol worshipers? Or God worshipers? Paul wrote this letter to the church he started in Ephesus. He wanted them to think of themselves in a whole new way. They were no longer idol worshipers but God worshipers. They had a whole new self in Christ. Then Paul went on to talk about how the believers in Ephesus were also part of a very special group of people—the church of Jesus Christ. Paul wrote this book while he was in a Roman prison during the years AD 57 to AD 61 or 62.

Writer:

Paul

Place:

Rome

Why Is It Important?

Paul wanted all believers—both those who were Jews and those who weren't—to understand that they were all part of Christ's church.

Some Teachings in Ephesians:

New Life in Jesus: Ephesians 2

Living in the Light: Ephesians 4:17–5:14

Living with Each Other: Ephesians 5:15–6:9

God's Armor: Ephesians 6:10–20

Ephesians 1 Spiritual Blessings

Paul began this letter with a strikingly clear outline of God's plan of salvation. Through Jesus, God would bless his people (Ephesians 1:3), adopt them as his own (Ephesians 1:5), and forgive them of their sins (Ephesians 1:7).

> **Ephesus** Ephesians 1:1
>
> Ephesus was a huge city in Asia Minor. It was the last city on the land routes through Asia. From Ephesus, trade goods were put on ships and brought to other cities on the Mediterranean Sea. Paul worked in Ephesus on his third missionary trip. (See the note on Acts 18:23–20:38.)

Ephesians 2–3 God's New Family

God first saved people—unworthy, sinful people. God's work would show everyone his wonderful kindness. Then God planned to take these people and, one by one, build his new family, the church. The link that had been broken between God's people would be repaired. God's plan was for his people to live at peace with him and at peace with each other.

Ephesians 4:1–16 One Church

The purpose of the church, said Paul, is not so its members can compete with each other. They are to help each other become more and more like Jesus (Ephesians 4:13–15). Together, as individual people and as a group, the church should grow up in Jesus (Ephesians 4:14). That will happen only when God's people treat each other with love (Ephesians 4:15–16).

Be Wise—Memorize!
Ephesians 3:20 God is able to do far more than we could ever ask for or imagine.

Ephesians 4:17–6:9 Changed

Because God's people lived in the light instead of the darkness, they no longer lived as they used to live. They lived a whole new way. Paul said they should live pure lives (Ephesians 5:3–14). They should spend time singing songs about Jesus instead of partying and getting drunk (Ephesians 5:18–21). They should honor and respect other people. That went for husbands and wives (Ephesians 5:22–33), children and parents (Ephesians 6:1–4), and slaves and masters (Ephesians 6:5–9).

Ephesians 6:10–20 God's Armor

Paul used a picture of armor to show how believers should prepare themselves to live. Only with God's help, and by wearing his armor, can believers live a good life in a sinful world.

PHILIPPIANS

A Letter of Joy

Paul's little letter to the church in Philippi is packed with power. In it, he covers a wide range of topics. But a common thread runs throughout. Believers should live joyfully. Imagine Paul writing this letter as he sat in prison in Rome. He must have wondered if he'd ever be released or if he'd be put to death. He wondered if anyone thought about him. Then a gift arrived. It was from the church in Philippi. Paul was deeply touched and wrote this letter to thank them for the gift. This book was written sometime between AD 59 and AD 61 or 62.

Writer:

Paul

Place:

Rome

Why Is It Important?

The book of Philippians is a very honest description of the Christian life. Paul doesn't deny the Christian life could be difficult, but he does say that no matter what life brings, Jesus is still enough.

Some Teachings in Philippians:

Paul Gives Thanks: Philippians 1:3–11

Thinking Like Christ: Philippians 2:1–11

Living Like Christ: Philippians 2:12–18

Reaching the Goal: Philippians 3:12–4:1

Always Be Joyful: Philippians 4:4

How to Think: Philippians 4:8

Finding Contentment: Philippians 4:12

Philippians 1 The Good News in Rome

Paul told the people in Philippi that going to Rome as a prisoner had turned out to be a good thing. He was able to tell many people in that city about Jesus, even those who were powerful officials in the Roman government. But Paul's life was difficult. He was old and worn out. He was ready to die. But living or dying, he was ready to serve Jesus (Philippians 1:21–26).

> **Philippi** Philippians 1:1
> Philippi was a Roman city on the main highway from Asia to Europe. Philippi had one of the early schools of medicine. It was the leading city in the area.

Philippians 2 Christ's Example

Jesus was the best example for believers of how to live and think. He wasn't proud. He was God, but he served his people by coming to earth to die. His example of humility was one all believers could see and follow. Jesus thought more about others than himself. That can be difficult for people to do, but Paul urged his readers to follow Jesus' example and think more about others than themselves.

Philippians 3 Only One Goal

Paul had only one goal in his mind: to know Christ. He had tried to gain salvation by obeying the law. He thought he was probably better at that than most other Jews. But all his efforts to be perfect now seemed like so much garbage to Paul. His only goal now—like a runner in a race—was to be in Christ, to know him better.

Philippians 4:1–9 On Joy

Paul asked two women, Euodia and Syntyche (Philippians 4:2–3), not to let their argument get in the way of love in the church. Paul jumped from that problem to the topic of joy. He didn't say be joyful when things are going great or when you feel good. He said to be joyful always (Philippians 4:4). All the awful things that had happened to Paul didn't make him bitter; it only gave him more reason to be joyful.

Be Wise—Memorize!
Philippians 3:1 Be joyful because you belong to the Lord.

Philippians 4:10–23 Thanks

Paul was very grateful for the visit of Epaphroditus and the gift he brought from the church in Philippi. Paul hadn't been unhappy with his situation. He had learned to be content no matter what. But the gift had brought him great pleasure.

COLOSSIANS

Jesus Saves Completely

Jesus and no one but Jesus has the power to save, Paul told the church in Colosse. The false teachers in Colosse had tried to make it seem as if they had special knowledge that no one else had. They taught that there was more to being a Christian than following Christ. Paul clearly and quickly set the believers straight. Jesus is all that is required. His work is enough to save anyone who will believe in him. Paul wrote this book while he was imprisoned in Rome from about AD 59 to AD 61 or 62.

Writer:
Paul

Place:
Rome

Why Is It Important?
This book reminds believers that even when others might come and try to teach something else, Jesus has done all that needs to be done to save his people from their sins.

Teachings in Colossians
Jesus Is Enough: Colossians 1:15–23
Freedom from Human Rules: Colossians 2:6–23
How to Live a Holy Life: Colossians 3:1–17

Colossians 1 Jesus Is God

Paul began this letter, like most of his others, by thanking God for the people of Colosse. He was always filled with thanks for all God was doing. He then gave clear instruction on Jesus as God. Jesus as God created everything (Colossians 1:16–17). Jesus as God is the head of the church (Colossians 1:18). Jesus as God lived and died so that sinners could be right with God (Colossians 1:21–22).

Colosse Colossians 1:2

Colosse was a very old city in what is Turkey today. It was located on a major east-west trade route. Later nearby Laodicea (Colossians 2:1) gained importance and Colosse declined in importance and size. No one lives on the site today.

Colossians 2 Jesus Is Enough

Paul told the believers not to let anyone or anything take Jesus' place in their lives. Their roots as Christians should go deeply into Jesus and Jesus alone (Colossians 2:7–8). Paul talked briefly about some of the lies that false teachers were spreading. The believers did not have to worry about obeying this law or that law, only Christ (Colossians 2:16–17).

Colossians 3:1–17 Life in Jesus

In this letter to the church in Colosse, Paul stressed the reality of a person-to-person relationship with Jesus (Colossians 3:3–4). A believer's whole life is rooted and found in Jesus (Colossians 3:3). Paul urged the people of Colosse to focus their lives on following and becoming more like Jesus Christ.

Colossians 3:18–4:6 Some Directions

In these verses, Paul gave a number of quick directions for living. Most of these directions were about relationships. Husbands and wives, children and parents, slaves and masters were all mentioned. He also encouraged the people to pray—a lot—and to be careful how they talked.

Colossians 4:7–18 Personal Matters

In the early years of the church, local groups had to meet wherever they could. Usually they met in the home of a church member. Paul mentioned several here. Then he closed with a reminder that he was in prison for serving Jesus.

Be Wise—Memorize!
Colossians 4:6 Let the words you speak always be full of grace. Season them with salt. Then you will know how to answer everyone.

1 & 2 THESSALONIANS

Jesus Is Coming Again

Paul wrote these two letters to the believers in Thessalonica shortly after he left their city in AD 51. He told them how thankful he was for their faith in Jesus, even though they were suffering for it. Then he answered their questions about when Jesus would return. After they received his first letter, it seemed that some of the believers quit working and just sat down to wait for Jesus to return. So Paul quickly wrote another letter and told them to keep working hard until Jesus came back.

Writer:

Paul

Place:

Corinth

Why Is It Important?

Jesus will return to earth, just as he promised.

Some Lessons in 1 & 2 Thessalonians

Living to Please God: 1 Thessalonians 4:1–12

He's Coming Back: 1 Thessalonians 4:13–5:10

Stand Firm: 2 Thessalonians 2:13–17

Work Hard: 2 Thessalonians 3:6–15

1 Thessalonians 1 Giving Thanks

Paul thanked God for the believers in Thessalonica. They had been faithful even though they were suffering for their belief in Jesus (1 Thessalonians 1:6). They were a good example for other churches and believers to follow (1 Thessalonians 1:7).

> **Thessalonica** 1 Thessalonians 1:1
>
> Thessalonica was a city in northern Greece. Thessalonica was the largest city and had the primary harbor in the area known as Macedonia. The city sat on the main road from Rome to the east. The city was within sight of Mount Olympus, supposedly the home of Greek gods.

1 Thessalonians 2 Paul's Work in Thessalonica

Paul reviewed the work he did when he was in Thessalonica. He had left earlier than he planned because his work set off riots. The people who opposed him continued to torment the believers in Thessalonica. Paul tried to comfort the believers by reminding them that others had suffered also. Paul himself had suffered. Paul planned to return to Thessalonica, but Satan stopped him. Paul didn't explain how this happened, just that he had wanted to come and couldn't.

1 Thessalonians 3 Timothy's Report

Paul so worried about the new church in Thessalonica that he sent Timothy to check on them. When Timothy came back to Paul, he told about the faith and love of the Thessalonians, even when they were suffering. Paul was happy with Timothy's report.

1 Thessalonians 4:1–12 Living to Please God

Paul included a whole list of ways that believers can live in order to please God. He encouraged the believers in Thessalonica to be pure (1 Thessalonians 4:3–6), to love each other (1 Thessalonians 4:9–10), and to work hard (1 Thessalonians 4:11).

1 Thessalonians 4:13–5:11 Jesus Is Coming Back

Paul now turned to his main reason for writing this letter. Jesus was coming again. His return was the great event that all Christians hoped for. It would be the crowning event of all of Jesus' work. Paul wanted believers to be sure about what happened to those who died. Christians who had died and Christians who were still alive would all be caught up together and meet Jesus in the air.

Then they would all go to live with him forever (1 Thessalonians 4:17). This event is sometimes called the rapture of the church.

1 Thessalonians 4:14–17 He's Coming Back

Jesus promised that he would come back. While he was on earth, he told his disciples about his return (Matthew 24:42; Luke 21:27–28). Paul told believers that it was true: Jesus would come again.

1 Thessalonians 5:12–28 Some Final Directions

Paul ended his letter with more than fifteen quick pieces of advice. He told the believers in Thessalonica—and believers everywhere—to be thankful, to live with others in peace and love, to be full of joy, and to pray often for Paul and for each other.

2 Thessalonians 1 The Day of the Lord

In his first letter, Paul stressed that Jesus would come back for believers. Now he talked about what would happen to those who refused to believe. Jesus would come for them also, but with blazing fire and powerful angels ready to punish. God is full of love and forgiveness for those who turn to him in faith. But those who do not believe will receive God's punishment.

2 Thessalonians 2:1–12 The Man of Sin

The main purpose of Paul's second letter to the Thessalonians was to make sure they knew that the Lord wouldn't be coming right away. It would not be until after the man of sin came and led many people away from God. (See the note on 1 John 2:18–29.)

Be Wise—Memorize!
2 Thessalonians 3:13
Brothers and sisters, don't ever get tired of doing the right thing.

2 Thessalonians 2:13–16 Stand Firm

Paul urged the believers to be strong and to hold on to what they had been taught.

2 Thessalonians 3 Everyone Should Work

Some of the Thessalonians had decided not to work since Jesus was coming soon. Paul told them that everyone should work while they waited for Jesus to return.

1 & 2 TIMOTHY

Help and Advice for Timothy

Paul wrote two letters to his young coworker Timothy. The first letter was written just after Paul got out of prison in Rome sometime during AD 61 or 62, and the second letter while he was in a Roman prison for the second time around AD 67. Both letters gave Timothy advice about how to work and lead in the church. Timothy had been having problems with the church in Ephesus. Paul tried to help him see how those problems should be handled. Paul also gave direction on how to live the Christian life, direction that was good for Timothy and for everyone who reads these books.

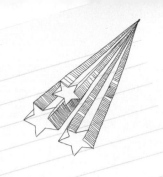

Writer:

Paul

Place:

Rome

Why Is It Important?

The church and its people will always face problems. Paul's words to Timothy can help anyone who is facing a problem in life or in the church.

Teachings in 1 & 2 Timothy:

False Teachers: 1 Timothy 1:3–11

On Worship: 1 Timothy 2

Church Leaders: 1 Timothy 3

The Church Family: 1 Timothy 5

Loving Money: 1 Timothy 6:3–10

Advice Just for Timothy: 1 Timothy 6:11–21

Be Faithful: 2 Timothy 1:3–2:13

Pleasing God: 2 Timothy 2:14–26

1 Timothy 1 False Teachers

When Paul had left the church in Ephesus seven years before, he warned that "wild wolves" would come among them (Acts 20:29–30). He meant that teachers who taught lies and led the people away from God would come to the church in Ephesus. What he had said would happen was now happening. Timothy was having a hard time dealing with these false teachers.

Timothy 1 Timothy 1:2

Timothy was from the city of Lystra (Acts 16:1), a town where Paul had been stoned and then left for dead (Acts 14:8–20). Timothy's mother and grandmother were both believers (2 Timothy 1:5). Timothy went with Paul on his second missionary trip, as well as many later trips. (See the note on Acts 15:36–18:22.) A shy young man, Timothy had trouble standing up to the false teachers in the church at Ephesus. Most people think that after Paul was put to death, Timothy continued to work in Ephesus and was later put to death himself.

Be Wise—Memorize!
1 Timothy 1:15 Christ Jesus came into the world to save sinners.

1 Timothy 2:1–8 Prayer for Rulers

When Paul wrote this letter, evil Nero was the ruler of the Roman Empire. Under him, Paul had been put in prison and would soon be put to death. Even so, Paul urged the people to pray for their rulers, whether they were good or bad.

1 Timothy 2:9–15 Women in the Church

Paul warned the women of Ephesus against wearing clothing that was improper or that drew unnecessary attention to them, especially in a worship service. Women, as well as men, should be more concerned about their good works than their good looks.

1 Timothy 3 Leaders in the Church

Paul listed for Timothy the type of men who should be chosen to lead the church. Church leaders should be honest—not pushy, not proud, and not married to more than one woman.

Deacons 1 Timothy 3:12

Deacons were church leaders who were helpers. They took care of the physical needs of the people. Deacons in Ephesus probably took care of the widows, making sure they had enough money and food.

1 Timothy 4 Direction for Timothy

Paul warned Timothy that some people would be led away from the truth and would take other believers with them. The best way to fight their lies would be to continue to tell people the simple truth of the good news.

1 Timothy 5:1–25 The Church Family

The church in Ephesus was about ten years old. It carefully took care of those who needed help. Some were getting so they depended on the church instead of their families for help. Paul said a person's help should first come from his or her family (1 Timothy 5:16). Older widows should be given help from the church, but younger widows should get married again, according to Paul (1 Timothy 5:14).

> **Be Wise—Memorize!**
> **1 Timothy 4:12** Don't let anyone look down on you because you are young. Set an example for the believers in what you say and in how you live.

1 Timothy 6:1–2 Slaves

Paul urged all those who are serving as slaves to be good slaves and obey their masters as a way of honoring God. Notice that Paul didn't say anything about not owning slaves. Slavery was an accepted thing in the world of Paul's day. Over the years, believers have fought to put an end to slavery by teaching people to love others as Jesus taught them.

1 Timothy 6:3–21 The Love of Money

The love of money was the motive behind a lot of the lies some leaders were teaching (1 Timothy 6:5). Through the years, the truths of the church had been twisted in order to produce more money. As Paul said, the love of money "causes all kinds of evil" (1 Timothy 6:10).

2 Timothy 1 Be Faithful

Paul was back in prison in Rome. From prison, he urged Timothy to be faithful to the truth. Paul had never been ashamed of the good news. And he didn't want Timothy to be ashamed either. He also didn't want Timothy to be ashamed of him, Paul. Though some in the church had turned against him, Paul wanted Timothy to know he was thankful for him and others who had not deserted him in his time of need.

2 Timothy 2 Advice

Paul gave Timothy good advice as an older person to a younger person. He knew what Timothy was like. He knew where Timothy needed help and encouragement. Paul now gave it freely.

2 Timothy 3 Terrible Times

Terrible times were coming. Those who would stop the spread of the good news were hard at work. Everyone who lived a godly life could expect to be mistreated (2 Timothy 3:12). Paul had been hurt many times; Timothy had suffered. So would many others. But even in terrible times, Paul urged believers to hang on to the truth of Jesus. By trusting God, they would gain strength to get through the hard times that were sure to come.

> **Be Wise—Memorize!**
> **2 Timothy 2:22** Run away from the evil things that young people long for.

2 Timothy 4 Paul's Last Words

Paul was in prison and was expecting to be put to death. He had some final words for Timothy—and for us. Paul was not sure he would ever see Timothy again or get to write him another letter. Paul begged Timothy to keep his mind on Jesus' coming and preach Jesus with zeal and fearlessness.

Paul then seemed to shout the words, "I have won!" This old worker for Jesus was about to die, and he knew for sure what was waiting for him: a crown (2 Timothy 4:7–8)! Paul didn't seem to fear what was ahead. He may have been sad because he was alone (2 Timothy 4:10–11), but he was not afraid.

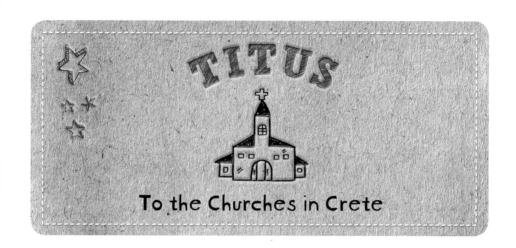

TITUS

To the Churches in Crete

Just as he wrote to Timothy to help him with his work in Ephesus, Paul wrote to Titus around AD 65 to help him with his work on the island of Crete. Titus helped Paul start the church there. He needed advice on how to handle the problems in those churches. Paul told Titus what qualities the church leaders should have and how to overcome arguments in the church.

Writer:

Paul

Place:

Around the Mediterranean Sea

Why Is It Important?

The problems Titus faced in the church are the same kinds of problems the church faces today. Paul's advice to Titus is just as good today as it was back in the early years of the church. Any church that is having problems with its leadership can look to Titus for direction.

Some Lessons in Titus:

The Church on Crete: Titus 1:5–16

Teaching God's People: Titus 2

Doing What Is Good: Titus 3

Titus 1 The Church on Crete

Paul gave Titus and Timothy much the same list of qualities of a good church leader (see 1 Timothy 3). Teachers who taught lies and twisted the truth about Jesus were troubling the church on Crete. Paul gave Titus some advice on how to handle these false teachers.

Titus Titus 1:4

Titus was Paul's friend and helper. Titus went with Paul to Jerusalem and worked with him in Ephesus and Corinth. Titus must have been a strong young man, able to handle the arguments that were hurting several different churches, including the one on the island of Crete.

Crete Titus 1:5

Crete is an island in the Mediterranean Sea. It was an island of mountains and fruitful valleys and many people.

Titus 2–3 Good Works

In his letter to Titus, Paul stressed the importance of good works. Believers are not saved by good works. They are saved by God's grace and mercy (Titus 3:5). They are made right with God by his grace (Titus 3:7). But because of God's good work in them, they respond by doing good works. They live good lives in front of others, no matter what their age (Titus 2:1–8). Believing slaves should always try to please their masters (Titus 2:9–10). By living good lives, believers make living the Christian life look good to others (Titus 2:10).

> **Be Wise—Memorize!**
> **Titus 3:1** Remind God's people to obey rulers and authorities. Remind them to be ready to do what is good.

PHILEMON

A Runaway Slave

Paul's other letters were sent to churches or to church leaders. This letter was a bit different. Paul, while imprisoned in Rome, sent this letter to a slave owner, Philemon, around AD 60. Philemon's slave Onesimus had stolen some money and run away. In Rome, Onesimus found Paul and became a believer. Now Paul was sending the slave back to his master, along with this letter asking Philemon to forgive. This short and very personal letter is a sweet appeal for grace and forgiveness for a person who had done something wrong.

Writer:

Paul

Place:

Rome

Why Is It Important?

The book of Philemon has an important lesson for believers on forgiving each other.

The Lesson in Philemon:

Forgiveness: Philemon 8–19

Philemon 1–7 Thanks

Paul as usual began his letter by thanking God for the person to whom he's writing. This time it's Philemon, the owner of the slave named Onesimus. Paul was sending the slave back to his master.

Philemon Philemon 1

Philemon was a friend of Paul from the church in Colosse. He must have been a rich man. He owned slaves and the church met in his home. He and Paul seemed to be good friends.

Philemon 8–25 Forgive Onesimus

Paul appealed to Philemon to forgive Onesimus and take him back—not as a slave but as a brother in the Lord. By law, Philemon could have Onesimus put to death for stealing and running away. But Paul urged Philemon to accept Onesimus back with love and forgiveness.

Be Wise—Memorize!
Philemon 7 Your love has given me great joy.

Onesimus Philemon 10

A slave who belonged to Philemon. He stole money from Philemon and then ran away. He ran to Rome and while there found Paul. Perhaps he remembered Paul from Paul's friendship with his master. While with Paul, Onesimus became a believer. Paul sent him back to his master along with this letter.

HEBREWS

The Old and the New

The writer of Hebrews carefully outlined the faith of the Old Testament. He then compared it with the faith of the New Testament. And he found the faith of the New far superior to the faith of the Old. All of the sacrifices and laws of the Old Testament point to and prepare the way for one thing: the coming of Jesus. The saving work of Jesus has made the rituals of the Old Testament no longer necessary. The letter was written sometime before AD 70, when Jerusalem was destroyed.

Writer:
Scholars disagree. Some say Paul, while others think Barnabas or Apollos wrote Hebrews.

Place:
Unknown

Why Is It Important?
The Jewish Christians in Jerusalem were suffering for their faith in Jesus and being drawn back to their Old Testament way of life—depending on sacrifices for their salvation. The writer of Hebrews wanted them to understand that Jesus' work was and is enough.

Some Lessons in Hebrews:
Jesus Is Greater: Hebrews 1
Jesus Is Our High Priest: Hebrews 4:14–5:10
God Keeps His Promises: Hebrews 6:13–20
Jesus Is Enough: Hebrews 10:1–18
Be Faithful: Hebrews 10:19–39
Heroes of the Faith: Hebrews 11
God's Training: Hebrews 12:4–13

Hebrews 1 Jesus Is God

The writer of Hebrews clearly explained that Jesus is higher than any angel—higher than Moses or any Old Testament priest. Jesus came to fulfill the Old Testament. His death on the cross was the sacrifice that paid the penalty for all our sins. The Old Testament system of sacrifices had helped teach the Jewish people about sin and the need for sacrifice and reconciliation with God. God commanded them to make sacrifices in the Old Testament so that they would eventually recognize Jesus' death as the perfect sacrifice for sin. After Jesus had sacrificed himself by dying on the cross—and then rose from the dead—the old system of sacrifices was no longer needed.

Hebrews 2 Jesus Was Made Like Us

Pay attention, said the writer to the Hebrews, as if to say that what was coming next was really important. Jesus had to become a human being in order to die for human beings. His life and death brought not only salvation but also an understanding of what human life was like. Because Jesus understands humans so completely, he can be a better high priest for them than any Old Testament high priest ever was.

Hebrews 3:1–6 Jesus and Moses

The Hebrews still seemed to think there was no one greater than Moses. The writer of Hebrews explained that Jesus was greater.

Hebrews 3:7–19 A Warning

Only those who are faithful to the end can hope to share all that Jesus offered. The author used the example of the Israelites. They had been freed from slavery in Egypt. But as they traveled in the desert, they disobeyed the laws of Moses. Their punishment? They died in the desert and didn't get to enter the Promised Land. If they failed because they disobeyed Moses, what hope is there for those who disobey Jesus—someone far greater than Moses?

> **Be Wise—Memorize!**
> **Hebrews 3:13** Build one another up every day.

Hebrews 4:1–11 Sabbath Rest

Those who trust in Jesus for their salvation no longer need to work to gain it. Jesus has done all the work. Believers can rest in the work Jesus has done for them.

Hebrews 4:12–13 The Power of God's Word

God's Word, the Bible, is alive. It's not just a bunch of words put on a page. God's Word has the life of the Spirit behind it. When people read God's Word, it enters not only their minds but also their hearts.

Hebrews 4:14–5:10 Jesus Our High Priest

This is the main theme of the book of Hebrews. The priests of Israel were from the tribe of Levi. There were hundreds of them over the years. There is only one Christ. They offered animal sacrifices over and over and over again for the sins of the people. Jesus offered himself once for all time. They died. Jesus lives forever.

Hebrews 5:11–6:20 Another Warning

The writer warned that only if believers "grow up" (Hebrews 6:1) will they be able to stand firmly in their beliefs and not fall away. Faith in Jesus and his death on the cross is the only way to salvation. The writer urged believers not to give up but to hold on tightly to the promises of God that had been fulfilled in Jesus.

> **Be Wise—Memorize!**
> **Hebrews 6:10**
> God is fair.

Hebrews 7:1–10 Melchizedek

Melchizedek was the king of Salem and a priest of God hundreds of years before Moses. He was a king and a priest. Years later, under Moses, the priests came from the tribe of Levi. Later still, the kings of Israel came from the family of David. One family supplied the kings of Israel. Another family supplied the priests of Israel. But Jesus was both a king (from the family of David) *and* priest (by sacrificing himself on the cross). In that way he was like Melchizedek.

Melchizedek Hebrews 7:1

Melchizedek was a priest and king of Salem, which is probably the early settlement of Jerusalem, in Abraham's time. Abraham saw Melchizedek as a priest of God. He gave the priest a tenth of everything he had won in a battle. Many Christians today follow Abraham's example by offering their *tithe*, a tenth of everything they earn, back to God so that his work can be done all over the world.

Hebrews 7:11–28 A Forever Priest

The Old Testament priests and sacrifices weren't perfect. They just pictured sin being covered. The sacrifices had to be made over and over again throughout the years. But Christ changed all that. Now a perfect priest had come. And he sacrificed himself once for all.

Hebrews 8 A New Covenant

The old covenant centered on the sacrifices and the Ten Commandments. Its laws had been written on tablets of stone (Hebrews 9:4). The new covenant under Christ, however, has been written on believers' hearts (Hebrews 8:10). The old covenant didn't last forever, but the new covenant would last forever.

Hebrews 9 A New Way

All through the Old Testament, God told the Hebrews to follow laws that would eventually help them understand his eternal plan. That plan was fulfilled in Jesus. When Jesus came, he made the Old Testament way of doing things no longer necessary. The old way was to sacrifice animals over and over again for people's sins. The new way is to accept Jesus' once-for-all-time sacrifice on the cross.

Hebrews 10:1–18 Sin Removed Forever

There is no need for sacrifices any longer. Jesus' death on the cross was enough. It took care of all the sins of the past and all the sins of the future. God can now forgive, and will forgive, those who put their trust in Jesus.

Hebrews 10:19–39 A Third Warning

The writer again warned his readers to be careful. The very people who had earlier stood firm—even when faced with suffering for their faith—were now wavering (Hebrews 10:32–35). The point the writer made was that there had been one sacrifice for sin. There would never be another. Those who did not believe in what Jesus did for them on the cross might as well say good-bye to God forever, go their own way, and suffer for their own sin (Hebrews 10:27–31).

Hebrews 11 Heroes of the Faith

Believers, living by faith, can be sure that God will keep his promises. The writer mentions the following Old Testament men and women. Their faith made them worthy to be included in this hall of fame of the faithful:

Abel—he offered the first sacrifice of faith for sin. (See the note on Genesis 4.)
Enoch—he walked with God.
Noah—he built an ark when nobody thought there would be any use for it.
Abraham—he left his homeland when God told him to and was willing to offer his son as a sacrifice.

411

Sarah—she came to believe what she at first had laughed at because she saw it as impossible.

Isaac—he blessed his sons and foretold their future by faith.

Jacob—he believed that God would keep his promises.

Joseph—he believed that his bones would someday return to the Promised Land.

Moses' parents—they hid Moses when they saw he was a special baby (Exodus 2:1–10).

Moses—he chose to suffer with Israel and turned his back on Egypt.

The people of Israel—they walked through a sea on dry land and saw the walls of Jericho fall down (Exodus 14:21–22; Joshua 6:20–21).

Rahab—she trusted in the God of Israel.

Gideon—he became a strong warrior.

Barak—he defeated an army. (See the note on Judges 4–5.)

Samson—his weakness became his strength.

Jephthah—he defeated armies (see Judges 11).

Samuel—he directed God's people by faith.

David—he ruled God's people by faith.

The prophets—they did many amazing deeds by their faith.

Hebrews 12 Keep Your Eyes on Jesus

The writer of Hebrews urged the runners in the race of faith to keep their eyes on Jesus. All of those who had already finished their race were around them, watching and cheering them on. He told his readers not to get tired or discouraged by difficult times. God would use those times to train them and make them perfect in him.

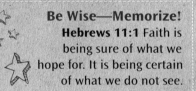

Be Wise—Memorize!
Hebrews 11:1 Faith is being sure of what we hope for. It is being certain of what we do not see.

Hebrews 13 Final Words

After all the difficult topics he had been covering, the author now finished his letter by giving some everyday advice. The writer of Hebrews told his readers that God would be with them as they followed Jesus in every part of their daily lives.

JAMES

Faith and Good Works

Bacon and eggs. Ice cream and summer. Birds and trees. Lots of things go together. When you have one, you usually have the other. Here's another one: faith and works. According to James, one of Jesus' brothers, you can't have one without the other. If you have only faith and no works, your faith is pretty much dead. The rest of James builds something like a fence around this faith/works truth. James gave many small pieces of advice on many parts of life as a Christian. He probably wrote this book near the end of his life around AD 60.

Writer:

James

Place:

Jerusalem

Why Is It Important?

There is no way believers can earn their way into heaven by doing good things. The only way is through faith in Jesus. But James points out that faith in Jesus and our love for him just naturally grow into doing good things.

Some Lessons in James:

Facing Trouble: James 1:2–18
Don't Play Favorites: James 2:1–13
Believing and Doing: James 2:14–26
Taming the Tongue: James 3:1–12
Living Right: James 4

James 1:1–8 Suffering

James told his readers to be joyful when they suffered. Now that's an amazing idea, isn't it? If you hurt, cheer. If others mock you because you believe in Jesus, jump up and down for joy. When you go through difficult times, remember that all of this happens because Jesus is working to make you more and more like him.

> ### James James 1:1
> James was Jesus' brother and a leader in the church in Jerusalem. At first, James and his other brothers didn't believe in Jesus. But after Jesus died and rose again, James and the others became believers and leaders. James stayed in Jerusalem until he was put to death for his faith in Jesus. (See the note on Mark 6:1–6.)

James 1:9–18 God's Work

James touched on a number of issues concerning Christian living in these verses. He ended by reminding his readers that everything they have is from God and that God is working in them to make them the best and greatest of all his creation.

Be Wise—Memorize!
James 1:17 Every good and perfect gift is from God.

James 1:19–27 Do What God Says

James again gave bits of advice on different areas of life. Then he stressed the fact that believers should do more than just read God's Word. They should do what it says.

James 2:1–13 Treat Everyone the Same

Compare these verses about special treatment for the rich with Acts 4:32 where everyone shared everything. James said selfish behaviors had to change.

James 2:14–26 Faith and Works

This was the central teaching in the book of James. Paul taught that the only way to be right with God was by faith in Jesus. James now adds that faith in Jesus will show itself in the good works we do. A person's *actions* show a person's *faith*.

James 3:1–12 Taming the Tongue

James urged his readers to tame their tongues. Such a small part of the body, but the damage it can do is amazing.

James 3:13–18 On Wisdom

True wisdom comes from heaven and shows itself in living a good life. People who are wise and understanding show it by the way they live every day.

James 4:1–17 Obey God

In all areas of life, obey God. Don't want what isn't yours. Be sure about what you believe. Be careful to depend on God's will, not your own. Lots of good advice from James can be found in these verses.

Be Wise—Memorize!
James 4:8 Come near to God, and he will come near to you.

James 5:1–6 Warning to the Rich

These are strong words again for the rich. James hit them between the eyes four times in this short book (James 1:9–11; 2:1–13; 4:1–10; 5:1–6). Their riches would get them nowhere with God. They would leave all their money and things behind. Quite a few rich people in the church in Jerusalem must have been living selfish and self-satisfied lives since James had to point this out so often.

James 5:7–20 Patience and Prayer

James reminded his readers that one day Jesus would return and their suffering would be over. He urged them to keep their eyes on Jesus. In his final words, James told believers to be sure to pray because God does hear and will answer.

Hope When Suffering

Peter, one of Jesus' disciples, wrote two letters to the believers living in Asia Minor. He most likely wrote the first letter shortly after Paul was put to death in AD 67. Christians were suffering for their faith everywhere. Peter told them not to be surprised by that. Jesus had suffered too. God would use suffering to make his people strong. Peter wrote a second letter a few years later just before his own death to warn believers about false teachers. He wanted them to be ready to stand up against those who were teaching lies.

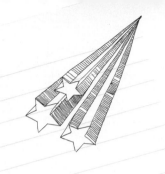

Writer:

Peter

Place:

Rome

Why Is It Important?

Hard times will come. God doesn't always take the trouble away, but he does go with the believer through it and makes the believer more like him in the process.

Some Lessons in 1 & 2 Peter:

A Living Hope: 1 Peter 1:3–12

Be Holy: 1 Peter 1:13–2:3

On Obeying: 1 Peter 2:13–25

Suffering for Doing Right: 1 Peter 3:8–22; 4:12–19

False Teachers: 2 Peter 2

The Day of the Lord: 2 Peter 3

1 Peter 1:1–12 A Living Hope

Jesus is alive. And the believers' hope in him is a living hope. That hope will be fulfilled when believers go to heaven and receive all God has prepared for them. Until then, he will be with them and keep them strong. Even the sufferings they go through will make them stronger and prove they have a living faith in Jesus.

1 Peter 1:13–2:3 Be Holy

Peter told the believers that their lives should be a clear sign of their faith in Jesus. They were to live holy lives, obeying God and leaving behind the empty lifestyles they had before they met Jesus.

1 Peter 2:4–12 A Living Stone

Peter called Jesus the "living Stone" and said believers "are like living stones" (1 Peter 2:4–5). These "stones" will be used to build a living church, not one of cold, dead wood and stone. The most important stone in it is, of course, Jesus (1 Peter 2:6). Many Old Testament prophecies speak of Jesus as "the stone" (check out Psalm 118:22; Isaiah 8:14; 28:16). Paul calls Jesus the "most important stone" in Ephesians 2:20.

> **Be Wise—Memorize!**
> **1 Peter 1:7** Your troubles have come in order to prove that your faith is real.

1 Peter 2:13–25 On Obeying

Peter taught that believers should obey those over them in government. Slaves should obey their masters.

1 Peter 3:1–7 Husbands and Wives

Peter taught about proper relationship between a husband and wife. By her kind and loving actions, a believing wife might win her unbelieving husband to the Lord. Women should concern themselves more with what they are like on the inside than the outside.

1 Peter 3:8–4:19 On Suffering

Peter wanted those who read his letters to know that suffering was coming. He wanted them to be ready for it. The one who caused believers to suffer hoped they would fall away from God during these tough times. But suffering often has just the opposite results. Christians are drawn closer to God during difficult times.

1 Peter 5 Older and Younger Men

Peter advised older leaders in the church not to be proud or pushy but to lovingly lead the young men, to teach them by their example. Then Peter turned to the younger men and advised them to willingly follow the older leaders in the church without complaining or arguing.

2 Peter 1:1–11 Leading a Godly Life

Peter expected a lot from believers! He didn't want them to just try to get by, to do as little or change as little as possible. Instead, they should try to add to their faith the seven good qualities listed in 2 Peter 1:5–7: goodness, knowledge, self-control, strength, godliness, kindness, and love. All of these good points should become more and more a part of a believer's life as that person grows closer to Jesus (1 Peter 1:8).

Be Wise—Memorize!
1 Peter 5:7 Turn all your worries over to him. He cares about you.

2 Peter 1:12–15 Peter's Death Is Near

Almost forty years before, Jesus had hinted that Peter would be put to death for his faith (John 21:18–19). Now Peter sensed that the time was near.

2 Peter 1:16–21 Prophecy from God

Peter reminded his readers that he had seen Jesus and that what he told them about Jesus was true. Everything that happened was in direct fulfillment of God's prophecies in the Old Testament.

2 Peter 2 False Teachers

Now it was Peter's turn to warn that false teachers would try to lead believers away from the truth of God's Word. Jesus (Matthew 7:15; 24:11) and Paul (2 Thessalonians 2:1–12) had warned of the same thing. Even angels who rebelled against God had been punished (2 Peter 2:4), and so would these false teachers.

2 Peter 3 The Lord's Coming

Peter reminded his readers of this truth—with God, one day is just like a thousand years (1 Peter 3:8). God's timing is very different from our timing. He will fulfill his promise. Jesus will return. But it will be when God says the time is right.

1, 2 & 3 JOHN

All about Love and Truth

As the ideas of false teachers spread throughout the church, John—one of Jesus' disciples—wrote three letters sometime between AD 85 and AD 95 to fight those lies. He wanted believers to remember the truths they had learned and to walk in the light of those truths. John urged believers to live close to God, to stand up to false teachers, and to be sure to love each other.

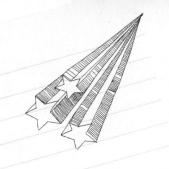

Writer:

John

Place:

Probably Ephesus

Why Is It Important?

These three short books are clear that it is just as important today as it was then to stand strong against false teachers.

Some Lessons in 1, 2, and 3 John:

Walking in the Light: 1 John 1:5–2:14

Loving Each Other: 1 John 3:11–24

More on Love: 1 John 4:7–21

Faith in God's Son: 1 John 5:1–12

Love One Another: 2 John 5–6

Do Good: 3 John 11

1 John 1:1–2:17 Walking in the Light

The light is God's kingdom of truth and joy and glory. Darkness is this world of sin and lies and evil. People have a choice. They can walk in the darkness of what the world teaches, or they can walk in the light of God and his love for them. Seems like a simple choice, doesn't it? Choose to walk in the light!

1 John 2:18–29 Enemies of Christ

John taught that these enemies of Christ were false teachers who would try to lead believers away from God. But believers, who have the Holy Spirit to teach them the truth, have the power to stand firmly against these false teachers (1 John 2:27).

1 John 3:1–10 Children of God

As children of God, believers just simply would not keep on sinning (1 John 3:6). John didn't deny that believers at times were weak and fell into sin. He meant instead that believers would do all in their power, with the help of the Holy Spirit, to stay away from sinning.

1 John 3:11–24 Love

Love. That word appears more than sixty times just in these three short books. John had a point to make. He wanted believers to know that love was the most important element in the Christian life. God loved us, so he sent us his Son. Jesus loved us, so he came to earth to die. We love God for sending his Son, and we love Jesus for dying for us. Then it follows that if God loves others, so should we.

Be Wise—Memorize!
1 John 4:11 Since God loved us that much, we should also love one another.

1 John 4:1–6 False Prophets

Some churches in John's time were targets of false teachers who said they had a special message from the Holy Spirit. John taught Christians that they could determine whether a teacher was teaching the truth by asking them if they believed that Jesus was God in human form. If a teacher did not believe this, he was a false teacher.

1 John 4:7–21 Love Again

John insisted that even though we're saved by Jesus' grace, we should still obey his commands. And Jesus' main commandment was that we love God and others.

1 John 5 Faith in God's Son

Many Christians get discouraged because they don't feel sure they are saved. Some may hear that if they do not *feel* or *know* they are saved, it is a sign they are not. But that's a sad mistake. A baby doesn't *know* it has been born. But it is still born. Being sure of salvation only comes with growth. You can be sure that if you have committed your life to Jesus, you are his for all eternity. His faithfulness will never let you go.

2 John 1–6 The Truth

John used the words "the truth" five times in these six verses. He meant the truth of the good news of Jesus—that Jesus came to earth, died, rose again, and saves all those who come to him.

Chosen Lady 2 John 1

This may have been a well-known woman who lived near Ephesus. Or John could have been calling a certain church a "chosen lady," just as the whole church was sometimes called the "bride" of Christ (Revelation 19:7).

2 John 7–13 False Teachers

These teachers went from church to church, teaching in the name of Jesus, but teaching lies. John wrote this letter to warn the people to be on their guard and refuse to support these false teachers.

> **Be Wise—Memorize!**
> **3 John 11** Anyone who does what is good belongs to God. Anyone who does what is evil hasn't really seen or known God.

3 John 1–14 Gaius and Others

John wrote to his good friend Gaius. He wanted to thank him for his work in supporting the true teachers and leaders of the church. And he wanted to warn him about another leader, Diotrephes, who was a troublemaker in the church.

Gaius 3 John 1

Gaius was a good friend of John and a kind man. He may have taken in some helpers of John when Diotrephes refused to let them work in his church.

Diotrephes 3 John 9

Diotrephes was a false teacher in the church. It appeared that he had refused to let some helpers of John work in his church.

JUDE

Sounding the Alarm

Jude, one of Jesus' brothers, writes this short letter to sound the alarm against false teachers. He is shocked when he discovers that some believers might be swayed to believe in the lies of these "godless people" (Jude 4). It seems these teachers were telling believers that since they were saved by grace, it didn't matter if they sinned. Jude writes to help the believers see that they must not give in but need to stand firm on the truth of God's Word. This book was probably written around AD 67.

Writer:

Jude

Place:

Asia Minor

Why Is It Important?

Some people think that because they are saved by God's grace they can live as they please, disobeying God. That's a lie! The truth is that God gives us his grace because he loves us. We show our love for God by being obedient and striving to live like Jesus.

Some Lessons in Jude:

Ungodly Teachers: Jude 3-16

Stay in God's Love: Jude 17-23

Jude 1–16 Godless People

Jude didn't use kind words to describe the people who were trying to lead
believers away from the truth. He called them "godless" (Jude 4), "dreamers"
(Jude 8), "wild animals" (Jude 10), "stains" (Jude 12), "wild waves" and "falling
stars" (Jude 13). God did not and does not take it lightly when someone feeds
his people lies instead of the truth.

> ### Jude Jude 1
>
> Jude was likely a brother of Jesus, the Savior. He didn't believe in Jesus until
> after Jesus died and rose again. He was also a brother of the writer of the book
> of James.

Jude 17–25 Remain in God's Love

Jude encouraged the people to remain in God's
love and to build themselves up in the faith. They
would then be able to withstand the lies of the
false teachers. Jude also encouraged the people to
carefully hold up the weak in the faith and even
to "pull others out of the fire" (Jude 23). He perhaps referred to people who
had already been misled by the false teachers.

Be Wise—Memorize!
Jude 21 The mercy of
our Lord Jesus Christ will
bring you eternal life.

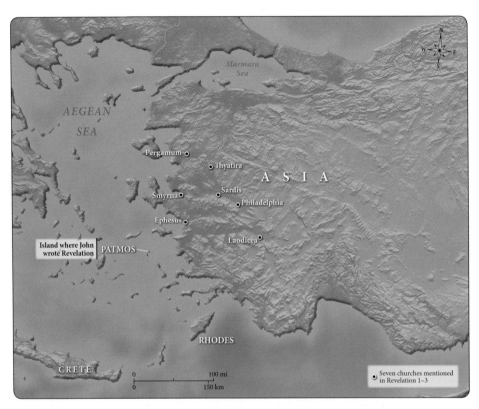

AEGEAN
SEA

Marmara
Sea

Pergamum ○

○ Thyatira

A S I A

Smyrna ○

Sardis ○

○ Philadelphia

Ephesus ○

Laodicea ○

Island where John
wrote Revelation | PATMOS

RHODES

CRETE

0   100 mi
0   150 km

Seven churches mentioned
in Revelation 1–3

Map 13. Churches of the Revelation

REVELATION

Jesus Wins!

When you think that the bad in the world is winning over the good . . . when you think there's no hope . . . when you wonder what the future holds, read this book. Revelation reveals what will happen in the last days just before Jesus returns. The stories in Revelation can be hard to understand and even frightening. But this book also reveals the final chapters in God's amazing plan to destroy our enemy, Satan, once and for all. So don't lose sight of Revelation's main message: In the end, Jesus wins! John, a disciple of Jesus, wrote this book based on a vision he had while he was on a prison island in AD 95.

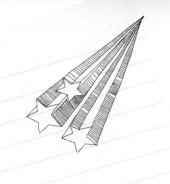

Writer:
John

Place:
Island of Patmos

Why Is It Important?
Revelation encourages all of those who are discouraged by the wickedness in the world today that no matter how bad it gets, in the end Jesus will be the winner.

Some Lessons in Revelation:
Letters to the Seven Churches: Revelation 2–3
The Winner!: Revelation 5
The Seal and Trumpet Judgments:
    Revelation 6; 8–9; 11:15–19
Two Witnesses: Revelation 11:1–14
Two Beasts: Revelation 13
Bowl Judgments: Revelation 15–16
Sin Will Be Punished: Revelation 18
A New Heaven and Earth: Revelation 21
Jesus Is Coming: Revelation 22

Revelation 1:1–3 The Revelation of Jesus

Right from the beginning, John made it clear that these were not his words. These were the words of Jesus. John had been commanded to write down what he saw in his visions.

Revelation 1:4–8 Greetings to the Seven Churches

A great highway connected the seven churches to which John wrote. These churches are named in Revelation 2–3 in clockwise order. Each church received its own copy of the complete book of Revelation. These seven churches probably represent typical churches throughout the years. They may also represent different types of believers.

Revelation 1:9–20 Seeing the Son of Man

John had been sent to the island of Patmos. The Romans often sent people there to punish them. While there, John had a vision of Jesus. Revelation 1:13–18 describes how Jesus now presents himself to his church. He's ready for battle. His show of strength is an encouragement to those who are fighting wickedness. It is also a warning to those who are getting involved in the sin of the world.

> **Patmos** Revelation 1:9
>
> Patmos is a small island off the coast of modern Turkey. The Romans used it as a place of punishment.

Revelation 2:1–7 The Letter to Ephesus

The church at Ephesus had one great problem. They no longer loved Jesus as much as they had in the beginning. They had become lazy in their faith. John warned them that in order to experience "paradise" (Revelation 2:7), they would have to stand firm in their faith.

Revelation 2:8–11 The Letter to Smyrna

The church in Smyrna was suffering for their faith in Jesus. John offered them comfort. Their faithful preaching of the good news had brought them terrible suffering, and with it, poverty. Jesus assured them that they would gain great riches in heaven. The church in Smyrna grew tremendously during their time of suffering.

Smyrna Revelation 2:8

Smyrna was an important port city with a well-protected harbor. It was one of the main cities of Asia Minor. It was famous for science, medicine, and the beauty of its buildings.

Revelation 2:12–17 The Letter to Pergamum

The church in Pergamum was faithful to Jesus, even to the point of dying (Revelation 2:13). But they also accepted false teachers. Those false teachers were saying that Christians could take part in their old idol worship and still be believers. John told them that they had better be careful because the Lord is not pleased when people accept such lies.

Pergamum Revelation 2:12

Pergamum was the capital of the ancient Greek kingdom of Pergamos until it became part of the Roman Empire. The first temple for worshiping an emperor was built in Pergamum.

Revelation 2:18–29 The Letter to Thyatira

The church at Thyatira had some good points. They were known for their love and faith, and they didn't give up easily. But they were also willing to accept false teachers. Even worse, they put up with "that woman Jezebel" (Revelation 2:20). This Jezebel was a well-known woman in Thyatira who was misleading people in the church. John warned that those who allowed her to teach in the churches and followed her evil lead should beware.

Thyatira Revelation 2:18

Thyatira was probably the least notable of the seven cities of Revelation. The history of Thyatira is barely mentioned by ancient writers.

Revelation 3:1–6 The Letter to Sardis

Sardis was a "dead" church. It was alive in name only. Its members called themselves Christians, but they did not really believe in Jesus Christ as their Savior. The words of this letter were almost like a shout, trying to wake up those sleeping in that church. If they didn't wake up and follow the truth, their names would not be found in the Book of Life (Revelation 3:5).

Sardis Revelation 3:1

Sardis was a city famous for its arts and crafts. It was the first city to make gold and silver coins. A great earthquake in AD 17 destroyed much of the city. The Romans sent a large amount of money in relief, but the city never fully recovered.

Revelation 3:7–13 The Letter to Philadelphia

The church in Philadelphia was a humble but faithful church. They were showing the life of Jesus right in the middle of their wicked city. The name Philadelphia means "brotherly love." The people in this church loved God's Word and were unshakable in their faith.

Philadelphia Revelation 3:7

The city of Philadelphia was located on a broad, low hill, which was easily defended. But the area was often hit by earthquakes, including the one that hit Sardis in AD 17. Built right on top of the fault line, the city suffered one earthquake after another for many years.

Revelation 3:14–22 The Letter to Laodicea

The church in Laodicea was a lukewarm church. It was described as being neither hot nor cold. The believers there were rich in possessions but poor in spirit. The words Jesus had for them were clear and sharp: I will "spit you out of my mouth" (Revelation 3:16). Jesus was looking for people who would follow him with their whole hearts, not just make a show of being religious. He still is!

Laodicea Revelation 3:14

Laodicea was a wealthy city in Asia Minor. It was on one of the great Asian trade routes, which brought lots of goods and money into the city.

Revelation 4
A Vision of the Throne of God

Before showing his people the horrible times that are ahead, God assures them that he is in control and on his throne. The terrible things that will happen are the final act in the story of salvation. Jesus will soon finish the work he began while he was on earth.

> **Be Wise—Memorize!**
> **Revelation 4:8** "Holy, holy, holy is the Lord God who rules over all. He was, and he is, and he will come."

Rapture Revelation 4:1

Many Christians believe that all believers will be caught up into the air with Jesus when he comes for them. This event is called the "rapture" of the church. It is expected to happen "in a flash" (see 1 Corinthians 15:51–54 and 1 Thessalonians 4:16–17).

Revelation 5 The Scroll and the Lamb

The scroll contains the secrets of the future, the final act in the story of salvation. All creation wants to know the outcome, but the only way to open the scroll is to break the seven seals. And the only person in all of creation who can do that is Jesus—not because he is strong but because he is worthy. He is free of sin and therefore the only one good enough.

In John's vision of the future, he saw Jesus break the seven seals—one by one. As each seal was broken, a terrible event happened on earth. Not until all the seals were broken did the future become clear: a new heaven and a new earth. John saw that God will live with his people in a revived and renewed creation.

Revelation 6 The Seals

The seals mark the events during a time of terrible suffering. The first seal (Revelation 6:1–2) reveals a vision of a white horse with a rider. Some think this means Christ. Others think it's the Antichrist, who falsely represents himself as Christ. The second seal (Revelation 6:3–4) reveals a red horse and rider, which means war. When the third seal is broken (Revelation 6:5–6), a black horse and rider appear. This horse shows the coming of a great famine, which will leave the inhabitants of the earth without food to eat. A pale horse appears when the fourth seal is broken (Revelation 6:7–8). It represents the death that comes from war and famine. The fifth seal unleashes a vision of the souls of those who died for their faith (Revelation 6:9–11). The sixth seal (Revelation 6:12–17) predicts a terrible, worldwide earthquake. The events of the sixth seal make people realize that these are acts of God's judgment and that the end is coming. Everyone runs to hide.

Revelation 7 Sealing the 144,000

The terrible events just described in Revelation 6:15–17 seem like they are so awful that no one could survive. But even in the middle of judgment, God shows mercy. The 144,000 are those who come to know Jesus as their Savior during this terrible time. They are "sealed" or marked with the mark of God on their foreheads. Some see this number as exactly 144,000 Jewish people, with

12,000 coming from each tribe of Israel. Some see this number as a symbol of all those who come to believe in Jesus during this time of suffering.

Revelation 8 The Seventh Seal and the Trumpets

The seventh seal contains the terrible plagues of the seven trumpets. These are even more horrible than those of the first six seals. When the seventh seal is opened, there is a time of quiet in heaven, as if all are waiting, holding their breath, for something huge to happen.

The first angel blows his trumpet, and hail and fire destroy a third of the earth. The second angel blows his trumpet and a third of the oceans turn to blood. The third angel blows his trumpet and a star falls from heaven, destroying rivers and waters and people. The fourth angel blows his trumpet and a third of the sun, moon, and stars turn dark.

Be Wise—Memorize!
Revelation 7:17 "God will wipe away every tear from their eyes."

Now an eagle appears, saying, "How terrible! How terrible!" (Revelation 8:13). Three more trumpets are to be blown. The worst is yet to come.

Revelation 9 The Fifth and Sixth Trumpets

When the fifth angel blows his trumpet, a falling star releases a plague of demon locusts from the Abyss, also called the bottomless pit, a place where evil spirits live. These demon locusts are terrifying. They don't eat the green things left on earth. Instead, they sting all those who don't have God's seal on their foreheads. The sting is so horrible that people wish they could die. But they can't.

Now the sixth angel blows his trumpet. Four fallen angels are unleashed and with them an army of two hundred million horses and riders. They kill a third of the people left on earth. But amazingly, all of this death and destruction has no effect on the people left. They continue to reject God.

Revelation 10 The Angel and the Little Scroll

Revelation 10–11 are a brief look at events that happen between the blowing of the sixth and seventh trumpets. An angel puts his right foot on the sea and his left foot on the land and gives a huge shout—a warning that the end is near. John is told to take and then eat the scroll the angel is holding in his hand. The scroll is sweet (a wonderful future awaits believers) and also bitter (judgment awaits those who don't believe).

Revelation 11:1–14 Two Witnesses

These two witnesses will preach in Jerusalem for three and a half years (1,260 days). They will call the people to turn away from their sin and believe in Jesus' saving work on the cross. Many will hate them. But those who try to hurt them will be killed by fire from the witnesses' mouths. When the three and a half years are over, the Beast (see Revelation 13) will attack and kill both of them. But that's not the end of these two men—far from it! After three and a half days, God will bring them back to life! God will call them to heaven in a cloud while their enemies watch. At the same time, a great earthquake will hit the earth, and seven thousand people will die.

Revelation 11:15–19 The Seventh Trumpet

The seventh angel blows his trumpet to signal that the end has come. Judgment has arrived.

Revelation 12 The Woman, Child, and Dragon

John now goes back and begins to tell the story with a new series of visions. A woman, who probably represents Israel, gives birth to a child. The child is Christ. The woman goes into the desert, and the child goes to heaven to be with God. Meanwhile, a battle begins in heaven. Michael and all of his angels fight a dragon—Satan. The angels defeat the dragon. Having lost in heaven, the dragon now turns his attention to the earth. He wants to keep as many people as possible from turning to Jesus.

Revelation 13 Two Beasts

This chapter now introduces the two beasts through which Satan begins to control the people of earth. The first beast seems to be a government official while the second beast seems to be a religious or church official. Both get their power and direction from Satan.

The first beast (Revelation 13:1–10) is usually thought to be the Antichrist. He has what seems to be a deadly head wound. But he has been healed. Many think the Antichrist will die and be brought back to life by Satan, a weak imitation of the events of Jesus' life. Those who don't belong to Christ, whose names are not written in the Book of Life (Revelation 13:8), will worship this Antichrist.

The second beast (Revelation 13:11–18) holds a place of power in the church. He is now revealed as the one who brings the first beast back to life again. He has the power to sway the people of earth to worship the Antichrist. He is the one who forces all people on earth to take the beast's mark. The only way to buy or sell food, clothes—you name it—is to take the beast's mark. This is another poor imitation of what God has done. This time, it is of the seal that was earlier put on the foreheads of the servants of God. (See the note on Revelation 7.)

Revelation 14 The Lamb and His Followers

John described seven visions in this chapter. These visions give the big picture while the following chapters fill in the details. The 144,000 sing praises to Jesus the Lamb. (See the note on Revelation 7.) As they sing, an angel goes out to tell all the earth the good news of Jesus. This appears to be sort of a last call to faith in Jesus before judgment arrives.

Another angel appears and says Babylon will fall. Babylon is the name given in Revelation to the working partnership of the two beasts. A third angel arrives to shout out the doom that awaits those who have taken the beast's mark. (See the note on Revelation 13.)

Revelation 15–16 Seven Bowls of Wrath

The angels of Revelation 15 set the stage for the coming of the seven bowls of God's wrath described in Revelation 16. These seven angels in heaven prepare to pour out the contents of the seven bowls on earth.

The first bowl is poured out on earth and causes terrible sores on all of those who have the mark of the beast. The second and third bowls are poured out on the oceans and rivers. The water turns to blood and everything that lives in the oceans and rivers dies. The fourth bowl turns up the heat of the sun. The fifth bowl is poured out onto the throne of the Antichrist. Darkness fills his kingdom. The sixth bowl dries up the Euphrates River. The seventh bowl is poured out on the air. With the pounding of hundred-pound hailstones and the greatest earthquake of all time, the kingdom of the two beasts—Babylon—falls!

Revelation 17 The Woman and the Beast

The woman, the "great prostitute" (Revelation 17:1), is the worldwide false religion headed up by the second beast of Revelation 13. Her name is "Mystery, the Great City of Babylon" (Revelation 17:5). She sits on many waters. These waters are the many people of earth who are led away from the truths of God's Word by the second beast. This woman rides on another beast (the Antichrist). Remember that Satan is the power behind these two beasts and that they work together.

In the end religious Babylon will fall because the Antichrist will turn his back and betray the second beast. He will strip all power from him and his religion.

Revelation 18 The Fall of Babylon

God uses the name Babylon, the nation that took God's Old Testament people captive, for the world power that will take the people of the world captive in the last days. "Babylon the Great" (Revelation 18:2), the city from which the Antichrist rules the world, is destroyed. With the fall of Babylon, all of the world's political and commercial systems also fall.

Revelation 19 The Destruction of the Two Beasts

Shouts of "Hallelujah," which means "Praise the Lord!" fill the air. John hears the roar of a great congregation in heaven lifting up God in glory and praises. They are happy because Jesus has won! A great supper—a wedding dinner—has been prepared for Jesus, the bridegroom, and for the church, Jesus' bride.

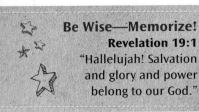

Be Wise—Memorize!
Revelation 19:1
"Hallelujah! Salvation and glory and power belong to our God."

At this moment, John sees the heavens open, and Jesus returns to the earth riding a white horse. He is followed by all the armies of heaven, which are also riding on white horses. This is the moment when Jesus reveals himself to the whole world. All the saved in heaven—including the Old Testament saints, the believers from the church age who were taken up to heaven in the rapture, and the believers from the tribulation—now return to fight with Christ at the battle of Armageddon. But in the end, Christ alone fights the battle and wins. John sees God deal out judgment. First, the Antichrist and then the false prophet, the second beast, are destroyed.

Revelation 20 The Thousand Years

During this thousand-year reign of Christ, Satan is bound with chains and thrown into the Abyss. He had been the ruler of this world, but he will not be allowed any power during this thousand years. After the thousand years have passed, Satan will be loosed from his chains for a short time. But he will not be able to regain his hold on the people of the earth.

Satan's final doom is sure. He is thrown into the "lake of burning sulfur" (Revelation 20:10), the same place the two beasts had been thrown. Satan and the beasts and all those who follow them will live on forever in that terrible place.

Heaven Revelation 20:1

Heaven is the place where God lives and where believers will one day go to live with him.

Abyss Revelation 20:1

The Abyss is the place of eternal pain where Jesus sends Satan, his demon helpers, and all those who have rejected God during their time on earth.

Revelation 21 Heaven

John now sees "a new heaven and a new earth" (Revelation 21:1), the eternal home of those who believe in Jesus and follow him faithfully. No one knows for sure if this means there will be a completely new heaven and earth or if this old one will be renewed and restored.

John then sees the "new Jerusalem" (Revelation 21:2) coming down out of heaven. The Bible talks about two Jerusalems. The first is on earth and becomes the home of Christ during his thousand-year reign. The second is in heaven. The second heavenly city is pictured here. An angel carries John to the city and shows him its beauty and glory.

Book of Life Revelation 21:27

The Book of Life is referred to six times in the book of Revelation (Revelation 3:5; 13:8; 17:8; 20:12, 15; 21:27). It is the book—whether a real physical book or something in the mind of God—where the names of those who believe in Jesus are recorded.

Revelation 22 Final Words

The Garden of Eden is restored in the middle of the city. After Adam and Eve sinned in the Garden of Eden, God posted an angel at the Tree of Life to prevent them from eating its fruit (Genesis 3:24) and living in their sinful state forever. In the final glory of heaven, believers will finally be free to eat from that tree.

In the closing of the book of Revelation we are encouraged with the wonderful words of Jesus, "I am coming soon!" Those are his last words, an invitation yet again to choose him and his way of life—eternal life in heaven with him.

Have you chosen Jesus as your Lord and Savior? Have you chosen to live your life for Jesus? Don't wait another day! Jesus loves you so much! Ask Jesus to be your Lord and Savior and receive his free gift of eternal life!

INDEX

Where Did *Halley's Bible Handbook for Kids* Come From?

This book has a long history—one that goes back to around the time your great-grandparents were born. *Halley's Bible Handbook for Kids* is named for Dr. Henry H. Halley, who was born in 1874. He was a teacher and preacher who wanted to help people read, understand, and love God's Word, the Bible.

Henry memorized huge parts of the Bible—some said he could quote Scripture from memory for twenty-five hours! Churches invited him to recite verses and then teach people about the Bible. He and his wife typed some notes to go along with his teaching, and that was the beginning of what would become *Halley's Bible Handbook*. Over the years, those few notes would grow into a book of several hundred pages—and more than six million copies would be sold.

The handbook was for grown-ups, but shortly before Henry died in 1965, he began work on a children's version. His family continued the work over many years, until *Halley's Bible KidNotes* became available in 2003. This updated edition, with the title *Halley's Bible Handbook for Kids*, was finished in 2016.

Dr. Henry H. Halley's family hopes this book will be helpful to students, parents, and kids' ministry leaders—to help everyone become, in Dr. Halley's words, "a constant and devoted reader of the Bible."